THE EMPRE
ROM

JOSEPH MCCABE

ZINC READ

Published by
This edition copyright © 2024 by Zinc Read
Design and setting By Zinc Read
Email- zincread@gmail.com
ISBN-978-93-6360-215-1

CONTENTS

INTRODUCTION

THE story of Imperial Rome has been told frequently and impressively in our literature, and few chapters in the long chronicle of man's deeds and failures have a more dramatic quality. Seven centuries before our era opens, when the greater part of Europe is still hidden under virgin forests or repellent swamps, and the decaying civilizations of the East cast, as they die, their seed upon the soil of Greece, we see, in the grey mist of the legendary period, a meagre people settling on one of the seven hills by the Tiber. As it grows its enemies are driven back, and it spreads confidently over the neighbouring hills and down the connecting valleys. It gradually extends its rule over other Italian peoples, bracing its arm and improving its art in the long struggle. It grows conscious of its larger power, and sends its legions eastward, over the blue sea, to gather the wealth and culture of Egypt, Assyria, Persia, and Greece; and westward and northward, over the white Alps, to sow the seed in Germany, Gaul, Britain, and Spain. A hundred years before the opening of the present era the tiny settlement on the Palatine has become the mistress of the world. Its eagles cross the waters of the Danube and the Rhine, and glitter in the sun of Asia and Africa. But, with the wealth of the dying East, it has inherited the germs of a deadly malady. Rome, the heart of the giant frame, loses its vigour. The strong bronze limbs look pale and thin; the clear cold brain is overcast with the fumes of wine and heated with the thrills of sense; and Rome passes, decrepit and dishonoured, from the stage on which it has played so useful and fateful a part.

The fresh aspect of this familiar story which I propose to consider is the study of the women who moulded or marred the succeeding Emperors in their failure to arrest, if not their guilt in accelerating, the progress of Rome's disease. Woman had her part in the making, as well as the unmaking, of Rome. In the earlier days, when her work was confined within the walls of the home, no consul ever guided the momentous fortune of Rome, no soldier ever bore its eagles to the bounds of the world, but some woman had taught his lips to frame the syllables of his national creed. However, long before the commencement of our era, the thought and the power of the Roman woman went out into the larger world of public life; and when the Empire is founded, when the control of the State's mighty resources is entrusted to the hands of a single ruler, the wife of the monarch may share his power, and assuredly shares his interest for us. Even as mere women of Rome, as single figures and types rising to the luminous height of the throne out of the dark and indistinguishable crowd, they deserve to be passed in review.

Some such review we have, no doubt, in the two great works which spread the panorama of Imperial Rome before the eyes of English readers. In the graceful and restrained chapters of Merivale we find the earlier Empresses delineated with no less charm than learning. In the more

genial and voluptuous narrative of Gibbon we may, at intervals, follow the fortunes and appreciate the character of the later Empresses. But, no matter how nice a skill in grouping the historian may have, his stage is too crowded either for us to pick out the single character with proper distinctness, or for him to appraise it with entire accuracy. The fleeting glimpses of the Empresses which we catch, as the splendid panorama passes before us, must be blended in a fuller and steadier picture. The tramp and shock of armies, the wiles of statesmen, the social revolutions, which absorb the historian, must fall into the background, that the single figure may be seen in full contour. When this is done it will be found that there are many judgments on the Empresses, both in Merivale and Gibbon, which the biographer will venture to question.

For the study of the earlier Empresses the English reader will find much aid in Mr. Baring-Gould's "Tragedy of the Caesars" (1892). Here again, however, though the Empresses are drawn with discriminating freshness and full knowledge, they are constantly merging in the great crowd of characters. The aim of the present work is to place them in the full foreground, and to continue the survey far beyond the limits of Mr. Baring-Gould's work.

It differs also in this latter respect from Stahr's brilliant "Kaiser-Frauen," which is, in fact, now almost unobtainable; and especially from V. Silvagni's recent work, of unhappy title, "L'Impero e le Donne dei Cesari," which merely includes slight and familiar sketches of four Empresses in a general study of the period.

The work differs in quite another way from the learned and entertaining book of the old French writer Roergas de Serviez, of which an early English translation has recently been republished under the title "The Roman Empresses, or the History of the Lives and Secret Intrigues of the Wives of the Twelve Caesars"--an improper title, because the work is far from confined to the wives of the Caesars.

The work is an industrious compilation of original references to the Empresses, interwoven with considerable art, so as to construct harmonious pictures, and adorned with much charm and piquancy of phrase, if some hollowness of sentiment. But it is so intent upon entertaining us that it frequently sacrifices accuracy to that admirable aim.

Serviez has not invented any substantial episode, but he has encircled the facts with the most charming imaginative haloes, and where the authorities differ, as they frequently do, he has not hesitated to grant his verdict to the writer who most picturesquely impeaches the virtue of one of his Empresses. Roergas de Serviez was a gentleman of Languedoc in the days of the "grand monarque." His Empresses and princesses reflect too faithfully the frail character of the ladies at the Court of Louis XIV. For him the most reliable writer is the one who betrays least inclination to seek virtue in courtly ladies.

It need hardly be said that the present writer is indebted to these authors, to the learned Tillemont, and to others who will be named in the course of the work. But this study is based on a careful examination of all the references to the Empresses in the Latin and Greek authorities, with such further aid as is afforded by coins, statues, inscriptions, and the incidental research of commentators. We

shall consider, as we proceed, the varying authority of these writers. We shall find in them defects which impose a heavy responsibility on the writer whose aim it is to restore those faded and delicate portraits of the Empresses, over which later artists have spread their sharper and more crudely coloured figures. One may, however, say at once that it is not contemplated to urge any very revolutionary change in the current estimate of the character of most of them. If a few romantic adventures must be honestly discarded, we shall find Messalina still flaunting her vices in the palace, Agrippina still pursuing her more masculine ambition, Poppaea still representing the gaily-decked puppet of that luxurious world, and Zenobia, in glittering helmet, still giving resonant commands to her troops.

But it will be well, before we introduce the first, and one of the best and greatest of the Empresses, to glance at the development of Roman life which prepared the way for woman to so exalted a dignity. The condition of woman in early Rome has often been restored. We see the female infant, her fate trembling in the hand of man from the moment when her eyes open to the light, brought before the despotic father for the decision of her fate.

With a glance at the little white frame he will say whether she shall be cast out, to be gathered by the merchants in human flesh, or suffered to breed the next generation of citizens. We follow her through her guarded girlhood, as she learns to spin and weave, and see her passing from the tyranny of father to the tyranny of husband at an age when the modern girl has hardly begun to glance nervously at marriage as a remote and mystic experience.

We then find her, not indeed so narrowly confined as her Greek sister, yet little more than the servant of her husband. Public feeling, it is true, mitigated the harsher features, and forbade the graver consequences, of this ancient tradition. For many centuries divorce was unknown at Rome. Yet woman's horizon was limited to

her home, while her husband boasted of his share in controlling the Commonwealth's increasing life.

In the second century before Christ we find symptoms of revolt. The wealthier women of Rome resent the

curtailing of their finery by the Oppian Law, now that the war is over (195 B.C.). Old-fashioned Senators are dismayed to find them holding a public meeting, besetting all the approaches to the Senate, demanding their votes, and even invading the houses of the Tribunes and coercing them to withdraw their opposition. The truth is that Rome has changed, and the women feel the pervading change. The passage of the victorious Roman through the cities of the East had corrupted the patriarchal virtues.

Roman officers could not gaze unmoved on the surviving memorials of the culture of Athens, or make festival in the drowsy chambers of Corinthian courtesans or the licentious groves of Daphne, without altering their ideal of life. The splendour of Eastern wisdom and vice made pale the old standard of Roman *virtus*. The vast wealth extorted from the subdued provinces swelled the pride of patrician families until they disdainfully burst the narrow walls of their fathers' homes. The hills of Rome began to shine with marble mansions, framed in shady and spacious gardens, from which contemptuous patrician eyes looked down on the sordid and idle crowds in the valleys of the Subura and the Velabrum. Rome aspired to have its art and its letters.

Roman women were not content to be secluded from the new culture, and could not escape the stimulation of their new world. The Roman husband must be kept away from the accomplished courtesans of Greece and the voluptuous sirens of Asia by finding no lesser attractions in his wife. So the near horizon of woman's mind rolled outward. An inscription found at Lanuvium, where the Empress Livia had a villa, shows that the little provincial town had a *curia mulierum*, a women's debating club. The walls of Pompeii, when the shroud of lava had been removed from its scorched face, bore election-addresses signed by women. The world was mirrored in Rome, and few minds could retain their primitive simplicity as they contemplated that seductive picture.

By the beginning of the first century of the older era the women of Rome had ample opportunity for culture and for political influence. In the great conflicts of the time their names are chronicled as the inspirers of many of the chief actors. They rise and fall with the cause of the Senate or the cause of the People. They unite culture with character, public interest with beauty and motherhood.

At last the conflicting parties disappear one by one, and a young commander, Octavian, the great-nephew of Julius Caesar, gathers up the power they relinquish.

A youth of delicate and singularly graceful features, of refined and thoughtful, rather than assertive, appearance, he hears that Caesar has made him heir to his wealth and his opportunities; he goes boldly to Rome, adroitly uses its forces to destroy those who had slain Caesar, forces Mark Antony to share the rule of the world with him and Lepidus, and then destroys Lepidus and Mark Antony. It is at this point, when he returns to Rome from his last victories, when the whole world wonders whether he will keep the power he has gathered or meekly place it in the hands of the Senate, that the story opens.

CHAPTER I

THE MAKING OF AN EMPRESS

ON an August morning of the year 29 B.C. the million citizens of Rome lined the route which was taken by triumphal processions, to greet the man who brought them the unfamiliar blessing of peace.

From the Triumphal Gate to the Capitol, past the Great Circus and through the dense quarter of the Velabrum, with its narrow streets and high tenements, the chattering crowd was drawn out in two restless lines, on either side of the road, ready to fling back the resonant "Io Triumphe" of the bronzed soldiers, bubbling with discussion of the war-blackened stretch of the past and the more pleasant prospect of the future. The hedges of spectators were thicker, and the debate was livelier, under the cliff of the Palatine Hill and in the Forum, through which ran the Sacred Way to the white Temple of Jupiter, towering above them and crowning the Capitol at the end of the Forum. There the conqueror would offer sacrifice, before he sank back into the common rank of citizens of the Republic. Would the young Octavian really lay down his power, and become a citizen among many, now that he was master of the Roman world?

Possibly one woman, who looked out on the seething Forum and the glistening temple of Jupiter from a modest mansion on the Palatine Hill, knew the answer to the eager question. Possibly it was unknown to Octavian himself, her husband. She heard the blasts of the leading trumpeters, and saw the sleek white oxen, with their gilded horns and their green garlands, advance along the Sacred Way and mount the

Capitol. She saw the people rock and quiver with excitement as painted scenes of the remote Dalmatian forests, where her husband's latest victories had been won, and the gold and silver of despoiled Egypt, and the very children of the witch Cleopatra, were driven before the conqueror.

She saw the red-robed lictors slowly pass, their fasces wreathed in laurel; she saw the band of dancers and musicians tossing joyful music in his path; and she saw at last the four white horses drawing a triumphal chariot, in which her husband and her two children received the frenzied ovation of the people.

Octavian was then in his thirty-fourth year. Fifteen years of struggle had drawn a manly gravity over the handsome boyish face, though the curly golden hair still seemed a strange bed for the chaplet of laurel that crowned it. His full impassive lips, steady watchful eyes, and broad smooth forehead gave a singular impression of detachment--as if he were a disinterested spectator of the day's events and the whole national drama, instead of being the central figure. The busts which portray him about this period seem to me, in profile, to recall David's Napoleon, without the slumbering fire and the hard egoism. Men would remind each other how, when he was a mere boy, fifteen years before, he had found his way through a maze of intrigue with remarkable dexterity.

Now, Mark Antony was dead, Brutus and Cassius were dead, Lepidus was dead, and the followers of Pompey were scattered. It was natural to assume that dreams of further power were hidden behind that mask of strong repose.

Behind Octavian went the body of Senators, with purple-striped togas, and silver crescents on their sandals.

The lines of spectators broke into gossiping groups when the tail of the procession had passed on. The white oxen fell before the altar of Jupiter. Octavian gave the customary address to the Senate, and joined Livia in the small mansion on the Palatine. But for many a day afterward Rome bubbled in praise of him. Not for years had such combats reddened the sands of the amphitheatre, such clowns and conjurors and actors filled the stage of the theatre, such sports fired the 300,000 citizens at the circus.

Never before had the uncouth form of the rhinoceros or hippopotamus been seen at Rome. Not since the beginning of the civil wars had so much money flowed through the shops of the Velabrum and the taverns of the Subura. Such wealth had been added to the public store by the despoiling of Egypt that the bankers had to reduce the rate of interest. To a people grown parasitic the temptation to make a king was overpowering; and it was easy to point out, to those who clung to the strict democratic forms, that Octavian was extraordinarily modest for a man who had reached so brilliant and resourceful a position. So within a few months Octavian was Imperator, and Livia became, in modern phrase, the Empress of Rome.[1]

Livia, unhappily for Rome, gave Octavian no direct heir to the purple, and we may therefore speak briefly of her extraction. She came of the Claudii, one of the oldest and proudest families of the Republic, one that numbered twenty-eight consuls and five dictators in its line. A strong, haughty race, more useful than brilliant, religiously devoted to the old Republic, they had helped much to make Rome the mistress of the world. Livia's father, Livius Drusus Claudianus, had taken arms against Octavian and Antony, and had killed himself, with Roman dignity, when Brutus and Cassius fell, and he saw the shadow of despotism coming over the city.

Livia was then in her sixteenth year,[2] and had early experience of the storms of Roman political life. Her husband, Tiberius Claudius Nero, had been promoted more than once by Julius Caesar, but, after the assassination of Caesar, he had passed into what he regarded as the more favourable current. He seems to have steered his course with some skill until the year 41 B.C., when, like many other small schemers, he came under the influence of Mark Antony's wife, Fulvia. Antony was caught at the time in the silken net with which Cleopatra prevented him from carrying out the ambition of Rome at the expense of her country. Fulvia, a virile and passionate woman, tried to draw Antony from her arms by provoking a revolt against Octavian. She induced her brother-in-law and other nobles to rebel, and Nero, who was then prefect of a small town in Campania, joined the movement.

Octavian swung his legions southward, and scattered the thin ranks of the insurgents. With her infant--the future Emperor Tiberius--in her arms the girl-wife fled to the coast with her husband, and endured all the horrors of civil warfare. So close were the soldiers of Octavian on their heels that at one point the cry of the baby nearly destroyed them. Octavian had little mercy on rebellious nobles before he married Livia. At last they reached the coast, where the galleys of Sextus Pompeius hovered to receive fugitives, and sailed for Sicily. They were cordially received there by the Pompeians, but went on to

Greece, and were again hunted by the troops. Long afterwards in Rome they used to tell how the delicate girl, the descendant of all the Claudii, fled through a burning forest by night before Roman soldiers, and singed her hair and garments as she rushed onward with her baby in her arms.

The troubled history of Rome for a hundred years was stamped on her mind by a personal experience that she could never forget. With worn feet and aching heart, she and her husband at last found shelter, until the feud between Antony and Octavian had been composed.

From the straits of exile they returned to their pretty home on the Palatine Hill, and the story of her adventures ran, and gathered substance, in Roman society. If the experts be right in assigning to Livia a small mansion which has been uncovered on the hill, we find that she was, in the year 38 B.C., living only a short distance from the house of Octavian. Among the palatial buildings which now whitened the slopes of the Roman hills, Nero's house--later, Livia's house--was poor, but its mural paintings

are amongst the most delicate that have been discovered under the overlying centuries of mediaeval rubbish. A small portico gave shelter from the summer sun, and the small, cool atrium (hall) led only to some half dozen modest rooms. But Livia was happy in her husband, and sober in her tastes. She was then in her nineteenth year, a young woman of regular and pleasing, though scarcely beautiful, features and rounded form, one of those who happily united the old matronly virtue to the new love of society and gaiety. All Rome discussed her adventures, and the generous feeling which her romance engendered made people give her an exceptional beauty and wit--qualities which neither her marble image nor her recorded career permits us to accept in any large measure. There was no whisper of slander against her until the days of her power.

From this peaceful and happy little world she was now to be suddenly removed.

Octavian, who mingled very freely with his fellows, and often supped with the literary men who were now multiplying at Rome, heard the gossip about the youthful Livia, and sought her. He was already married, and a word may be said about the *imperatrices manquees* before we unite him to Livia.

In early youth he had been affianced to the girlish daughter of Publius Servilius Isauricus, but a mere betrothal had little strength at a time when even the marriage bond was so frail. When he came to face Mark Antony, with many grim legions at his command, and a fresh civil war was threatened, peacemakers suggested that the storm might be turned from the fields of Italy by a matrimonial alliance. The soldiers, weary of slaying each other, acclaimed the proposal. Servilia was sacrificed, and Octavian was married to the young and hardly marriageable daughter of Fulvia. As we saw, there was a fresh

rupture with Antony in the year 41, and Octavian sent back the maiden, as he described her, to her infuriated mother. Some of our authorities declare that Fulvia had tried to draw Antony from the arms of Cleopatra by making love to his handsome rival, but one can only suppose that Antony would smile if he were told that his unpleasant spouse--the woman who is said to have gloated over the bloody head of Cicero, and thrust her hair-pin through his tongue--was offering her heart to Octavian. We cannot, therefore, accept the rumour that, when Octavian sent back her daughter to Fulvia, he maliciously explained that he was anxious to spare Fulvia the mortification of thinking that he had preferred the pretty insipidity of Clodia to her own more assertive qualities.

The marriage with Clodia had been frankly political, and it naturally broke down in the new political dissolution.

The second marriage had the same origin, and the same welcome termination. He had married Scribonia, a woman older than himself, during the rupture with Antony, because her brother was one of the chief members of the Pompeian faction. The leader of this party, Sextus Pompeius, held Sicily, and not only welcomed fugitives from Octavian's anger, but commanded the sea-route to Rome. Through his devoted friend Maecenas, the famous patron of letters, Octavian proposed a marriage with Scribonia. It would not be unnatural for a woman in her thirties, who had already outlived two husbands, eagerly to espouse, and probably love, so graceful, ambitious, and advancing a youth as Octavian; but to him the alliance was only one more move in the great game he was playing. He could bear the strain of a diplomatic marriage with ease, since there is no reason to reject the statement of Dio and Suetonius that he found affection among the wives of his nobler friends.

It has been commonly held that Octavian masked a tense and unwavering ambition with an affectation of simple joviality, and his irregularities have been excused on the ground that he used them as means to detect political whispers in Roman society. But this view of Octavian's character may be confidently questioned. His tastes, we shall see, remained extremely simple when he might safely have indulged any feeling for luxury, when every rival had been removed. That he was ambitious it would be foolish to question; but his ambition must not be measured by his success. There are few other cases in history in which fortune so wantonly smoothed the path and drew onward an easy and vacillating ambition. Octavian could well believe the assurances of the Chaldaean astrologers that he was born to power.

With all his simplicity, however, Octavian had some sense of luxury in love-matters, and his imagination wandered. Scribonia's solid virtue was unrelieved by any of the graces of the new womanhood of Rome, her sparing charms had already faded under the pitiless sun of Italy, and she had a sharp tongue. Moreover, his marriage with her had proved a superfluous sacrifice. Fulvia's stormy career had come to a close shortly after the return of her daughter, and Antony and Octavian had divided the Roman world between them. Antony married his colleague's sister, but the pale virtue of Octavia had no avail against the burning caresses, if not the calculated patriotism, of Cleopatra. At the second rupture between Antony and Octavian she was driven from Antony's palace at Rome, where she was patiently enduring his distant infidelity, and sent back to her brother. In the meantime Octavian had discovered a pleasanter way of obtaining peace with the Pompeians than by the endurance of Scribonia's jarring laments of his infidelity. He found, or alleged, that Sextus Pompeius did not curb the pirates of the Mediterranean as he ought, and he determined to wrest from him the rich appointments that he held. He was in this mood when, in the year 38 B.C., the young Livia came to Rome, and the exaggerated story of her adventures and her beauty began to circulate among the mansions of the Palatine.

Some of the authorities describe Octavian as hovering about her for some time, and say that the splendour with which he celebrated his *barbatoria*, or first shave of the beard, was due to the generosity of his new passion. It is more probable that he at once informed Nero of his resolution to marry Livia. Tacitus expressly says that it is unknown whether Livia consented or not to the change of husband. Great as was the liberty then enjoyed by Roman women, they were rarely consulted on such matters. Scribonia received a letter of divorce, in which it was suggested that the perversity of her character made her an unsuitable spouse for so roving a husband. She had given birth to a daughter a few days before, and we shall find the later chapters of this chronicle lit up more than once by the lurid hatred which was begotten of this despotic dismissal. For the moment I need only point out that later Roman writers borrowed their estimate of the character of Livia from Scribonia's great-grandchild, the Empress Agrippina, and we must be wary in accepting their statements. Scribonia herself, who came so near to being an Empress, we must now dismiss, save that we shall catch one more glimpse of her when she follows her dissolute daughter into exile.

Roman law imposed a fitting delay on the divorced wife before she could marry again, but Octavian was impatient.

He consulted the sacred augurs, and, if the legend is correct, the diviners gave admirable proof of their art.

They gravely reported that the omens were auspicious for an immediate marriage *if* the petitioner had ground to believe that it would be fruitful. The verdict entertained Rome, because Livia was well known to be far advanced in pregnancy, and Octavian was widely regarded as the father.

Whether that be true or no, Octavian intimated to Nero that he must divorce Livia, and we cannot think that she felt much pain at being invited to share the mansion in the Palatine to which all Roman eyes were now directed. An anecdote of the time lightly illustrates the ease with which such matrimonial transfers were accomplished at Rome.

Dio says that, during the festive meal, one of those bejewelled boys who then formed part of a Roman noble's household, and whose vicious services were rewarded with an extraordinary license, said to Livia, as she reclined at table with Octavian: "What do you here, mistress? Your husband is yonder." The pert youngster pointed to Nero at another table. He had given away the bride, and was cheerfully taking part in the banquet.

Livia's second son, Drusus Nero, was born three months after her marriage, and was sent by Octavian to Nero's house. Nero died soon afterwards, and made Octavian the guardian of his sons, so that they returned to the care of their mother. The extreme fondness of Octavian for the younger boy lends no colour to the rumour that Drusus was his own son. The probability is that Octavian, in his impetuous way, married Livia as soon as his fancy rested on her. The accepted busts of Drusus do not give any support to the calumny that Octavian was his father. He loved both the boys, and assisted in educating them, in their early youth. It is only when his daughter Julia brings her handsome children into the household that we detect a beginning of an estrangement between him and his successor, Tiberius.

The household in which these first seeds of tragedy slowly germinated was, in the year 38 B.C., one of great simplicity and sobriety. They lived in the comparatively small house in which Octavian had been born, and

Livia adopted his plain ways with ease and dignity. In that age of deadly luxury, when the veins of Rome were swollen with the first flush of parasitic wealth, Octavian and Livia were content with a prudent adaptation of the old Roman ideal to the new age. The noble guests whom Octavian brought to his table found that his simple taste shrank, not only from the peacocks' brains and nightingales' tongues which were served in their own more sumptuous banquets, but even from the pheasant, the boar, and the other ordinary luxuries of a patrician dinner. Rough bread, cream cheese, fish, and common fruit composed his customary meal. Often was he seen, as he came home in his

litter from some fatiguing public business, such as the administration of justice, to munch a little bread and fruit, like some humble countryman. Of wine he drank little, and he never adopted the enervating nightly carousal which was draining away the strength of Rome. While wealthy senators and knights prolonged the hours of entertainment after the evening meal, and hired sinuous Syrian dancing girls and nude bejewelled boys and salacious mimes to fire the dull eyes of their guests, as they lay back, sated, on the couches of silk and roses, under fine showers of perfume from the roof, sipping choice wine cooled with the snow of the Atlas or the Alps, Octavian withdrew to his study, after a frugal supper, to write his diary, dictate his generous correspondence, and enjoy the poets who were inaugurating the golden age of Latin letters. When there were guests, he provided fitting dishes and music for them, but often retired to his study when the meal was over.

After seven hours' sleep in the most modest of chambers he was ready to resume his daily round.

Since Octavian retained these sober habits to the end of his life, years after they could have had any diplomatic aim, it is remarkable that so many writers have regarded them as an artful screen of his ambition. Nor can we think differently of Livia. If Octavian presents a healthy contrast to the sordid sensuality of some of his successors, his wife contrasts no less luminously with later Empresses, and is no less unjustly accused of cunning. How far she developed ambition in later years we shall consider later.

In the fullness of his manhood, at least, she was content to be the wife of Octavian. With her own hands she helped to spin, weave, and sew his everyday garments. She carefully reared her two boys, tended the somewhat delicate health of Octavian, and cultivated that nice degree of affability which kept her husband affectionate and the husbands of other noble dames respectful. Dio would have us believe that her most useful quality was her willingness to overlook the genial irregularities of Octavian; but Dio betrays an excessive eagerness to detect frailties in his heroes and heroines. We have no serious evidence that Octavian continued the loose ways of his youth after he married Livia. The plainest and soundest reading of the chronicle is that they lived happily, and retained a great affection for each other, even when fate began to rain its blows on their ill-starred house.

But before we reach those tragic days, we have to

consider briefly the years in which Octavian established his power. His first step after his marriage with Livia was to destroy the power of the Pompeians. Livia

followed the struggle anxiously from her country villa a few miles from Rome. Sextus Pompeius was experienced in naval warfare, and, as repeated messages came of blunder and defeat on the part of Octavian's forces, she trembled with alarm. Her confidence was restored by one of the abundant miracles of the time. An eagle one day swooped down on a chicken which had just picked up a sprig of laurel in the farm-yard. The eagle clumsily dropped the chicken, with the laurel, near Livia, and so plain an omen could not be misinterpreted. Rumour soon had it that the eagle had laid the laurel-bearing chick gently at Livia's feet. As in all such cases, the sceptic of a later generation was silenced with material proof. The chicken became the mother of a brood which for many years spread the repute of the village through southern Italy; the sprig of laurel became a tree, and in time furnished the auspicious twigs of which the crowns of triumphing generals were woven.

Whether it was by the will of Jupiter, or by the reinforcement of a hundred and fifty ships which he received

from Antony, Octavian did eventually win, and, to the delight of Rome, cleared the route by which the corn-ships came from Africa. Only two men now remained between Octavian and supreme power--the two who formed with him the Triumvirate which ruled the Republic. The first, Lepidus, was soon convicted of maladministration in his African province, and was transferred to the innocent duties of the pontificate, under Octavian's eyes, at Rome.

Octavian added the province of Africa to his half of the Roman world, and found himself in command of forty-five legions and six hundred vessels. Fresh honours were awarded him by the Senate, in which his devoted friend Maecenas, who foresaw the advantage to Rome of his rule, was working for him.

Then Octavian entered on his final conflict with Mark Antony. I have already protested against the plausible view that Octavian was pursuing a definite ambition under all his appearance of simplicity. Circumstances conspired first to give him power, and then to give him the appearance of a thirst for it. He really did not destroy Antony, however: Antony destroyed himself. The apology that has been made for Cleopatra in recent times only enhances Antony's guilt. It is said that she used all that elusive fascination of her person, of which ancient writers find it difficult to convey an impression, all her wealth and her wit, only to benumb the hand that Rome stretched out to seize her beloved land. The theory is not in the least inconsistent with the facts, and it is more pleasant to believe that the last representative of the great free womanhood of ancient Egypt sacrificed her person and her wealth on the altar of patriotism than that her dalliance with Antony was but a languorous and selfish indulgence in an hour of national peril. But if it be true that Cleopatra was the last Egyptian patriot, Antony was all the more clearly a traitor to Rome. The quarrel does not concern us. Octavian induced the Senate to make war on Egypt; and we can well believe that when, in a herald's garb, he read the declaration of war at the door of the temple of Bellona, the thought of his despised sister added warmth to his phrases. The pale, patient face and outraged virtue of Octavia daily branded Antony afresh in the eyes of Rome.

Livia and Antonia followed the swift course of the last struggle from Rome. They heard of the meeting of the fleets off Actium, the victorious swoop of Octavian, the flight of Antony and Cleopatra. What followed would hardly be known to Livia. It is said that Cleopatra offered to betray Antony to Octavian, and such an offer is in entire harmony with the patriotic theory of her conduct. While his able but ill-regulated rival, deserted by his forces, drew near the edge of the abyss, Octavian visited Cleopatra in her palace. Her seductive form was displayed on a silken couch, and from the slit-like eyes the dangerous fire caressed the young conqueror. Cleopatra probably relied on Octavian's weakness, but his sensuous impulses were held in check by a harder thought. He felt that he must have this glorious creature to adorn his triumph at Rome. Cleopatra saw that she had failed, and she went sadly, with a last dignity, before the throne of Osiris. Octavian returned to Rome with the immense treasures of Egypt, to enjoy the triumph I have already described and to await the purple.

The domestic life of Livia and Octavian lost none of its plainness after the attainment of supreme power. Some time after the Senate had (27 B.C.)

strengthened his position by inventing for him the title of "Augustus"--a title by which he is generally, but improperly, described in history after that date[3]--he removed from the small house which his father had left him to a larger mansion, built by the orator Hortensius, on the Palatine. This was burned down in the year 6 B.C., and the citizens built a new palace for Livia and Octavian by public subscription. At the Emperor's command the contribution of each was limited to one *denarius*. If we may trust the archaeologists, it was modest in size, but of admirable taste,

especially in the marble lining of its interior. On one side it looked down, over the steep slope of the hill, on the colonnaded space, the Forum, in which the life of Rome centred. On the other side it faced a group of public buildings, raised by Octavian, which impressed the citizens with his liberality in the public service. The splendid temple of Apollo, the public library and other buildings, adorned with the most exquisite works of art that his provincial expeditions had brought to Rome, stood in fine contrast to his own plain mansion, of which the proudest decoration was the faded wreath over the door--the Victoria Cross of the Roman world--which bore witness that he had saved the life of a citizen.

In this modest palace Livia reared her two children in the finer traditions of the old Republic, while Octavian made the long journeys into the provinces which filled many years after his attainment of power. Livia was no narrow conservative. She took her full share in the decent distractions of patrician life, and, like many other noble women of the period, she built temples and other edifices of more obvious usefulness to the public. A provincial town took the name Liviada in her honour. We have many proofs that she was consulted on public affairs by Octavian, and exercised a discreet and beneficent influence on him.

One of the anecdotes collected by later writers tells that she one day met a group of naked men on the road. It is likely that they were innocent workers or soldiers in the heat, and not the "band of lascivious nobles" which prurient writers have made them out to be. However, Octavian impetuously demanded their heads when she told him, and Livia saved them with the remark that, "in the eyes of a decent woman they were no more offensive than a group of statues." On another occasion she dissuaded Octavian from executing a young noble for conspiracy.

At her suggestion the noble was brought to the

Emperor's private room. When, instead of the merited sentence of death, Cinna received only a kindly admonition, an offer of Octavian's friendship, and further promotion, he was completely disarmed and won. We shall see further proof that the wise and humane counsels of Livia contributed not a little to the peace and prosperity which Rome enjoyed in its golden age.

LIVIA AS CERES

STATUE IN THE LOUVRE

For it was in truth an age of gold in comparison with the previous hundred years and the centuries to come.

The flames of civil war had scorched the Republic time after time. The best soldiers of Rome were dying out; the best leaders were perishing in an ignoble contest of ambitions. Corruption spread, like a cancerous growth, through all ranks of the citizens of Rome, and far into the provinces. The white-robed (*candidati*) seekers of office in the city now relied on the purchase of votes by expert and recognized agents. Hundreds of thousands of the citizens lived parasitically on the State, or on the wealthy men to whom they sold their votes, and from whom they had free food and free entertainments. The loathsome spectacle was seen of vast crowds of strong idle men, boasting of their dignity as citizens of Rome, pressing to the appointed steps for their daily doles of corn. Large numbers of them could hardly earn an occasional coin to buy a cup of wine, a game of dice, or a visit to the *lupanaria* in the Subura.

By means of other agents the wealthy refilled their coffers by extortion in the provinces, and paraded at Rome a luxury that was often as puerile as it was criminal. Rome, once so sober and virile, now shone on the face of the earth like some parasitic flower, of deadly beauty, on the face of a forest.

No man, perhaps, could have saved Rome from destruction, but Octavian did much to clear its veins of the poison, and its chronicle would have run very differently if he had not been succeeded by a Caligula, a Claudius, and a Nero.

He chastised injustice in the provinces, purified the administration of justice at Rome, fought against the growing

practices of artificial sterility and artificial vice, and genially pressed on the senators his own ideal of sober public service. From his mansion on the Palatine he looked down without remorse on the idle chatterers in the Forum, from whom he had withdrawn the power, of which they still boasted, of ruling their spreading empire. Nor were there many, amongst those who looked up to his unpretentious palace on the edge of the cliff, who did not feel that they had gained by the sale of their tarnished democracy.

There was more than literal truth in Octavian's

boast that he had found Rome a city of brick, and had left it a city of marble.

Yet all the augurs and soothsayers of Rome failed to see the swift and terrible issue that would come of this seemingly happy change. Corrupt and repellent as democracy had become, monarchy was presently to exhibit

spectacles which would surpass all the horrors of its civil wars, and outshame the sordid reaches of its avarice. The new race of rulers was to descend so low as to use its imperial power to shatter what remained of old Roman virtue, and to embellish vice with its richest awards.

From the sobriety and public spirit of Octavian we pass quickly to the sombre melancholy of Tiberius, the wanton brutality of Caligula, the impotent sensuality of Claudius, the mincing folly of Nero, and the alternating gluttony and cruelty of Domitian, before we come to the second honest effort to avert the fate of Rome. From the genial virtue of Livia we are led to contemplate the dissolute gaieties of Julia, the cold ambition of Agrippina, the robust vulgarity of Caesonia, the infectious vice of Messalina, and the insipid frippery of Poppaea. Had there been one syllable of truth in the divine messages which augurs and Chaldaeans saw in every movement of nature, not even the beneficent rule of Octavian would have lured men to sacrifice even the effigy of power that remained to them, and that they had lightly sold for a measure of corn and the bloody orgies of the amphitheatre.

CHAPTER II

THE END OF THE GOLDEN AGE

IN tracing the further career of Livia we enter upon the opening acts of the tragedy of the Caesars, and we have to consider carefully if there be any truth in the charge that Livia herself initiated the long series of murders that now make a trail of blood over the annals of Rome. With the coming of the Empire we more rarely find legion pitted against legion in the horrors of civil war, but we have nerveless ambition stooping to the despicable aid of the poisoner, autocracy paralysing the best of the nobility with its murderous suspicions, and folly growing more foolish with the increasing splendour of the imperial house. We already know that the germs of this disease were found in the quiet home of Livia and Octavian on the Palatine. Scribonia had received her letter of divorce a few days after the birth of her daughter Julia. As Livia bore no direct heir to the Emperor, while Julia became the mother of many children, we have at once the promise of a dramatic struggle for the succession. When we further learn that the strain of Imperial blood, which takes its rise in Julia, is thickly tainted with disease, we are prepared for a bloody and unscrupulous conflict. And when we reflect that on this unstable pivot the vast Empire will turn for many generations, we begin to understand the larger tragedy of the fall of Rome.

Let us first glance at the interior of the modest household on the Palatine. Besides Livia and Octavian, with whom we are now familiar, there is Octavia, sister of the Emperor and divorced wife of Mark Antony, a gentle lady with the matronly virtues of the time when a Roman could slay his wife or daughter for irregular conduct.

With her were her children, Marcellus and Marcella, of whom we shall hear much. Then there were Livia's two sons--the elder, Tiberius, a tall, silent, moody youth, with little care to please; the younger, Drusus, a handsome, buoyant, fair-headed boy, threatening the elder's birthright.

Octavian closely watched the education of the boys. He taught them to write on the wax-faced tablets in the fine script on which he prided himself, kept them beside him at table, and drove them in his chariot about public business.

But the most interesting and fateful figure in the group was Julia. Octavian had removed her at an early age from the care of Scribonia, and adopted her in the palace.

She learned to spin and weave, and helped to make the garments of the family, under the severe eyes of Livia and Octavia. The Emperor was charmed with the pretty and lively girl, and would make a second Livia of her.

Knowing well, if only from his own youth, the vice and folly that abounded in those mansions on the hills of Rome, and roared in its dimly-lighted valleys by night, he kept her apart. None of the young fops who drove their

chariots madly out by the Flaminian Gate, and sipped their wine after supper to the prurient jokes of mimes, were suffered to approach her. And, not for the first or last time in history, the veiling of the young eyes had an effect quite contrary to that intended. A Roman girl became a woman at fourteen, a mother at fifteen. At that early age, in the year 25 B.C., Julia was married to her cousin Marcellus, who was then seventeen. Marcellus was so clearly a possible successor to the throne that courtiers hung about him, and taught him the art of princely living. The doors of the hidden world were opened, and the tender eyes of Julia were dazed.

The authorities are careless in chronology, and we may decline to believe that Julia at once entered on the riotous ways which led her to the abyss. Her marriage concerns us in a very different respect. All the writers who adopt the view that Livia was a hard and unscrupulous woman--a view that Tacitus must have taken

from the memoirs of her rival's granddaughter, the Empress Agrippina, which were made public in his time--consider that this marriage of Julia and Marcellus marks the beginning of her career of crime. She is supposed to have been alarmed at the marriage of two direct descendants of Caesar, seeing that she herself had no child by Octavian. Most certainly she was ambitious for her elder son. The boy whom she had clasped to her breast, when she fled along the roads of Campania and through the burning forests of Greece, was now a clever and studious youth, and she wished Octavian to adopt him. Unfortunately, Tiberius was of a moody and solitary nature,

and was easily displaced in Octavian's affection by the handsome and popular Marcellus and the beautiful and witty Julia.

The first cloud appeared in the year 23 B.C. Octavian fell seriously ill, and Livia's hope of securing the succession for her son was troubled by two formidable competitors.

One was Marcellus, the other was Octavian's friend and ablest general, M. V. Agrippa. He was of poor origin, but of commanding ability and character, and was suspected of entertaining a design to restore the Republic. He was married to Marcella, and had some contempt for the spoiled boy, her brother Marcellus--a contempt which Marcellus repaid with petulance and rancour. Octavian recovered, sent Agrippa on an important errand to the East, and made Marcellus AEdile of the city. Marcellus was winning, the eager observers thought, when suddenly he fell seriously ill and died. The death was so opportune for Tiberius that we cannot wonder that a faint whisper of poison went through Rome when his ashes were laid in the lofty marble tower that Octavian had built in the meadows by the Tiber.

But we need not linger over this first charge against Livia. Even Dio, who is no sceptic in regard to rumours which defame Empresses, hesitates to press on us so airy and improbable a myth. It was a hot and pestilential summer, and Marcellus seems to have contracted fever by remaining too long at his post, before going to Baiae on the coast.

The death of Marcellus, far from promoting the cause of Tiberius, brought a more formidable obstacle in his way. Octavian sent for Agrippa, and directed him to divorce Marcella and wed Julia. The general, who was in his forty-second year, thought it immaterial which of the two young princesses shared his bed, and Octavia consented to the divorce of her daughter--as some conjecture, to thwart Livia's design. To the delight of

Octavian the union of robust manhood and amorous young womanhood was fruitful. During the ten years of their marriage Julia gave birth to three sons and two daughters.

Happily unconscious of the tragedies which were to close the careers of these children in his own lifetime, Octavian welcomed them with great enthusiasm. During his whole reign he was engaged in a futile effort to induce or compel the better families of Rome to take a larger share in the peopling of the Empire. When he penalized celibacy, they defeated him by contracting marriages with the intention of seeking an immediate divorce. When he made adultery a public crime, there were noblewomen--few in number, it is true; the facts are often exaggerated--who enrolled themselves on the list of shame, and noblemen who took on the degrading rank of gladiators, in order to escape the penalties. He created a guild of honour for the mothers of at least three children; but the distinction seemed to the ladies of Rome to be an inadequate reward for so onerous an accomplishment, and they scoffed when Livia was enrolled in the guild, though the only child she had conceived of Octavian had never seen the light.

Far greater, however, was the amusement of Rome when Octavian held up Julia as a model of maternity, and ostentatiously fondled her babies in public. A coarse and witty reply that she is said to have made, when some one asked her how it was that all her children so closely resembled her husband, was then circulated in Roman society, and is preserved in Macrobius.[4] Beautiful, lively, and cultivated, the young girl had exchanged with delight the dull homeliness of her father's mansion for the rose-crowned banquets of her new world. Her marriage with Agrippa restrained her gaiety for a time, but her husband was often summoned to distant provinces, and she was left to her dissolute friends. Octavian was curiously blind to her conduct, but when Agrippa was compelled to undertake a lengthy mission in the East, he ordered Julia to accompany him. The journey would not improbably foster her vicious tendencies. There is truth in the old adage that all light came to Europe from the East, but it is hardly less true that darkness came to Rome from the East. Julia would not be ignorant how the ancient Roman puritanism had been corrupted by the introduction of Eastern habits and types--the poisoner, the Chaldaean astrologer, the Syrian dancer, the eunuch, the cultivated Greek slave, the priests of orgiastic Eastern cults. A mind like hers would seek to penetrate the depths from which these types had emerged. In Greece she would find the remains of its perfumed vices lingering at the foot of its decaying monuments. In Antioch there would not be wanting freedwomen to gratify her curiosity in regard to its unnatural excesses and the world-famed license of its groves. In Judaea she was long and splendidly entertained at the court of Herod, a monarch with ten wives and concubines innumerable.

They returned to Rome in the year 13, and in the

following year Agrippa died of gout, and Julia was free. One of the most surprising features of her wild career--one that would make us hesitate to admit

the charges against her, if hesitation were possible--is that Livia was either ignorant of her more serious misdeeds, or unable to convince Octavian of them. Livia would hardly spare her, as Julia was inflaming Octavian's dislike for Tiberius. Refined, sensitive, and studious, the young man avoided the boisterous amusements in which other young patricians spent their ample leisure, and his cold melancholy made him distasteful to them.

One of the Roman writers would have us believe that Julia made love to him during the life of Agrippa, and that she incited Octavian against him in revenge for his rejection of her advances. The story is improbable. We need only suppose that Julia, in speaking of Tiberius, used the disdainful language which was common to her friends. Neither Livia nor Tiberius seems to have

attempted to open the Emperor's eyes to Julia's conduct.

Octavian disliked her luxurious ways, but was blind to her vices, though the names of her lovers were on the lips of all. One day Octavian scolded her for having a crowd of fast young nobles about her, and commended to her the staid example of Livia. She disarmed him with the laughing reply that, when she was old, her companions would be as old as those of the Empress.

One writer says that Octavian compelled her to give up a too sumptuous palace which she occupied. One is

more disposed to believe the story that, when he remonstrated with her for her luxurious ways, she replied

"My father may forget that he is Caesar, but I cannot forget that I am Caesar's daughter."

In spite of their mutual aversion Octavian now ordered Tiberius to marry her. He was already married to

Vipsania, the virtuous and affectionate daughter of Agrippa, and this enforced separation from one whom he loved with an ardour that was fading from Roman marriage, and union with one who contrasted with Vipsania as the wild flaming poppy contrasts with the lily, further soured and embittered him. We may dismiss in a very few

words his relations with the woman who ought to have been the second Empress of Rome. After a few years spent, as a rule, in distant frontier wars, he returned to Rome in the year 6 B.C., to find that his wife had passed the last bounds of decency and Octavian was as blind as ever. In intense disgust, and in spite of his mother's entreaties, he begged the Emperor's permission to spend some years in literary and scientific studies at Rhodes.

Not daring to open the eyes of Octavian to the true character of his daughter, he had to bow to his anger and disdain, and seek consolation in the calm mysteries of the planets and the fine sentiments of Greek tragedians.

JULIA

BUST IN THE MUSEUM CHIARAMONTI

Julia now cast aside the last traces of restraint. A half-dozen of the young nobles of Rome are associated with her in the chronicles, and, gossipy and unreliable as the records are, in this case the issue of the story disposes us to believe the charges. Round such a repute as hers legends were bound to grow, and the conscientious biographer must be reserved in giving details. Dio tells us,

for instance, that she expected her lovers to put crowns, for each success she permitted them to attain, at the foot of the statue of Marsyas--a public statue, at the feet of which Roman lawyers were wont to place a crown when they had won a case. However that may be, it is certain that in the nightly dissipation of Rome, when plebeian offenders sought the darkness of the Milvian Bridge, or wantoned in the taverns and brothels of the Subura, Julia's party was one of the boldest and most conspicuous.

Not content with the riotous supper, which it was now the fashion to prolong by lamp-light, in perfumed chambers, until late hours of the night, Julia and her friends went out into the streets, and caroused in the very tribunal in the Forum--the Rostra, a platform decorated with the prows of captured vessels--from which her father made known his Imperial decisions.[5]

The thunder of the Imperial anger scattered this licentious band some time in the second year before Christ.

In the earlier part of the year Octavian had entertained Rome with one of the thrilling spectacles which he often provided. To celebrate the dedication of a new temple of Mars, which he had built, he had the Flaminian Circus flooded, gave the people a mock naval battle, and had thirteen crocodiles slain by the gladiators. Julia had hoodwinked the Emperor so long that she and her friends seem to have abandoned all restraint, and their adventures came to the knowledge of the Emperor.

The charges against Julia must have been beyond

cavil, since Octavian, who loved her deeply, at once yielded her to the course of justice. A charge of conspiracy was made out against her companions. One of

the young nobles killed himself, and the rest were banished.

Julia was convicted of adultery--the evil that her father had fought for ten years--and from the glitter of Rome she was roughly conducted to the barren rock-island of Pandateria (Ponza), in the Gulf of Gaeta. In that narrow and depressing jail, with no female attendants, no wine and no finery, accompanied only by her unhappy mother, the fascinating young princess spent five years, looking with anguish over the blue water toward the faint outline of the hills of Italy, or southward toward those rose-strewn waters of Baiae, where she had dreamed away so many brilliant summers. Rome, touched with pity for the stricken woman, implored Octavian to forgive her; and when he swore that fire and water should meet before he pardoned her, the people naively flung burning torches into the Tiber. Hearing, after a few years, that there was a plot to release her, Octavian had her removed to a more secure prison in Calabria. There she dragged out her miserable life until her father died, and Tiberius came to the throne. When he in turn refused to release her, she sank slowly into the peace of death.

There is no charge against Livia in connexion with this tragic fate of Julia, but another possible rival of Tiberius had disappeared during these years, and there is the usual vague accusation that the Empress assisted the action of nature. Drusus, her younger son, died in the year 9 B.C., and Livia is charged with sacrificing him to her affection for her elder son. The charge is preposterous.

Drusus had, it is true, been much more popular than Tiberius at Rome. His genial and engaging manner gave him a great advantage over the retiring and almost sullen Tiberius. But the brothers loved each other deeply, and when Tiberius, who was making a tour in the north of Gaul, heard that Drusus was dangerously ill in Germany, he at once rode four hundred miles on horseback, and held Drusus in his arms in his last hour.

Livia was at Ticinum, in the north of Italy, with Octavian when the news reached them. That either Livia or Tiberius--for both are accused--should have in any way promoted the death of Drusus is a frivolous suggestion.

The epitomist of Livy, Tacitus, and Suetonius, describe the death as natural. Drusus was thrown and injured by a frantic horse. The libel that his death was in some mysterious way accelerated may have been set afoot by his partisans. It was generally believed that he favoured a restoration of the Republic, and the corrupt officials who, at his death, lost their faint hope of returning to the days of peculation and bribery, may have begun the charge. No evidence is offered for it. Livia and Octavian accompanied the remains to Rome with great sorrow.

Seneca says that the Empress was so distressed that she summoned one of the Stoic philosophers to console her.

The next charge against Livia requires a more careful examination. By the beginning of the present era, when the poor health of Octavian gave occasion for many speculations as to the succession, there were only two rivals to the chances of Tiberius. These were the elder sons of Julia, and Livia must have reflected gloomily on their fortune.

While Tiberius remained in retirement at Rhodes the young princes were idolized by Octavian and by the people.

Tiberius had proposed to return to Rome after the banishment of Julia, but Octavian peevishly told him to remain in Greece. Every astrologer in Rome must have read in the planets that either Caius or Lucius was born to the purple. They were spoiled by Octavian, enriched with premature honours, and, glittering in silver trappings, appeared in the spectacles as "Princes of the youth of Rome." Let those youths be removed from the scene by any accident, and so prurient a city as Rome will be bound to discover some insidious action on the part of Livia; and later writers, brooding over a chronicle in which ambition leads freely to the most brutal murders, will be disposed to believe her guilty.

It is somewhat surprising to find more recent writers caught by the fallacy. We are not puzzled when the scandal-loving Serviez opens his chapter on Livia with a glowing enumeration of her virtues, adopts nearly every libel against her as he proceeds, and closes with a very dark estimate of her character; but we are entitled to expect more discrimination in Merivale. Even Mr. Tarver, in his recent "Tiberius the Tyrant" (1902), does much injustice to the mother in vindicating the son. He speaks of her as "hard, avaricious, and a lover of power," and, without the least evidence--indeed, against all probability--suggests that it was Livia who urged Octavian to keep

Tiberius in retirement at Rhodes. He makes Livia hostile to Tiberius in favour of Julia's sons, on the ground that she would find them more pliant than Tiberius. Every other writer suggests precisely the contrary. They make her murder Julia's sons in the interest of Tiberius.

The death of the younger son, Lucius, is obscure. He was sent on a mission to Spain in the year 2 A.D., and died at Marseilles on the way. Since the only ground for the rumour that he was poisoned is the indubitable fact that he died, we need not delay in considering it. Octavian then sent the elder brother Caius on a mission into Syria under the care of his old tutor Lollius. His counsellor unhappily died in the East, and the young prince was left to the vicious companions who regarded him as the future dispenser of Imperial favours. He fell into

Oriental ways, and was at length (A.D. 3) treacherously wounded by a Syrian patriot.

Instead of returning to Rome, he remained in the unhealthy atmosphere of the East, indulged in its habits of languor and vice, and died eighteen months after the death of his brother. There is no obscurity about his death. It is beyond question that he was severely wounded by a Syrian.

But the deaths of the two brothers happened so opportunely for Tiberius that one cannot wonder at the suspicion, in certain minds, that Livia had had the youths poisoned.

Nothing more than this vague rumour is given us by Tacitus, Dio, Suetonius, or Pliny; and it is from a sheer pruriency of romance that later writers, like Serviez, have accepted and emphasized the suspicion recorded in the Roman historians. Not on such slender grounds can we be

asked to sacrifice the conception of Livia's character which is forced on us by the plainer facts of her career.

The youths were delicate; Caius, at least, had undermined his frail constitution by luxury, if not by vice;

and the Roman world harboured death in a hundred

forms.

If we still hesitate to choose between the artifice of Livia and the unaided action of natural causes in this removal of the obstacles to the advancement of Tiberius, we have only to glance at the fate of the rest of Julia's children. The third son, Agrippa, was as robust in body as his brothers were weak, but he was defective in mind and devoid of moral control. His boorish conduct as a boy gave great pain to Livia and Octavia, and his great physical strength broke out in uncontrollable gusts of passion. In his adolescence he readily adopted the worst vices that Rome could teach him, and Octavian was obliged to condemn him to imprisonment and exile. There remained the

two daughters, Julia and Agrippina. The younger, the sanest of Julia's children, lived to intrigue for power, and greatly to embarrass Livia's later years; though we shall find the same tragic fate befalling her after the death of the Empress, who protected her. The elder, Julia, was banished (A.D. 9) for incest, and, like her mother, lacking the courage or virtue to end her shame as the nobler Romans did, she protracted her miserable life for twenty years, her hard lot only alleviated by the charity of Livia.

Fate had removed every possible competitor to the

succession of Tiberius. He returned to Rome, and his judicious and sedulous activity removed the last traces of the Emperor's resentment. Peace returned, after many years of storm, to the mansion on the Palatine. But Octavian had suffered profoundly from those terrible and persistent storms. The Rome of his manhood was gone. All his friends and counsellors had disappeared, and the future of his people filled him with apprehension. The patrician stock was decaying from luxury and vice; the ordinary citizens clamoured for free food and free entertainment with a blind disregard of the laws of national health. He shrank from the public gaze, and leaned affectionately on Livia and Tiberius.

In the year 14 he remained at Rome in the early heat of the summer, and became seriously ill. Livia and Tiberius went down with him to the coast, where he rallied, and some pleasant days were spent on the island of Capreae (Capri), which he had bought. They passed to the mainland, where Tiberius left them, but he was soon recalled by a message from his mother that the Emperor was sinking. On the last morning of his life Octavian dressed with unaccustomed care, and summoned his friends to his bedside. Was Rome tranquil on receiving the news of his dangerous condition? Did they approve of his conduct and accomplishments? They gave him the assurance he desired, and were dismissed. Could they have foreseen the line of rulers who were to stain the purple robe with blood, and load it with shame, for so many decades to come, they would have wept. The last moments were for Livia. He died kissing her, and murmuring: "Be mindful of our marriage, Livia. Farewell." So ended, peacefully, a union that had lasted fifty-two years in a city where divorce was as lightly esteemed as marriage. There can be little serious doubt about the character of the first Empress of Rome.

Livia probably concealed the death of Octavian until Tiberius arrived from Dalmatia. A report was given out that Tiberius arrived in time to receive the last injunctions of the Emperor. This may be doubted without any serious reflection on her character; if, indeed, it was she, and not Tiberius, who spread the report. There were grave fears--well-founded fears, as we shall see--that a plot, in the interest of corruption, had been framed to prevent the succession of Tiberius. In the coolness of the night, so as to avoid the intense heat of August, they bore the remains with great pomp to the capital. There, on a bed of ivory and purple, preceded by wax effigies of Octavian and of earlier rulers of Rome, the body was carried to the temple of Julius, where Tiberius read a funeral oration. The cortege went on to the Field of

Mars, by the Tiber, through lines of black-draped citizens. The pile was fired, and zealous eyes saw the soul of Octavian mount toward heaven in the outward form of an eagle.

Livia, on approved custom, remained by the sacred

ashes for five days, and then returned to face the new life which opened for her. With the especially wild suggestion that she had accelerated the death of her husband we may disdain to concern ourselves. It was owing to her devoted care that the ailing and delicate Octavian had lived to old age. But a second libel in connexion with the death of Octavian must be briefly considered.

The apprehension, or the secret information, of the dying Emperor was correct. No sooner was his death announced than a servant of the imprisoned son of Julia hurried to the coast, and set sail for the island of Planasia, with the intention of bringing Agrippa to Rome as a candidate for the purple. He arrived only to find a bleeding corpse. The centurion in charge had dispatched

Agrippa as soon as the Emperor's death was made known to him.

Who gave the order for this execution? One cannot call it murder, for Agrippa was unfit to be restored to society, and any attempt to raise him to the throne would have been disastrous to Rome. The authorities, as usual, merely give us the rumours that circulated at the time, and leave us to choose between Octavian, Livia, and Tiberius. We can have little difficulty in choosing. It would be so natural for either Octavian or Tiberius to crush the conspiracy by executing Agrippa that the introduction of Livia is superfluous. Most probably Octavian

had left directions with Agrippa's custodian. There is a curious story, in several contradictory versions, but credible in substance, that Octavian in his later years paid a secret visit to Planasia, to see personally what Agrippa's real condition was. Quite the most plausible theory is that, after personal verification of his madness, Octavian felt it best for Rome, and not inhuman to Agrippa, to have him put to death as soon as the question of succession was opened.

We come to the last phase of Livia's career. Tiberius was now a tall, handsome man, though slightly disfigured, with long fair hair and features strangely delicate for one of his exceptional physical strength. A better soldier than his predecessor, and not an inept statesman, he was well enough fitted to wield the power which Octavian had virtually bequeathed to him. But a retiring disposition, an unhappy youth, and long years of study, had made him shrink from the society of any but scholars, and he long hesitated to ascend the throne to which the Senate invited him. We have not good ground to regard this reluctance as feigned. At last he consented, and the critics of Livia would have it that her ambition now passed such bounds as had been set to it by the ability of Octavian. We may freely admit that she looked forward to being closely associated in power with the son whose career she had followed with such devotion and helpfulness. On the other hand, we shall see how advantageous to the State her influence was; the evils that at once begin to darken the life of Rome when Tiberius rejects her counsels will plainly show this. Nor is there any evidence that she sought power from any other motive than the good of the State. She might take pride in what she did, and even exaggerate it, but such a pride is not inconsistent with the view that she was ever gentle, humane,

and generous.

The first searching test of her character occurs a few years after the accession of Tiberius. As the news of the death of Octavian slowly travelled over the Empire, there were mutinous movements among the legions in many

provinces. In Lower Germany, especially, the troops considered that their commander, Germanicus, the nephew of Tiberius, was entitled to the purple, and they asked him to lead them to Rome. He was a handsome, engaging young general, of imperial blood, with moderate ability and much conceit, and had won the regard of the soldiers by visiting the sick and wounded, advancing their pay out of his own purse, and other popular acts. He was married to Julia's daughter, Agrippina, who lived in camp with him. They dressed their little son Caius in soldier's costume, and his quaint appearance in miniature military boots won for him the pet-name Caligula ("Little-boots") by which he is known to history. The legionaries thought that they had with them a model Imperial family, and promised to wrest the throne from Tiberius. Germanicus weakly composed the mutiny--mainly by forging a letter in the name of Tiberius and then treacherously executing the leaders--and endeavoured to cover his blunders by vigorous and rather aimless attacks upon the Germans. Tiberius recalled him to Rome to enjoy a "triumph," and to keep him out of further mischief.

Merivale acknowledges that his conquests were

"wholly visionary," but Germanicus had inherited the charm and popularity of his father, Drusus, and Rome was easily won for him. People streamed out from the gates to meet him, and gazed with awe on his gigantic blue-eyed captives and on the large highly-coloured paintings of his victories in Germany. It was a new source of concern for

Livia and Tiberius, and, to the satisfaction of Livia's critics, the danger ended like all the others.

Germanicus and Agrippina were sent on a mission to the East. Tiberius seems to have had some disdain for his spoiled and conceited nephew, and he was well aware of the interested aims of those who affected to see in him a restorer of the old republican liberty. He chose an older statesman, Cn. Calpurnius Piso, to go out as Governor of Syria, to watch and prudently direct the movements of Germanicus. With Piso was his wife Plancina, an intimate friend of Livia. From these Tiberius and Livia shortly heard exasperating accounts of the progress of Germanicus and Agrippina. Piso found, on calling at Athens, that Germanicus had been flattering the Greeks for their ancient culture, instead of pressing the dominion of Rome.

He made free comments on the young general's conduct, pushed past his galleys, as they dallied in Greek waters, and was hard at work in Syria when Germanicus arrived.

The wives conducted the quarrel with more asperity than their husbands.

Rome had now its party of Germanicus and party of

Tiberius, and the news from the East was heatedly discussed.

Germanicus has gone to Egypt, without asking

the Emperor's permission, and is patronizing the Greek and Egyptian cults, which Tiberius represses, and going about in Greek instead of Roman dress. Piso has had a violent quarrel with Germanicus, and left Syria. And before they have time to discuss this important intelligence there comes a report that Germanicus is dangerously ill; that bones of dead men, half-burnt fragments of sacrificial victims, leaden tablets with the name of Germanicus scrawled on them, and other deadly charms, have been found under the floors and between the walls of his house.

At length the news comes that Germanicus is dead, and that with his last breath he has urged his friends to avenge him. Rome goes into mourning. All the shops are closed, and crowds gather everywhere to discuss this fresh tragedy of the Imperial house. In the middle of the night a rumour spreads that Germanicus is not dead, and people fill the streets with the glare of their torches, and break into the temples. But the fatal news is confirmed, and, when at last Agrippina comes with the golden urn containing his ashes, such mourning is seen as no living man can

remember.

People observed that neither Livia nor Tiberius appeared at the funeral. Livia had no reason to be present, and Tiberius knew that the demonstration was due largely to a spirit of hostility to himself. For the rest, it was merely the feeling of a frivolous people for a handsome and unfortunate youth. But Livia incurred more serious censure

during the trial of Piso which followed. The ex-governor of Syria defended himself resolutely for a day or two, and then, hearing that his wife had deserted him, committed suicide. The anger of the citizens now turned on the wife, Plancina. The Empress, with whom she had been in close communication throughout, begged Tiberius to save her, and he reluctantly checked the prosecution. Livia was, of course, accused of sheltering a murderess. It must be recollected that the accounts of the story are taken in part from the memoirs of Agrippina's daughter, and are coloured with prejudice against Tiberius and his mother. One cannot see anything more serious than indiscretion in Livia's conduct. Her conviction of the innocence of Plancina is intelligible enough, and one can equally understand how she would distrust a trial held at Rome in the inflamed state of public feeling. There is no serious reason to suspect, in the death of Germanicus, the action of any other poison than the tainted atmosphere of the East.

But the interference of Livia annoyed Tiberius, and the ten years that follow are full of differences between mother and son. The Emperor's resentment of his mother's share in public affairs had begun with his reign. Livia had proposed to erect a statue to the memory of Octavian.

Tiberius interfered, and referred her to the Senate for permission. She then proposed to give a commemoratory banquet to the Senators and their wives. Tiberius restricted her to the wives, and entertained the Senators himself. He reduced her escort, frowned on the public honours that were paid to her, and resented her interference in public affairs. On one occasion her friend

Urgulania was summoned for debt, and, presuming on her intimacy with the Empress, treated the process with contempt.

Livia asked Tiberius to quash the proceedings, and he deliberately lingered so much on his way to the Forum that the case was allowed to proceed.

These are a few of the stories which illustrate the want of harmony between them. For this Livia was largely to blame. It was not unnatural that she, who had been so often and so profitably consulted by Octavian, should expect a larger power under the young Emperor, but she failed to take discreet account of the extreme sensitiveness of Tiberius. If a story given in Suetonius is correct, she so far lost her discretion in one of their quarrels as to produce old letters in which Octavian had made bitter reflections on the defects of Tiberius. The fault was not wholly on her side, however. Tiberius was jealous when he contrasted the honour and respect paid to her with the general feeling of reserve and distrust toward himself, and he pleaded the old-fashioned idea of woman's sphere as a pretext to restrain her. He grumbled when he one day found her directing the extinction of a fire, as she had done more than once in Octavian's time, and he was seriously angry when he found that she had placed her name before his on a public inscription.

But we may leave these lesser matters and come to the next tragedy in the Imperial chronicle, the shadow of which darkened Livia's closing years. She had retired from the palace to the house which she had inherited from her first husband, Tiberius Nero. Here she remained a saddened and helpless spectator of the coming disaster.

Tiberius, whom she saw only once more before she died, had become a peevish and gloomy old man. His tall spare frame was bent, his head bald, his face, which had always been disfigured with pimples, now hideous with eczema, or concealed with bandages. His large melancholy eyes so startled people that they believed he could see in the dark. Astrologers and students of the occult gathered about him in the palace he had built on the Palatine, and the way lay open for adventurers.

The two chief aspirants for power were Agrippina, the widow of Germanicus, and Sejanus, Tiberius's favourite general. Julia's younger daughter seems to have concentrated in her person all the masculinity of her family.

"Implacable," as Tacitus says, proud, and ambitious, she added to the gloom that was deepening on the Palatine.

Merivale calls her the "she-wolf." It seems probable that she sought marriage with the aged Tiberius in order to secure power for herself or her son. The only son of the Emperor had been poisoned by Sejanus, as we shall see presently, and her son had a plausible title to inherit the purple. The authorities tell us that Tiberius one day found her in tears, and was entreated, when he asked the reason, to find her a husband. She thought it expedient to forget the supposed share of Tiberius in the death of her husband.

Her innocent manoeuvres were met, however, by the

sinister intrigues of Sejanus, one of the most unscrupulous characters we have yet encountered. Under a cloak of friendliness he was countering her schemes and ruining her house. He had seduced her daughter Livilla, the wife of Tiberius's son Drusus, and had, with her connivance, poisoned the young prince, and kept the secret

from the Emperor for many years. It is said that he then made proposals to Agrippina to unite their ambitions, and, when these were rejected, he determined to destroy her and secure the supreme power for himself. He put his great ability astutely at the service of the Emperor, and once had the good fortune to save his life, by arching his herculean body over Tiberius when the roof of a cave fell on them. It is probable that he inflamed the resentment of Tiberius against his mother, and then used the

estrangement to increase the unpopularity of the Emperor. Scurrilous libels on "the ungrateful son" were current in Rome. These are sometimes attributed to writers in the service of Livia, but it would be a natural part of the scheme of Sejanus to spread them. On one occasion a noble lady, Appuleia Varilia, was charged by the Senate with accusing Tiberius and Livia of incest. Tiberius consulted his mother, and declared to the Senate that they wished to treat the libel with contemptuous

indifference.

To Sejanus also we must, on the authority of Tacitus, attribute a plot against Agrippina, which other writers assign to Tiberius or to Livia. At a banquet in the palace it was noticed that Agrippina, pale and sullen, passed all the dishes untouched. Tiberius at length invited her to eat a fine apple which he chose. Under the eyes of all she handed it to a servant to throw away, and Tiberius not unnaturally complained of her unjust suspicions.

Tacitus, who gives the most credible version of the story, says that the agents of Sejanus had warned her that she was to be poisoned at the banquet, so that she would act in a way that the Emperor would resent.

Tiberius, weary of the violent passions of the capital, now lived chiefly in Campania. It is not improbable that his disfigurement made him sensitive. Rome would not spare the feelings of so unpopular a ruler. It is not at all clear that he shrank from his Imperial duties--Suetonius expressly says that he thought it possible to rule better from the provinces--or that he wished to indulge in the wild debauches which some attribute to him. Probably Sejanus, to secure more power for himself, persuaded him that he could best discharge his duties from a provincial seat.

At this juncture, in the year 29, saddened by the

estrangement from her son, by his helpless surrender to an unscrupulous adventurer, and by the increasing degeneration of Rome, Livia died. She had, by sober living--Pliny adds, by the constant chewing of a sweetmeat containing a certain medicinal root, and by the use of Pucinian wine--attained the great age of eighty-six. She had seen her husband dispel the long horrors of civil war, refresh the Empire, and adorn Rome; and she had felt the gloom and chill of a coming tragedy in her later years. Few of the Empresses have been so differently estimated as Livia. Merivale regards her as "a memorable example of successful artifice, having obtained in succession, by craft if not by crime, every object she could desire in the career of female ambition." He adds: "But she had long survived every genuine attachment she may at any time have inspired, nor has a single voice been raised by posterity to supply the want of honest eulogium in her own day."[6]

The more concentrated research of the biographer has often to reverse the verdict of the historian, and in this case it must acquit Livia of either craft or vice. It is a singular error to say that Livia had no "honest eulogium" in her own day. The Roman Senate is exposed to the disdain of historians for its obsequiousness to the reigning Emperor, yet, at the death of Livia, it sought to honour her memory in spite of the resentment of Tiberius. The Emperor had refused to go to Rome, either to see her before death or to attend her funeral. He gave to Rome an example of silent indifference. Yet he had to use his authority to prevent the Senate from decreeing divine honours to Livia, building an arch to her memory, and declaring her "mother of her country." Dio remarks that the Senators were moved to do these things out of sincere gratitude and respect. Few of the less wealthy members of the Senate had not profited by her generosity.

Their children had been educated, and their daughters had received dowries, from her purse. Her generosity is recognized by all the authorities. Her humanity is made plain by the contents of this chapter.

The adverse estimate of Livia's character is chiefly based on the "Annals" of Tacitus, and it has long been recognized that Tacitus drew his account largely from the memoirs of the younger Agrippina, daughter of the woman who hated Livia. Yet Tacitus adds, when he has recorded the death of Livia: "From this moment the government of Tiberius became a sheer oppressive despotism. While Augusta lived one avenue of escape remained open, for the Emperor was habitually deferent toward his mother, and Sejanus dared not thwart her parental authority; but when this curb was removed, there was nothing to check their further career."[7]

We have seen that Livia had used the same restraining influence on the impetuosity of Octavian. With her died the attribute, or the wise policy, of Imperial clemency, only to be revived by Emperors who adopted that Stoic creed in which she found consolation after the death of her son.

That she was "hard" and "unscrupulous" is entirely at variance with the most authenticated facts of her career.

To say that she was "avaricious" is a sheer absurdity.

She maintained her sober personal habits to the end, and took money only to bestow it on the indigent and worthy, or expend it in raising public buildings. We may grant that she had some ambition, but may claim that it was well for Rome that she had it. She fell into many errors of judgment in her later years, when Roman life was confused by such strong undercurrents of intrigue; but these very errors tend to discredit the notion that she employed a consummate art and strong intelligence in the furthering of her own interests. In a word, it is the vices and follies of later Empresses that have disposed historians to regard her sober virtues as a mere mask.

* * * * *

NOTE

For the guidance of the general reader it is advisable to add a few words on the Latin authorities, whom we now constantly quote. Tacitus, the chief source of our knowledge down to the year 70 A.D., is not only weakened as an historian by the very strength of his morality, but he has too lightly followed the memoirs in which the later Agrippina defamed the rival Imperial family. Suetonius, who takes us as far as Domitian, is no less honest, but he has too genial and indulgent a love of anecdotes to discard any on the mere ground that they are untrue or improbable. Dio Cassius, who covers the first two centuries, is usually described as malignant; but one may question if he does more than indulge still further the same amiable preference of piquancy to truth. The "Historia Augusta," which is our chief authority for the greater part of the Empresses and the richest source of scandal, has been much and profitably discussed since Gibbon placed such reliance on it. It is now thought by some experts that the original writers of this series of biographical sketches of the Roman Emperors lived at the beginning of the third century, and had a comparatively sober standard of work. Toward the close of the third, or beginning of the fourth, century the work was written afresh by the group of less scrupulous writers whose names, or pseudonyms, actually stand at the head of its chapters. But a still later writer once more recast the work, and lowered its authority. He wrote frankly from the point of view of the piquant anecdotist, omitting much that would interest only the prosy student of exact facts, and filling up the vacant space with such faint legends of Imperial vice or folly as still, in his time, lingered without the pale of history, or arose in the field of romance.

The question is fully discussed by Otto Schultz, "Leben des Kaisers Hadrian" (1905), and Professor Kornemann, "Kaiser Hadrian" (1906).

---

* * * * *

CHAPTER III

THE WIVES OF CALIGULA

THE remainder of the reign of Tiberius does not properly concern us, but a very brief account of it will serve at once to confirm our estimate of the influence of Livia, and to prepare us for the almost incredibly degraded scenes that were witnessed under his successor. We saw that two persons were intriguing for the purple mantle which must soon fall from the shoulders of the aged and unhealthy Emperor. One was a woman of great ability and masculine courage, who sought the succession for one of her sons. The other was a strong soldier and an astute minister, a man of the most unscrupulous and hypocritical character. The change in the form of government had already betrayed its evil. The fate of the vast Empire seemed but a ball tossed from player to player. But the issue was even worse than the most sober observer anticipated. Before Tiberius died both the strong man and the strong woman were to be destroyed, and the Imperial power was to pass to one who was grossly unfit to exercise it.

AGRIPPINA THE ELDER

BUST IN THE MUSEUM CHIARAMONTI

Less than a year after the ashes of Livia had been laid in the marble tower by the Tiber, the Senate received a letter from the court impeaching Agrippina and her two elder sons. According to Tacitus, it was "commonly believed" that this letter had been written some time before, and had been withheld through the influence of Livia. The only reasonable interpretation that we can put on this rumour is that people were so convinced of the humanity of Livia that they did not think the letter would have been written or sent if she were still alive.

However that may be, Agrippina and her sons were put on trial and condemned to exile, in spite of the angry crowds that gathered about the court-house. Agrippina passed with dramatic suddenness from her dream of ruling the world to a dreary exile in Herculaneum, and, after a time, to the far more terrible prison of Pandateria, where her mother had spent four years of agony. There, with all the strength of her proud and ambitious nature, she awaited the death of Tiberius. But the only messages which came over the sea to her gradually broke her spirit.

Her sons, Drusus and Nero, had been convicted of unnatural vice, as well as conspiracy; and although we may entertain some doubt about the conspiracy, the other charge is only too credible when we know the habits of the class to which the youths belonged. Nero was imprisoned on one of the islands of the Ponza group, and it was not long before his mother, on the neighbouring island, heard that he had starved himself, or been starved, to death. After some time she learned that Drusus had followed his example, and the despairing woman refused food in her turn, and went into the kindlier exile of death. The last of Julia's children did not escape the tragic fate which hung over the family.

We have yet to see how the curse falls on the third generation.

Sejanus, whose action we may confidently see in the ruin of Agrippina, now stood near the steps of the throne, waiting impatiently for the passing of the despised Emperor.

He was betrothed to Livilla, the widow of Tiberius's only son Drusus, whom he had poisoned, with Livilla's assistance.

With a consort of Caesarean blood he felt that he could easily fill the place of Tiberius. And in the height of his corrupt power and criminal hope the vengeance of the fates fell on him like a stroke of lightning. It is said that the wife he proposed to divorce disclosed to Tiberius that Sejanus was the murderer of his only son. Within a few hours he was impeached, condemned, and put to death. All who had gathered about him in the hope of his coming power were scattered or destroyed by the frantic anger of Tiberius. Livilla was urged by her mother to bury her shame in the grave. She refused, and was banished. We shall meet her again in the chronicle of vice and violence.

After this terrible ordeal Tiberius withdrew to Capreae, where he had built a palace. Wandering, some years ago, among the ruins of what is believed to have been the palace of Tiberius, I found that the echoes still lingered there of the dark stories which men told in Rome of his later years. Men said that he had shut himself in that sea-girt palace only to indulge, unseen, in the grossest perversions of a sensual nature, and that a new profession of ministers to lust, of which a description may be found in Tacitus, had grown out of his weariness even of unnatural vice.

One does not readily admit such orgies in a man between his seventy-second and seventy-eighth year, and it seems to me that one may offer an explanation of the myth, which will also serve to introduce the third Emperor of Rome and his wives.

Suetonius describes Tiberius as surrounded by learned men and absorbed in obscure problems of astrology, mythology, and letters. The most resolute adherent of the more romantic story must have some difficulty in reconciling this band of prosy pedants with the sensual orgies which popular rumour located in the lonely palace.

When, however, we learn that two young princes of the least intellectual and most immoral character formed part of the household, we see that there may have been two entirely distinct lives sheltered by the palace at Capreae.

If we suppose that these young men and their sycophantic attendants freely indulged in the vices which were then common to Roman youths, while their elders were intent on the glorious planets of a Neapolitan sky, we have a satisfactory explanation of the legend. The horror of Rome at the Emperor's bloody avenging of the murder of his son would not dispose people to discriminate conscientiously.

One of these princes was Herod Agrippa, son of the King of Judaea, whom Octavian had brought to Rome for security. The other, a year younger, was "Caligula," as the soldiers had nicknamed the surviving son of Agrippina and Germanicus. Caius Caesar--to give him his real name--was in his nineteenth year when his mother was banished.

Tiberius a few years later took him to Capreae, where he would prove an apt pupil to Herod in Oriental ways. The vein of moral perversity, if not insanity, which we trace in all the descendants of Julia, is most clearly exhibited in Caligula, and the tragedy of the Caesars deepens when, in the year 37, Tiberius dies, and Caligula is called to the throne.[8]

He had been married in 33 to Junia Claudilla, daughter of Junius Silanus, a proconsul of eminent services and distinguished family. She was happily spared the fate of sharing the throne with Caligula by dying in childbirth.

What her life in Capreae must have been is not obscurely suggested by her early death. No prospect in Europe is more pleasant than that which unfolds its superb and far-lying beauty to the spectator on the green summits of Capri, from which the eye may wander over the broad blue bay, with its silver fringe of surf, or round the crescent of evergreen land that begins with Sorrento, and sweeps majestically, past the foot of Vesuvius, to the distant haze in which Baiae once lived. Yet to a refined and sensitive young woman this splendid palace must have been a deathly jail. Repelled alike by the purblind scholars and the licentious princes, the heavy monotony of learning and vice unrelieved by visits to Rome, she sank under her burden in three years--just missing by one year the title of second Empress of Rome. Her father, a grave and illustrious Senator, endeavoured to check Caligula's extravagance in the first year of his reign. The brutal Emperor bade him "take his greeting to the spirit of the dead." With a last sad glance at the future of his country, Junius Silanus obeyed.

We are credibly told that Caligula then made love to Ennia, wife of the Prefect of the Guard. Sejanus had persuaded Tiberius to form a corps of "Praetorian Guards,"

an Imperial body-guard which was destined to have a disastrous influence on the future of Rome. The actual prefect or commander of this regiment, Macro, was the most powerful person in the suite of Tiberius. With or without his connivance, his wife yielded to Caligula, on the condition that he should marry her when he became Emperor. Macro and Ennia accompanied Caligula when he bore the will and the ashes of Tiberius to Rome. A gloom had settled over Italy during the later years of Tiberius's reign, and men hailed the young Caligula as the sun and the blue sky are hailed after days of dark tempest at sea. Standing by their flower-girt altars, coming out with torches at night, people greeted him with frantic epithets of affection. He was their "star,"

their "chicken," their "dear child," as he had been to the soldiers in Germany years before. Not that he was a handsome youth. His frame was thin and lanky, and his movements awkward. He was prematurely bald, and his sunken eyes looked out with a scowl from his pallid face. But he was the son of Germanicus, the grandson of Julia. All the follies which the family had perpetrated were forgotten.

For a month or two he fulfilled the hope of his people.

The reign of terror was ended at once. He recalled his sisters from exile, and brought to Rome, with great respect, the ashes of his mother and brothers. The circus and the amphitheatre rang once more with the cheers of the populace. The golden age of Octavian had been restored, men said. But the emasculated system and feeble mind of Caligula were unequal to the nervous strain.

Early in his reign Ennia reminded him of his written promise to marry her, and Macro had an air of patronage in advising him. In a sudden blaze of ferocity he ordered Ennia and her children to be executed, and graciously permitted Macro to end his own life. He had found a wife--his sister Drusilla.

His incestuous relation with Drusilla was soon the topic of Rome. It had probably begun before she was banished, and when he recalled her to his palace, a young and beautiful girl of about twenty summers, he conceived a violent passion for her, divorced her from her husband, and announced that he intended to marry her. The Emperor was above all laws, he said. Rome laughed the laughter of fools. He was providing it with stupendous entertainment. The games of the circus ran for twelve hours, day after day, and the night was turned into fresh day with illuminations, banquets, and such pleasures as they could get with the money he freely distributed. In the midst of it all he fell ill; not improbably he was paying with epilepsy the price of his wild excesses. There was such sorrow in Rome as had rarely been felt at the illness of its greatest citizens. Men vowed their lives for the life of the beloved Emperor; and Caligula, when he recovered, saw that they kept their vows. He was ill for many weeks, and, when his strength returned, he had lost the little sanity and sobriety that nature had ever put in his ill-compacted frame. The rest of his reign was a nightmare.

Drusilla died during his illness, or soon after his recovery. Some writers suggest that her malady was a feeling of deep shame, but the description which Dio gives of her does not support this view, nor does the single virtue of remorse seem to be known among the descendants of Julia. The grief of Caligula was no less insane than his passion had been. No illustrious Roman was ever honoured with such pomp of funeral as this woman, whose incestuous life he cried over the world. A Senator saw her soul mount to heaven from the burning pile, and was rewarded with a million sesterces. The degraded Senate declared her a goddess, and it was decreed that henceforward women should swear by the divinity of Drusilla. Earth and heaven resounded with his demented moans; and even before Drusilla was put among the gods he had married again.

Livia Orestilla, the second Empress of Rome, is one of those ladies who are known to us only in the familiar phrase, that she was a young woman of great beauty and illustrious family. In her case we need no ampler portrait, as she was Empress only for a few days. Before the end of the first year of his reign (37), and in the midst of his lamentation over Drusilla, Caligula was invited to the wedding of Calpurnius Piso, a noble of rank and wealth. Caligula fancied the bride, and at once made her his Empress. With equal license he divorced her a few days afterwards, and she learned what it was to fall from the height of a throne. He forbade her to have any commerce with the husband of whom he had robbed her, and then, alleging that his order had been disregarded, banished both of them to remote and distinct parts of the Empire.

The next lady on whom his unbridled imagination rested was Lollia Paulina. Caligula was probably more attracted by her wealth than by the remarkable beauty, the high character, and the distinguished ancestry which the chronicles ascribe to her. The rich spoils of conquered provinces had accumulated in her family, and her husband, the Governor of Macedonia and Achaia, was industriously adding to their wealth. People told at Rome that she once went to a marriage-supper in pearls and emeralds that were valued at fifty million sesterces. Her high virtue seems to have been consistent with a display that made her a topic of table-talk, and that brought upon her a lamentable fate. Caligula, piqued by the stories of her wealth and beauty, ordered her husband to bring her to Rome, and she was soon afterwards established in his palace as the third Empress of Rome. Within a year Caligula divorced her on the ground that she gave no promise of perpetuating his line.

It is often said that Caligula had only married her for the purpose of seizing her fortune, as his prodigal expenditure was rapidly emptying the treasury. This seems to be an error, as we shall find her in the next chapter incurring a miserable fate on account of her immense wealth. The truth was that Caligula had in the meantime discovered a lady whose temper wholly suited his own, and of whose fertility he was actually assured.

In the spring or early summer of the year 39 we find him perpetrating one of his stupendous acts of folly at Baiae. He was accustomed, in the warmer weather, to cruise about the coast of Campania with his wife and suite.

He had two great Liburnian galleys built, each with ten banks of oars, their prows blazing with gold and jewels, their decks adorned with vines, colonnades, and divers freaks of irresponsible wealth. As they cruised by the bay, some one reminded him of an old proverb which spoke of riding from Baiae to Puteoli, across an arm of the bay, as one of the most certain impossibilities. At once he ordered a bridge to be built across the water and elaborately decorated. In what was supposed to be the armour of Alexander the Great, over which was thrown a mantle of purple silk, the conqueror of impossibilities rode from Baiae to Puteoli. On the following day he drove his chariot across; and far into the night, the hills around being lit up with immense fires, he carried the debauch which celebrated his glorious feat. In their intoxication numbers reeled from the bridge into the scented waters.

Eager for fresh victories, he transferred his delirious court to Gaul, and declared that he was proceeding against the fierce Germans. The tribes were not in revolt, and the whole expedition was a comedy; some of the Roman writers say that a few tame captives were conveyed across the river and hunted, so that the Emperor might truthfully inform the Senate that he had gained a victory and merited a triumph. Suetonius even adds that, when he did eventually return to Rome and celebrate his triumph, a few slaves were forced to learn a little German and dye their hair, to pose as conquered tribesmen before his chariot. In the meantime, events which concern us more closely were happening at Lyons.

The extravagance of Caligula was rapidly emptying the treasury. In twelve months he spent 2,700 million sesterces.

His baths were of the most precious ointments; his banquets were especially designed to waste money--one alone cost PS80,000, in modern coinage--and, when the flow was not fast enough, he drank pearls dissolved in vinegar, and had gold fashioned in the shape of food and served to his guests. He disdainfully swept the palaces of Octavian and Tiberius, with other mansions, from the Palatine, and erected a palace of extraordinary proportions and barbaric splendour. Such habits drew about him a crowd of ignoble parasites, and one can well believe that he had discovered a conspiracy against him at Lyons. He had prostituted the honour of Rome in a manner so childish and base that few could be unmoved. Observing the wealth of the Gauls--for Lugdunum (Lyons) was then the centre of a prosperous and cultivated region--he began to sell to them the possessions of the Imperial house. He was present at the auction, and the proceeds were so satisfactory that he sent to Rome for wagon-loads of furniture, heirlooms, and curios from the Imperial palaces, and, as they were offered for sale, pointed out himself the historical value of each object.

In his suite was the first husband of his sister Drusilla.

This distinguished noble, Lepidus, may have exchanged views on the insanity of the Emperor with the disgusted Gauls. At all events, Caligula sent word to the Senate that he had discovered a plot against his life, and added that his sisters, Livilla and Agrippina, had been convicted of adultery with Lepidus. He put Lepidus to death, and compelled Agrippina, a proud and spirited young princess, to carry on foot to Rome the urn containing the ashes of her alleged lover. We shall see how, on his return to Rome, Caligula made atonement to vice for this drastic punishment of adultery. In fact, he already had a mistress in the Court at Lyons, and this lady now displaces Lollia Paulina, and becomes the fourth Empress of Rome.

Milonia Caesonia is one of the oddest figures in the very varied gallery through which our story conducts us. Julia and Messalina are imperial in their vices. Caesonia, whose vices are so little discussed, stands entirely apart from the other Empresses--at least of the first century. Wholly destitute of character or culture, already worn with the bearing of three children, she seems to have won and retained the fancy--one cannot call it affection or regard--of Caligula by a handsome figure, a robust masculinity, and an entire lack of refinement. He often exhibited her nude to his friends, and encouraged her to dress as an Amazon and ride her horse before the army. His disordered mind puzzled at times over the charm by which she held him.

He would stroke her strong white throat, and murmur pleasantly that at one word from him the knife of the executioner would sink into it; and he would sometimes, with the same brutal humour, threaten to have her tortured, in order to discover what philtre she secretly administered to him. She had much tact and no scruples. Their daughter Drusilla was born on the day of their marriage, according to Suetonius, or thirty days afterwards, according to more credible authorities. As the child grew, it showed the temper of a wild cat. Caligula watched its frenzies with delight, as it screamed and bit its nurse; there was, he said, no room for doubt about the paternity.

With such a spouse, and with his favourite courtesan Pyrallis, whom also he had established in his new palace, Caligula indulged his insane impulses without the least restraint. Within a few months of inflicting so terrible a punishment on his sister, he was giving imperial lessons in incest and adultery. So low had much of the Roman nobility fallen that no sword was drawn on the Emperor, or employed on its possessor, when he concluded his banquets with a command of promiscuous intercourse to the men and women of patrician rank whom he entertained.

Nor were his excesses confined within the walls of his palace, and known only by uncertain rumour. He developed a passion for driving chariots, and frequented the company of grooms and gladiators. Rome genially applauded, since it implied more and longer shows in the circus and amphitheatre. The struggles of the different factions in the races--of whom Caligula supported the Greens--more than ever enlivened the dull days of an idle populace. Caligula forced nobles to exercise the base and dangerous profession of the gladiator, and to drive chariots before the mob in the circus.

But the amusement of Rome reached its height when Caligula, in the year 39, discovered his divinity. Other Emperors were content to leave it to the flattery of their people to detect a divinity in them after their very human careers were over. "I am turning into a god," said one of them ironically, as he died. Caligula believed that his splendour was already divine. Vitellius, a contemptible courtier, father of the later Emperor, shrewdly borrowed the idea from Oriental monarchs, and suggested it to Caligula. Then were witnessed scenes in Rome which even the wildest extravagances of Nero cannot rival. Its citizens had, at the peril of their lives, to restrain their laughter, and bend in respectful worship, when the slim, ungraceful youth--he was yet only in his twenty-seventh year--with the weariness of dissipation on his pale face, trod their streets in the garments of Jove, with a beard of gold thread, or marched past them with the bow and quiver and golden halo of Apollo, or dressed to the more congenial part of Venus. A machine was made by which he could, in a puerile way, imitate the thunder of the rival god; and he ordered the heads to be struck off the statues of the Greek deities and replaced by copies of his own.

A deity must have a cult. Caligula appointed himself and his horse, for which he provided a marble palace and an ivory manger, the high priests of his cult. Caesonia was associated in the priesthood, and the position of ordinary priest of the cult was sold to various nobles at the price of eight million sesterces each. Poor men were forced to ruin themselves and put an end to their lives; wealthier men meekly posed as the ministers of a divinity who gorged himself with food and wine at each meal, and resorted to the vomit that he might return to the table.

How long nature would have suffered this madness to debase the fallen city one cannot tell, but the exhaustion of the treasury now led Caligula to do things which roused a few Romans from their lethargy. He repeated in Rome the auctions he had held at Lyons, and many stories are told of his brutal irresponsibility. The truth of these stories is always doubtful, but one may be quoted as an illustration of the popular feeling. It is said that a Senator fell asleep during one of the sales.

Caligula malignantly called the auctioneer's attention to the fact that the sleeping man was nodding at every bid, and the Senator awoke to find that he had bought thirteen gladiators and other property at fabulous prices. Caligula even stood at his palace door to receive gifts, pleading that the addition to his family had impoverished him.

He then discovered a new source of funds in the execution of the wealthier nobles. Brutal and sanguinary from the first, his growing madness and his delight in gladiatorial shows fostered his cruelty. He had an actor burned alive in the Forum for venturing even to hint, in an ambiguous phrase, that the Imperial behaviour was reprehensible. Others he had tortured and executed in his presence, in order that he might enjoy the sensation of seeing them suffer. But it was mainly in quest of money to maintain his terrible expenditure that he stooped to the lowest excesses. No man of wealth in Rome was safe. Informers were eager for the fourth part of a victim's property, to which they were entitled after a successful impeachment; Caligula hungered for the remaining three-fourths.

Every ten days he would "clear his accounts,"

as he put it, or doom to death any wealthy Senators whom he had chosen to put on his list of suspects. He would return from the court boasting to Caesonia of the heavy work he had done while she slept. A great terror brooded over the city, and men talked of the Emperor in whispers.

Omens and signs multiplied. The statue of Jupiter Olympus had been brought to Rome, and one day the workmen rushed in alarm from the temple in which it was placed, crying that the marble god had burst into a fit of laughter.

On January 24th, in the year 41, this appalling gloom came to an end, and the third Emperor and fourth Empress of Rome were justly removed. The long hesitation of the Romans must not too readily be ascribed to cowardice.

The Praetorian Guards were now encamped at the edge of the city, and were richly paid for personal loyalty to the Emperor; so that there was very faint hope of a successful rising of the citizens. For the greater part these formidable soldiers were mercenaries, caring nothing for the honour of Rome, faithful as dogs to the liberal master. It was not until an officer of this regiment headed a conspiracy that any action could be taken with a prospect of success. This officer was a favourite of Caligula, but the Imperial friendship was expressed in such coarse and stinging epithets that he was driven to rebel. He and his associates determined to assassinate Caligula when he attended the Palatine games in the later part of January. A large wooden theatre had been erected for the occasion, and Caligula presided with delight at the repulsive spectacles. Such was the popular enthusiasm that the conspirators surrounded Caligula day after day without daring to touch him. His German guard, insensible to the grievances of the Romans, would at once and blindly oppose a rising, and the people seemed to have forgotten his tyranny in the blood-reeking show he had provided for them.

They came to the fifth and final day of the games.

Caligula was unwell, and wished to remain in the palace, but he was persuaded to make an effort to attend the final performance. Before a vast audience the actors represented the crucifixion of a band of robbers, and the stage was washed with blood. The chief actor of the time had a trick of pouring blood from his mouth, and the other actors clumsily imitated him. When it was over, Caligula, elated with the wild applause of the citizens, entered the narrow passage which led from the theatre to his house on the Palatine. The conspirators seized their last chance, and fell upon the Emperor with their swords. Within a few hours Rome so far changed that it was the turn of the partisans of Caligula to tremble. His body was removed and stealthily buried by Herod Agrippa.

Caesonia seems to have remained in, or preceded Caligula to, the palace, with her little daughter. There the cries of the guard and the noisy confusion in the palace would soon announce the disaster to her. She had no time to escape, or devise any policy. A centurion rushed to her room and stabbed her to death. Her infant was roughly seized by a soldier, and its brain was shattered on the walls of the palace, where the brief infamies of its father and mother had degraded the civilization of Rome.

CHAPTER IV

VALERIA MESSALINA

THE fall of Caesonia was hardly less romantic than the succession to her position of the woman who is known to every reader of Roman history, and to many others, as Messalina. When Caligula entered the narrow passage leading to the Palatine, after the performance in the theatre, a few members of his suite walked before him. One of these was his uncle Claudius, a slow-witted and despised man, in his fiftieth year, whom Caligula had rescued from humiliation and put in office. He had already entered the palace when the raucous cries of the German guard and the flash of weapons informed him of the assassination of the Emperor. The guards were cutting down such of the conspirators as they could reach. In instinctive terror Claudius hid behind a curtain, nor was he reassured when he saw the soldiers pass with the heads of the nobles they had slain. Presently a soldier of the Praetorian Guard noticed his feet below the curtain, and drew him out. Claudius fell to the ground in terror, and implored them to spare his life. The soldiers had recognized him, however. They put him in a litter, and carried him on their shoulders to the camp. Citizens whom they passed in the street pitied the harmless and, as was generally believed, half-witted prince. At last some one learned, or divined, the purpose of the guards, and Claudius awoke from his terror to hear the strange cry of "Salve, Imperator," and realized that he was to be made Emperor of Rome.

He had been married three years before to Valeria Messalina, who thus became the fifth Empress. As the youngest son of Drusus, brother of Tiberius, and Antonia, daughter of Mark Antony and Octavia, he was the natural heir to Caligula. The Imperial power was in no sense hereditary, but the attachment of the Praetorian Guards to the ruling family, and their irresistible domination over Rome, for some time ensured a kind of hereditary succession. There had, however, been no deliberate proposal to put Claudius on the throne. While the future of the Empire was being determined by the rough mercenaries in the Praetorian camp, where Claudius promised a substantial largess for his elevation, the Senate was actually discussing the question of restoring the Republic. Somewhat deformed in person, clumsy in gait and corpulent, stuttering in speech, deficient at least in the power of expression, Claudius had always been regarded as a negligible offshoot of the Julian stock. His mother had spoken of him as "a little monster," Octavian had genially treated him as half-witted, and, when he arrived at early manhood, Tiberius had refused to give him any rank or office. Caligula, however, had given him consular rank, and promoted him in the palace, though he treated his uncle with the brutal jocularity which his mental infirmity was held to justify.

We shall see that this treatment was far from just, for Claudius had some excellent qualities; but the disdain of his family threw him upon the society of his servants, and led him to seek consolation in the pleasures of the table and the dice-board. He had in early youth been betrothed to a daughter of Julia. This contract was dissolved when Julia's vices were discovered, and he was married to a young lady of distinguished and wealthy family, Livia Medullina Camilla. She died on the wedding-day, and he married Plautia Urgulanilla, a daughter of the Empress Livia's intimate friend, Urgulania. Suspecting, after a few years, that her friendship with his emancipated-slave friends was warmer than he intended, he divorced her, and married AElia Paetina, who in turn was shortly divorced.

In the year 38 he married the notorious Valeria Messalina, whose name conveys to every student of history or morals a summary impression of the worst features of the early Empire. The spirit of our time is so resolutely bent on visiting the sins of the children on their fathers--so determined to seek the secret of character in heredity--that the older biographical practice of drawing out

genealogies cannot be entirely abandoned; though one may wonder whether the tainted atmosphere of Rome may not have been more deadly than a tainted stock. It is enough to say that both her parents were of the Julian family, and were first cousins of Claudius. Her father, Valerius Messala Barbatus, was a Senator of distinction.

He is known to us as the Senator who, in the old Roman spirit, made a futile effort to restrain women from invading public life and the camp. Her mother has a less reputable record. We shall see that she eventually falls under a charge of conspiracy and magic; but we may find that her more serious offence was an intense hatred of the Empress Agrippina, who brought the charge against her.

Messalina, as we may now briefly call her--with a passing protest against that uncouth expression, "the Messaline"--was in her sixteenth year at the time of her marriage. An indulgent imagination will be able to appreciate the dangerous situation of the young girl.

Entering, in her teens, a world of the most seductive pleasure and the utmost license, with so responsive and impulsive a nature as she had, she needed the guidance of a man whom she could at least respect. Instead of this, she found herself mated to a man of forty-eight years, whose full paunch and long thin legs and tremulous head were the jest of the Palatine, and who spent his hours in the company of Greek freedmen, or in too prolonged an enjoyment of rich dishes and costly wines. Claudius, it is true, adored her, but his adoration only made him the surer dupe of her craving for indulgence. Her misconduct probably began early. When, after the evening meal, she left her spouse intoxicated and snoring over the emptied dishes, when his throat had been tickled with a feather, so that he might disgorge and return to the Imperial dainties, the young girl would naturally yield to the counsels of the unscrupulous courtiers who abounded in such a palace.

The path to the abyss was made smoother for her by her husband's reliance on his freedmen. In the later years of the Republic, when the dominion of Rome was extended over the East, the practice had grown of employing the more accomplished slaves of Greece and Syria in the patrician palaces. Equally expert at keeping accounts or pandering to vice, they won their emancipation and acquired large fortunes in the service of their new masters.

They were usually regarded with disdain, but, as we saw, Claudius had been driven to associate familiarly with them, and they attained great power when he ascended the throne. Rome now discovered a new evil in the Imperial rule it had adopted. All who wished to approach the Emperor with a petition had to flatter or bribe the freedman Callistus, to whom this part of Claudius's duties was entrusted. His steward of finances, Pallas, his secretary, Narcissus, and his adviser in letters, Polybius, stood at one or other avenue of the palace, and exacted toll of all who approached. Offices were distributed through their avaricious hands, and it was soon noticed that they built magnificent villas in the neighbourhood of Rome. Whether the rumour was true or not, it was believed in Rome that some of the noblest ladies paid an ignominious price to these men for the favours they sought, or were surrendered to them by the Empress.

It is at all events clear that Messalina soon came to an understanding with them. Both they and she needed to dupe the purblind Emperor, and it was felt that a friendly co-operation would be better than a precarious contest for supremacy.

Before the end of the first year of Claudius's reign this corrupt collusion began to show its influence. Claudius had begun well. He set to work at once to redress the injustice and follies of Caligula. A general amnesty was granted, the courts of justice were purified, the administration was opened to the abler provincials, and the public funds were expended on public works of solid usefulness.

How far the freedmen were responsible for these measures it is difficult to say, but it seems that we must grant Claudius, not only good will, but some quality of judgment.

At the same time, there is evidence from the first of some infirmity of mind. His work as a judge seems to have been more remarkable for industry than enlightenment. On one occasion an angry knight (*eques*) threw books at him in the court-house; on another, during a shortage of corn, the people pelted him with mouldy crusts in the Forum.

Humane he was, apparently, in those early months, but he does not seem to have shaken off his earlier repute and exhibited any personal dignity.

It was not long before even his humanity was warped by the malignant persuasions of his wife and the corrupt connivance of his freedmen. In our age of apologists there has been some effort to relieve the character of Messalina from its heavy burden of infamy, or at least to discredit the evidence adduced for it. I have already said enough about the Roman authorities to justify one in making some reserve in regard to the details transmitted to us about Messalina. When we read Tacitus we have to remember that he had before him the memoirs of her bitter enemy and successor, Agrippina. When we read Suetonius and Dio and later writers we must not forget their love of vivid colours and romantic details. Yet these writers had in their time official records, and something like public journals, belonging to the earlier period, which put the malignant and unscrupulous action of Messalina beyond question; of the less startling stories of her infidelities we have proof enough in the remarkable and authentic episode which will close her career. It cannot reasonably be doubted that the traditional estimate of the character of Messalina is substantially just, though we must use some discretion in admitting particular statements about her.

With this reserve we may follow, in fair chronological order, the career of this young girl of nineteen, who is dazed by the sudden attainment of Imperial wealth and power, until, in her twenty-fifth year, her childish efforts to pierce her bosom with a dagger are ended by the manly thrust of a soldier's sword. She had borne a daughter, Octavia, before the accession of her husband, and she was far advanced in child-bearing when Caligula was assassinated.

Claudius, unable to believe his good fortune,

expecting daily that some fresh movement would dislodge him from the throne, kept in the palace with her. A month after his accession she bore a son, Tiberius Claudius Germanicus (later known as Britannicus), and Claudius ventured out, to exhibit his heir to the people and express his joy. He never entirely lost his fear. Soldiers served him at table, and all who approached him were searched.

But his clement and comparatively enlightened rule won him some popularity, his gluttony and weak wit were genially overlooked, and he gave promise of a prosperous reign.

The first indication of the evil of his feeble dependence on Messalina and the freedmen occurred before the end of the year 41. Claudius had recalled from exile Caligula's sisters, Julia Livilla and Agrippina, and restored their property. Agrippina, whose character and career will occupy the next chapter, was in her twenty-fifth year, Livilla in her twenty-third. Both had the beauty of the Julian women in its ripest development. Agrippina quickly realized her situation and discreetly concealed her ambition, but the younger woman was too proud to be diplomatic, and she was suspected of an ambition which she possibly did not entertain. Messalina became jealous, and denounced her to Claudius for adultery. Claudius was persuaded that an open trial would entail scandal on the Imperial family, and the unfortunate woman was exiled without the chance of defence. She was starved to death in her prison shortly afterwards, and, when the further course of this story has been read, one will hardly hesitate to accept the assurance of the chroniclers that this grave crime was committed by the orders of Messalina.

That the charge against Livilla was malignant cannot be doubted when we learn that her lover was said to be the famous Stoic moralist, Seneca.

The disease of Rome had already evoked a natural remedy. The austere code of morals which Zeno had formulated some centuries earlier in the marble colonnade at Athens was now adopted by the best of the Romans. Pointing to the enfeeblement and degradation which this epidemic of Eastern vice and luxury had brought on their city, the philosophers argued that the curb must be placed once more on sensual impulse, and the old virility of Rome restored. Seneca was the most distinguished representative of this growing school at Rome, and, ambiguous
or even reprehensible as his conduct may seem to us at a later stage, we should in this case prefer to attribute his punishment to the known vice of Messalina rather than to a frailty on his part of which we have no indication.

The wise and just counsel that he gave to Claudius was probably distasteful to Messalina and the freedmen.

Without trial or defence he was banished to Corsica. It is sometimes said that, as Seneca nowhere impeaches the virtue of Messalina, we may distrust the charge of vice against her which we find in all the later chroniclers; but Seneca also fails to refer to her greater and quite indisputable misdeeds, so that the omission has no significance.

Seneca remained in exile six years, and had no
more personal knowledge than Suetonius of the debauches of Messalina.

Her first success emboldened the Empress. Within a few months she selected another lady, Julia, the daughter of Drusus, and denounced her to Claudius. Such virtue or discernment as Claudius may have possessed was now attenuated by the sensual excesses in which his wife and his ministers encouraged him to indulge, and his humanity was contaminated by the passion for gladiatorial displays which he gradually contracted. We must not too hastily admit the lowest estimate of his powers. If Octavian could be so long and so easily duped by Julia, we may admit that Claudius's ignorance was consistent with some measure of good sense, which he still displayed in provincial administration and the accomplishment of public works. But from the end of the first year of his reign he lends himself so basely and ignobly to the schemes of Messalina that it is impossible to defend him. No sooner did his wife accuse Julia than she was banished, without trial, and it is easy to believe that her speedy death at the hands of the centurion in charge of her was due to the orders of Messalina. It was said that Julia had excited the Empress's suspicions by too tender a regard for Claudius.

The more prudent Agrippina now sought the protection of a husband. She is said to have chosen the future Emperor, Sulpicius Galba, and urged him to divorce his ailing wife; but the wife's mother took her part, and ended the intrigue by boxing Agrippina's ears in public.

The wife died soon afterwards, but Galba feared the resentment of Messalina too much to wed Agrippina.

She then induced Crispus Passienus, a wealthy and distinguished noble and a famous orator, to divorce his wife

and marry her. She had inherited a moderate fortune from an earlier husband--the father of her son, the future Emperor Nero--and the great wealth and distinction of Passienus put her in a much stronger position. Passienus died soon afterwards, leaving his fortune to Agrippina and Nero. How the fortune was used for the advancement of mother and son, and how Agrippina was

eventually murdered by her son, will be told in the next chapter. Serviez repeats without hesitation a rumour, lightly reproduced in one of the chronicles, that she murdered Passienus to secure the wealth. The charge is of the most frivolous character. Her husband had afforded her some protection: a fortune without a husband would rather attract than divert the passion of Messalina.

The year 42 was marked by a conspiracy that unhappily disposed Claudius more than ever to confide in

Messalina and the freedmen. The troops in Dalmatia were to be employed in the dethronement of Claudius.

At the last moment, however, the soldiers were startled by so many and such undeniable signs of the anger of the gods that they returned to their loyalty and slew their officers. The standards could not be dragged out of the ground--a not unnatural event, one would think, in a Dalmatian winter--and the wreaths had fallen from the eagles.

The plot was reported to the palace, and Messalina and the freedmen drew up long lists of men whom it was desirable to remove or despoil. Wealthier men redeemed their lives by paying considerable sums; others were put to the torture, or were consigned to prison or the grave.

A story is told in the record of this persecution which should guard us from admitting the common fallacy that the older spirit of Rome was quite extinct. A distinguished patrician heard that his name was on the list

of the condemned. His wife urged him to escape the ignominy of a public execution by ending his own life, and, when he hesitated, she buried the dagger in her own bosom, and then handed it to him with the words, worthy of a Corneille: "It does not hurt." Another victim was Appius Silanus, who had married Messalina's mother, Domitia Lepida. The chroniclers say that his crime was to have rejected the advances which Messalina made to him. Whatever the motive was, she induced the freedman Narcissus to tell Claudius that he saw, in a dream, Silanus thrusting a dagger into the Emperor's heart.

Claudius nervously consulted his wife, who confessed, with artistic horror, that the same dream had frequently tormented her. They had meantime summoned Silanus to the palace, and, as he entered at that moment, the Emperor ordered him to be executed at once.

Such are a few of the dark crimes attributed to Messalina that we cannot seriously question, and that fully prepare us to believe the less inhuman misdeeds which it might otherwise be possible to doubt. In the following year (A.D. 43) Claudius went to Britain, leaving his Empress at Rome. It seems to have been at this time that, unless we are arbitrarily to set aside one group of charges in the records and admit another, Messalina indulged in the practices which have secured for her an unenviable immortality. The perfectly authentic sequel of the story will show that she had so extraordinary a disregard for even the pretence of moral feeling that the statements of the chroniclers cannot for a moment be set down as improbable.

In a word, Messalina surpassed Caligula both

in her own misconduct and in the propagation of vice.

Envying the trade of the lowest women of Rome, she had one of the rooms at the palace equipped on the model of the chambers of the *meretrices* in the tenements of the Subura, put over the door the name of one of the most notorious women of that caste, Lycisca, and offered the lascivious embrace of an Empress to any who cared to pay the price for which she stipulated. Others place the scene in an actual brothel. Not content with her own abasement, she compelled the most distinguished ladies of Rome to follow her example. She bestowed the honours and offices, which Claudius left at her disposal, on the husbands who would complacently witness the defilement of their wives, and offered the alternative of her deadly lists to those who refused. Uncertain as we must always be whether these statements are not mere exaggerations of her conduct in the popular mind of the time, they are consistent enough with the accredited facts of her career.

In the year 44 Claudius returned with joy to what he still regarded as the chaste and tender arms of his young Empress. So lively was his esteem of her virtue that he obtained from the Senate permission for her to ride in the ceremonious car (*carpentum*), an honour which was restricted to the priestly rank and rigorously forbidden to women. He granted her, also, the signal distinction of riding in his chariot on the day of his triumphal procession.

The ease with which she duped him led her to fresh excesses. It is said that when she saw his wine-soaked body laid to bed at night, she placed one of her maids with him, and went with the companions of her debauches. If we may believe a story which has no inherent improbability, and has some confirmation later, she made the

blind Emperor himself purvey to her vices. She one day complained to Claudius that the popular actor, Mnester, would not obey her when she commanded him to leave the stage and enter her private service. Claudius forced him to do so; and three years later, when Messalina's conduct was exposed, Mnester exhibited to the Emperor the scars on his body which gave proof of Messalina's brutal familiarity. Even when she used the bronze coinage of Caligula, which had been withdrawn from circulation, to make a statue to Mnester, Claudius suspected nothing.

This licentious conduct continued until the year 47.

Messalina was only in her twenty-fifth year when her long impunity led her to take the step which ruined her. A bust of her that is preserved at Florence, and a cameo at Vienna, give a representation of her that we have no inclination to distrust. The curly golden-yellow hair--Juvenal tells us its colour--is elaborately dressed over the low forehead, and the large deep-set eyes are abnormally close. There is some irregularity in the undeniable beauty of the face; and the thin lips and small mouth, drooping weakly at the corners, would irresistibly suggest a record of adventure, if such a story were not assigned to her in the chronicles of the time. With that record before us it is, no doubt, easy for physiognomists to detect a moral distortion in the features, and to discover unknown, as well as verify the known, vices of the Empress in the truthful marble. Yet any thoughtful observer will be disposed to see in those pitiless lineaments a revelation of the truth about Messalina and her race. It is a picture of strength worn to decay by reiterated storms of passion, of beauty fading with the disease which foreruns death.

MESSALINA

BUST IN THE UFFIZI PALACE, FLORENCE

One last crime must be added to the record of Messalina before we come to the crowning folly of her career. There remained one woman in Rome more beautiful than she; and one distinguished patrician whose virtue rebuked her, and whose wealth allured her. She resolved to bury the two under a common ruin.

Valerius Asiaticus, a patrician of consular rank and great merit, had withdrawn from Rome to Crete as the madness of Messalina and the blindness of Claudius increased. Unhappily for him, he owned the beautiful and famous garden which Lucullus had laid out on the summit of the Pincian Hill, and Messalina was now eager for it. She employed the tutors of her children to declare to the Emperor that Asiaticus was at the head of an important faction at Rome, and had gone to fire the Eastern provinces with his rebellious spirit. The omens which were reported from the East seemed to Claudius to make mere human testimony superfluous. The moon had been darkened by an eclipse, and a new island had risen from the AEgaean Sea. The Chaldaean sages interpreted these signs with their customary art, and Asiaticus was brought to Rome.

He listened in disdain to the charge of conspiracy and adultery which the tutors, Sosibius and Suillius, brought against him, but, when they proceeded to accuse him of unnatural vice, he broke into an angry denial of the whole accusation. Messalina was present at the trial--a wholly irregular proceeding, in Claudius's chamber--and saw that the Emperor was moved. She whispered to Vitellius, the sycophant who had first discovered Caligula's divinity and shaded his eyes from the blaze, that Asiaticus must on no account escape, and left the room. Vitellius, with ready wit, fell at the feet of the Emperor. He enlarged at length on the great merits of the accused, and concluded with an artful plea that Claudius would grant Asiaticus the favour of being allowed to take his own life, instead of handing him over to the public executioner. Easily confused by this stratagem, and fancying that he was showing some clemency, Claudius assented. Asiaticus, true to the finest traditions of his fathers, returned to his palace, bathed and supped in perfect tranquillity, and then opened his veins. Messalina secured the gardens of Lucullus.

The lady with whom Asiaticus is said to have offended was Poppaea Sabina, the only woman in Rome who surpassed Messalina in beauty. That would be quite enough to arouse the jealousy of Messalina, but we are told that she had the still greater mortification of believing that Poppaea was too intimate with the actor Mnester, whom the Empress had appropriated. The daughter of Poppaea will presently come before our eyes in the gallery of Roman Empresses, and, if we may infer from her conduct the nature of her mother's precepts and example, we cannot set aside the charge as improbable. There is, however, no need for us to discuss it. No sooner was Asiaticus condemned than Messalina sent the news to Poppaea, and she put an end to her own life. Sosibius received a million sesterces, in the form of a special reward for his service in instructing the young princes; and other ministers to the cruelty, avarice, and passion of the Empress were richly endowed.

Messalina now ventured upon so flagrant a violation, not merely of decency, but of the moderate discretion that had hitherto concealed her conduct from her husband, that her career of infamy was brought to a violent close. She had for some time entertained and indulged a passion for Caius Silius, one of the most handsome men among the Roman nobility. Tacitus assures us that there was no secrecy in the amour. She persuaded Silius to divorce his wife, visited his house with a large retinue, and made him repeated gifts of slaves and other property belonging to the Imperial house. An obscure passage in Tacitus seems to imply that her impatience of all laws led her to form the design of marrying Silius while married to Claudius, and the details of what immediately followed have come down to us in contradictory versions. It is said by some that Silius proposed to her to remove Claudius and share the throne with him, and that she hesitated only from fear that Silius might divorce her as soon as he had secured the purple. Other writers say that the phoenix appeared in Egypt, as it had done before the death of Tiberius, and that the nervous Emperor was further told of a prediction that the husband of Messalina would die before the end of the year.

In order to cheat this decree of the fates, Suetonius says, Claudius signed the divorce of Messalina, and went down to the coast, leaving her free to marry Silius. He intended to return and recover her as soon as Silius had fulfilled the prophecy by dying.

It is clear that a good deal of legend has mingled with the true account of the events which led to Messalina's downfall, and one can merely try to construct a plausible story out of the discordant versions. Tacitus, the highest authority, knows nothing of the prophecy, or the divorce which it is said to have occasioned. His silence is not conclusive, and the course attributed to Claudius, however extravagant it may seem, is not inconsistent with his abnormally timorous nature. On the whole, however, one is disposed to agree with Merivale, that Claudius heard of no prophecy, signed no divorce, and knew nothing of the liaison until a later stage, as Dio implies. But Merivale is plainly wrong in suggesting that the marriage of Messalina and Silius is a libellous legend borrowed from Agrippina's memoirs. When he submits that such a marriage could not have taken place without the Emperor's knowledge, he forgets that, as all the authorities state or imply, Claudius had left Rome and gone down to the coast. The Emperor returned to the city as soon as he heard of the marriage.

The real course of events seems to be that Claudius was vaguely informed of the existence of a conspiracy against him. He complained bitterly to the Senate, confined himself for some time to the palace, and then, in October, went to Ostia to inspect certain public works which were in progress there. Delighted at his removal, Messalina went through the form of marriage--the laxer, not the more solemn, form (*confarreatio*)--with Silius, and cast aside the last shade of reserve. Base as her nature was, she must have been weary of the nightly spectacle of the repulsive old man sinking back in satiety on his couch, while slaves tickled his throat with a feather to induce a vomit. Silius was young, handsome, and not without wit. A better future seemed to open before her.

Perhaps the slow-witted Emperor would make no struggle for his throne; perhaps the city and the guards would gladly sacrifice him for this handsome young Imperial pair.

There is calculation in the carven face of Messalina. But the news was speeding to Ostia, and the dreadful end was near.

Shortly after the marriage came the festival of the vintage, the Bacchanalia, which was celebrated by the bride and bridegroom and their friends with the wildest merriment.

That last scene in the licentious career of Messalina must have made a deep impression on the feeling of Rome, and it is lit up for ever by one of Tacitus's most vivid flashes of description. Messalina had bestowed on Silius the Imperial palace and its contents, and in the garden of the palace they paid full honour to the orgiastic cult of Bacchus. Wine-presses were set up, and the women of Messalina's company, their white limbs and bosoms scantily covered with strips of fawn skin, sang and danced the Bacchic dance round the large vats of grape-juice.

Messalina, her golden hair flowing loose under her ivy wreath, shook her thyrsus and led the wild dance. Silius lay at her feet, crowned with ivy, nodding his head to the air of the lascivious chorus. Wine flowed freely on that autumn afternoon, and the gay world and distant Ostia were forgotten; or so little heeded that when Vettius Valens, one of Messalina's discarded lovers, had, in boyish exuberance, climbed a high tree, and they crowded round and asked what he saw, he gaily cried: "A hurricane from Ostia." But before the evening was out the hurricane came from Ostia and scattered the revellers in terror. News was brought to the garden that Claudius was hurrying to Rome to avenge his dishonour.

The freedman Narcissus had disliked the idea of Silius obtaining power, especially as Messalina had recently taken the ominous step of securing the execution of his colleague Polybius. In the suite of Claudius at Ostia were two female attendants, to describe them courteously, Calpurnia and Cleopatra, who were taken into counsel by Narcissus, and learned their parts in his scheme. Calpurnia flung herself at the feet of the Emperor, crying, "Messalina is married to Silius." Cleopatra and Narcissus were summoned by the Emperor, and they assured him that his life was in danger, and he must hasten to Rome.

Other advisers, who had been trained to their part by Narcissus, were drawn into the group, and the dazed and vacillating Claudius yielded to their guidance. He was at once placed in his chariot, and Vitellius and Narcissus rode with him. Claudius feebly discussed the news as they travelled, and Vitellius, not sure which party would triumph, remained silent; but the freedman assiduously fed the slow-kindling anger of the Emperor.

Silius had fled from the Bacchanalian garden to the Forum, and tried to conceal his part by a zealous absorption in business. Messalina saw all the companions of her revels fly for safety, and leave her to face the storm alone in the palace-garden. From the disordered relics of the feast she hurried to her Lucullan gardens on the Pincian. There her courage seems to have revived, and she determined to make an effort to disarm her husband.

Directing the head of the Vestal Virgins to follow with her children, she went out upon the road which entered Rome from Ostia. The news had now spread over Rome.

With three companions only out of the gay throng of her followers, and Vibidia, the Vestal Virgin, whose person was sacred, she braved the pitiless gaze of the citizens, who had so long seen her chariot flash by in triumph, and walked on foot to the gate of the city. There her strength failed, and she was forced to mount the common cart of a gardener. When they had covered a short distance from the gates, they saw the Emperor's chariot approaching, and she dismounted. Whether from real affection for her, or from an indolent dislike of trouble, Claudius hesitated once more when the piteous figure of his young wife appeared in his path; but Narcissus reminded him of her marriage, and ordered the charioteer to drive on.

Her last despairing appeal was unheeded. The chariot galloped on, and left her standing on the road. A little further on the Vestal Virgin, relying on her high position, demanded that Claudius should grant his wife an opportunity of defending herself, and thrust his children before him. The sight of his beloved Octavia and Britannicus again moved the wavering Emperor. Narcissus bade the charioteer drive onward, and Messalina slowly turned to meet her fate in Rome.

In order to dispel the last shade of tenderness from the Emperor's mind, Narcissus conducted him first to the house of Silius, and showed him the treasures of the Imperial palace which Messalina had showered on her lover. He then led him to the camp of the Praetorian Guards, and induced him to make a speech to the soldiers.

The feeble spirit of the Emperor was cowed by the full revelation of Messalina's perfidy. Now completely docile to the masterful freedman, he took his place at the tribunal, and passed sentence of death, which was at once carried out, on Silius, Mnester, Vettius Valens, and all Messalina's accomplices. Mnester vainly stripped off his robe, to show that he had received from the Empress rather the imprint of her anger than the embraces of which he was accused. The Emperor signed the doom of all, and returned wearily to the palace. Restored by food and wine, he began to resist the dictation of Narcissus, and ordered him to inform Messalina that he would hear her on the morrow. The freedman knew that a delay would ruin his design. He left the room, and told the guard that the Emperor had commanded the immediate execution of his wife.

Messalina had returned to her garden on the Pincian, where she was joined by her mother. Night had come on, and they sat in an arbour debating the mad brilliance of the past and the terrible gloom of the future. Domitia Lepida felt that there was no hope of recovering the favour of Claudius, and urged her daughter to end her life as Roman tradition prescribed. Strong only in her clinging to life, like most of the other frail women of the Julian house, Messalina fell at her mother's feet and sobbed.

Presently the stillness of the deserted garden was broken by the tramp of soldiers and a summons at the gate. Still Messalina shrank from the eternal darkness which she had so suddenly confronted. Only when the officer of the guard told her the order that Narcissus had given him, and the freedman who had come with the guard began insolently to revile her for her crimes, did she take the dagger from her mother's hands. In the light of the single lamp of the arbour the little group looked on with pity and disdain, as the nerveless hands of Messalina lacerated her white bosom with futile gashes. Then the tribune mercifully drove his sword through her heart.

Her children came up, and found their mother's lifeless body in a pool of blood.

This authentic closing of the career of Messalina must dispose us to think that there may be little or no exaggeration in the stories that are told of her. Stahr, in his brilliant apologetic study of the Empresses, ventures to say that Seneca did not reproduce these stories about Messalina because he knew that they came from the pen of an embittered libeller; and it is safe to assume that Tacitus did derive much of his material from the memoirs of the woman who had shrunk from the vindictive cruelty of Messalina, and came in time to replace her. But so much crime is authoritatively laid to the account of the Empress, and her last adventure reveals so shameless a disregard of either law or decency, that not a single detail is incredible or improbable. We shall find such excesses ascribed to later Emperors, by writers who were not merely recording rumours that may have gathered volume during decades of passage from mouth to mouth, that nothing can be deemed impossible to a Messalina. The humane biographer can but plead that she entered a world of the most dazzling allurement of vice and crime with a nature already tainted and distorted by the sins of her fathers, and that the horror of that last scene in the gardens of Lucullus may be left as a merciful shroud over her unhappy memory.

CHAPTER V

THE MOTHER OF NERO

TACITUS has given us a spirited picture of life in the Imperial palace during the months which followed the execution of Messalina. Claudius himself had sunk into a state of drowsy indifference when the storm excited by his discovery had spent itself. "Where is the Empress?" he asked, as he sat at supper the night after her death, and noticed the empty place on the couch.

Narcissus told him that she was dead, and he asked no more. But the palace about his slumbering figure soon began to hum with conflicting intrigues for the succession to her chamber. Ladies who had visited the Palatine with nervous prudence while Messalina lived now came to display their charms, and express their tenderness, to the doting Emperor. From the sombre night of the tragedy Rome passed with relief to the light enjoyment of the new comedy. The freedmen, who surrounded and controlled Claudius, selected their candidates.

Claudius had inserted one sentiment of his own in the speech which Narcissus had induced him to make to the Praetorian Guards. He had sworn that he would not marry again. There were ladies in his household, such as Calpurnia and Cleopatra, who would encourage the resolution; but the freedmen decided that he was bound to capitulate under so fair a siege, and it would be better to have some share in the making of the new Empress.

Each of the Greeks chose a different lady. Narcissus, who had been promoted to high public service for his zeal, favoured the suit of AElia Paetina, whom Claudius had lightly divorced twenty-one years before. Callistus took up the cause of Lollia Paulina, the wealthy and beautiful woman whom Caligula had torn from her husband and used so unjustly. The steward, Pallas, was more fortunate in his choice. He advocated marriage with Agrippina; and, as the mind of Agrippina coincided more decisively with that of her champion than seems to have happened in the case of her rivals, his campaign succeeded. She discovered a most tender and considerate affection for her uncle, visited him assiduously, and persuaded him to betroth his daughter Octavia to her son Lucius Domitius (later Nero).

Octavia was already betrothed, and Agrippina is said to have removed the first obstacle to her designs by a cruel and unscrupulous act. We are told that she induced, and it is at least clear that she permitted, the sycophantic courtier Vitellius, who favoured her suit, to accuse the young man, to whom Octavia was betrothed, of incest with his daughter-in-law. Tacitus has so mean an estimate of the young people and their generation that he does not regard the charge as a serious libel. He insists, however, that Agrippina had the case against them forged, and thus opened her dark Imperial career with a crime.

We are now approaching the generation in which the great historian lived, and we are considering the very woman whose memoirs furnished him with his more serious charges against her rivals and predecessors. It may therefore seem strange that, if we are to follow our authorities with docility, we must ascribe a very vicious and unscrupulous character to Agrippina herself. We have rejected the rumour that she poisoned her second husband, but that is by no means the only charge that is brought against her before she married Claudius. The authorities uniformly assert that she had had incestuous relations with Caligula in her early teens, had been notorious for her amours during the life of Messalina, and now very flagrantly placed such honour as she had at the disposal of Claudius. These charges we cannot control. We shall find even more serious accusations against her later, and shall have to regard them with reserve or frank incredulity. It was the literary fashion to make a consort of the Caesars imperial in her vices. On the whole, however, we are compelled to think that the eldest daughter of Agrippina and Germanicus had the taint of her stock. She inherited the virile ambition of her mother, and she had even less scruple in pursuing it. The best that can be said for her is that she aimed rather at making the future of her son than her own. And when that son proves to be the Emperor Nero, the murderer of his mother, we are disposed to read her record with the lenient eye of pity.

When the elder Agrippina had been banished by Tiberius, as we saw, in the year 12 A.D., her children were brought up in the house of their grandmother Antonia. In this plain home of old Roman virtue Caligula is said to have infected and corrupted all his sisters. Agrippina left it, in her thirteenth year, to marry Cn. Domitius Ahenobarbus. As the authorities are sharply divided in regard to his character, we cannot trace his influence in the development of her character.

He died in the year 40, leaving her with a three-year-old boy, Lucius Domitius. Agrippina was still a young and beautiful woman, and is said to have availed herself of the loose morals of Roman society until, as we saw, the attitude of Messalina forced her to marry. She was soon a widow for the second time, with considerable wealth. Her ambition revived at the death of Messalina, and she paid the most winning and flagrant attentions to Claudius. We should go beyond the letter of the chronicles if we suggested that she bribed Vitellius and Pallas to promote her suit. It is enough to say that they overcame the reluctance of Claudius, and they profited materially by her accession to the throne.

Claudius professed that he had a scruple about marrying his niece, and proposed to adopt her as his daughter.

That empty honour was hardly recompense enough for the daily contemplation of his senility and sensuality.

Vitellius induced him to submit his delicate feeling to the Senate and the people, and then artfully represented to the Senators that, if Claudius married Agrippina, she might rid them of the hated influence of the freedmen.

Tacitus, whose disdain for the obsequious Senate of the early Empire always aggravates his comments on their conduct, describes how they raced each other to the palace to inform Claudius of their decision, and how the people not improbably incited by Vitellius, assembled below the Palatine Hill and clamoured for the marriage. The obtuse and weak-willed Claudius assented, and a few days later, in the year 49, Agrippina became the sixth Empress of Rome. Little did she dream that she was entering upon the last decade of her eventful life, and that it would close with the most ghastly horror.

She was in her thirty-third year, Claudius in his fifty-eighth.

Years of sensual indulgence had not improved his character or his intelligence, and no one in Rome can have expected him to live more than the few years which remained for him. Agrippina was looking to the time when she would be sole mistress of the Empire.

The fine statue of her which is exhibited in the Lateran Museum has a moral physiognomy so concordant with the authentic record of her career that we picture her to ourselves with confidence. In face and figure she is all that the word imperial suggests to the imagination.

Haughty, strong, and reposeful in her self-reliance, she has lost the last shade of apprehension with the passing of Messalina, and has the majestic air of a mistress of the world. Her low brow and large, finely-carved oval face are said by some physiognomists to have every mark of purity and refinement, but the close observer will discover in her features only such a refinement of passion as her ambition would lead us to expect. In a word, it is the face of a woman who will not stoop to vice or crime to gratify a sensual impulse, but may have recourse to either when her ambition lends it a certain expediency.

AGRIPPINA THE YOUNGER

BUST, MUS. NAZ., NAPLES

The career of Agrippina shows that she really was a moral opportunist of this character. We need not pass any censure on her ambition. Unhappy would be the State in which men and women were not at times fired by the impulse to exert their powers more energetically than their fellows. But it is impossible to ignore the persistent and harmonious statements of the Latin historians in regard to the way in which Agrippina pursued her ambition. We may overlook the amorous adventures of her earlier years; we may reject, as a light and implausible rumour, eagerly caught up by prurient diarists, the charge that she made any dishonourable advances to Claudius before her marriage, or to the steward Pallas or her son Nero at later dates; and we may hesitate to admit that she was concerned in the murder of Claudius. But we cannot find any other motive than a not too nice ambition in her marrying the aged and repulsive Emperor, and we have strong reason to suspect her of conduct that is little short of criminal in many of the events that follow.

The most formidable of her rivals for the throne had been Lollia Paulina. Beautiful, wealthy, and popular, the former wife of Caligula seemed to threaten Agrippina's security. In their eagerness to avoid the rock of hereditary power the Romans had steered their vessel into the Charybdis of intrigue, and any prominent man or woman was regarded with concern by the one who wore the purple, or aspired to wear it. Agrippina had a strong and legitimate hope, but no guarantee, that her son would succeed. Messalina's son, young Britannicus, was ailing and epileptic, and was generally ignored in the speculations as to the succession. It was, therefore, quite natural that Roman gossip should accuse Agrippina of destroying Paulina, and Tacitus is not less generous in recording the charges against her than in admitting her slanders against Livia. He affirms positively that it was the Empress who persuaded Claudius to have Paulina prosecuted on the charge of consulting oracles and astrologers as to the duration of his marriage, and that, when her property was confiscated and she was sent into exile, Agrippina sent a soldier to compel her to commit suicide. Dio, as usual, improves upon the narrative. He describes Agrippina gloating over the bleeding head of her rival, as Fulvia had rejoiced over the head of Cicero, and opening the mouth to see certain peculiarities of the teeth by which it might be identified.

The fatal defect of Dio's more vivid account is that, as we know from Pliny, the double canine teeth, of which he speaks, belonged to Agrippina herself, not to Paulina, and were regarded as a sure presage of good fortune. The substance of the story, however, we cannot lightly reject.

A beautiful and happy woman was driven to death for no graver cause than, at the most, an idle patronage of the Oriental charlatans who then abounded in Rome; and, since this consultation of oracles was common, there must have been a special reason for the selection of Paulina. The motive suggested by Tacitus is only too probable. He adds that Agrippina also banished a lady named Calpurnia.

If we may identify this lady with the Calpurnia whose services to Claudius were so amiable as to embolden her to disclose to him the crimes of his beloved Messalina, she would hardly remain long in the palace of Agrippina.

Apart from such episodes as these, in which jealousy or avarice led her to make an unworthy use of her power, she ruled judiciously and serviceably. Claudius was in his sixtieth year. His poor mind was in complete decay, and it was both fitting and useful that Agrippina should rule in his name. The coinage of the time bears witness of her activity. There is, in fact, a living memorial of her rule in the city of Cologne, which, under the title of Colonia Agrippina, she established as an outpost of civilization on the farthest confines of the Empire. She gave dignity and etiquette to the easy-going court of Claudius, had the right to enter the precincts of the Capitol and to ride in the gilded imperial chariot of ceremony, and, when the famous British prince Caractacus was brought to Rome, her throne was raised by the side of that of the Emperor. The older Roman idea of woman's sphere was now discredited by the philosophers and contemptuously ignored by the women themselves, but the citizens moved slowly, and there was much discontent and consulting of astrologers.

They were expelled from the city, but in the guarded chambers of patrician families they continued, in imposing Chaldaean dress, to scan horoscopes and wave preternatural wands over their symbolical tripods--much as they do in Bond Street to-day. The more enlightened reader, who is disposed to regard the superstition with leniency, must reflect that the prophets might at times, for the vindication of their art, be tempted to lend a little human aid when nature tarried in bringing about the deaths which the planets had so plainly foretold.

Within the palace the whole care of Agrippina was centred in the education of her son for the purple. To the delight of Rome, she recalled the philosopher Seneca from exile, and gave him charge of her son's studies. When the real character of Nero was revealed in later years, it was said that Seneca had always disliked his task, and had even predicted that the boy would become a savage monster.

Seneca himself merely says that the boy was spoiled, and his training thwarted, by his mother. Nero would fly to Agrippina when Seneca had made some attempt to check his wayward impulses, and the whole lesson would be lost in her injudicious caresses. Apart from this not unnatural weakness, Agrippina made the most commendable efforts to prepare her son for the throne. The corrupt tutor whom Messalina had brought to the palace was dismissed--Dio says that he was executed for attempting the life of Lucius Domitius--to make way for the most distinguished moralist of the time, and the military instruction was entrusted to Burrus, whose integrity we shall learn presently. Pallas was rewarded with such honours as no freedmen had ever borne before, and Vitellius was rescued from some obscure charge of conspiracy and restored to his rank.

Agrippina was now in a position of very great wealth and power. She drove about Rome in a superb chariot, flaunted the stored jewels of the Imperial house, and received presents from the ends of the earth. A white nightingale, which had cost 6,000 sesterces, and a talking thrush were amongst the rare presents sent to conciliate her. The lingering of Claudius must have been irksome to her, but it was necessary to secure the succession of her son before the Emperor died. The one apparent obstacle was the boy Britannicus, who, as the son of Claudius and Messalina, had a juster title to be chosen.

He was, however, subject to epileptic fits, delicate in health, and peevish in temper. Agrippina had little difficulty in thrusting him aside in favour of her own handsome and engaging boy. The *toga virilis*, or garment of the man, was usually donned by the Roman youth in his seventeenth year, but the age was anticipated in the case of princes, and Domitius was to receive it at the end of the year 50. During the year, however, the convulsions of nature so plainly portended some momentous event, probably the passage of Claudius to join his divine forerunners, that Agrippina pressed for the immediate performance of the rite. Three suns were seen in the sky, an earthquake shook the solid earth, and birds of evil omen rested on the temple. Claudius assented, and manhood and other high distinctions were prematurely conferred on the future Emperor, whose name was changed to Nero.

He joined the priestly college, received the authority of a proconsul, marched at the head of the guards, and drew the attention of all at the games by the insignia of his manly dignities, while Britannicus sat in the *praetexta* and *bulla* of the boy. It was Nero who pleaded in the Senate for distressed cities, Nero who was made praetor when Claudius was absent from Rome. In the year 52 he was married to Octavia, and all Rome regarded him as the virtual heir to the throne.

There can be no serious doubt that Agrippina had no affection for Claudius, and must have waited impatiently for his removal when the succession was secured for her son. Certainly Rome held that view, and interpreted the events of the succeeding years in accordance with it.

We must therefore be prepared to find much libellous conjecture in the chronicles about this time. Serviez, who can never resist the fascination of scandal, gives us a lively picture of Agrippina stooping to any expedient course of vice or crime in the furtherance of her ambition.

We may have to tell a less romantic story, but it will be romantic enough.

It is clear that the Empress now entered into a conflict with Narcissus, the freedman who had ruined Messalina, and had then favoured the suit of AElia Paetina in opposition to her own. Her critics suggest that she wished to remove this faithful servant in order to attempt the life of the Emperor more easily, but the suggestion is superfluous.

Narcissus had found the rival freedman Pallas raised to such high honours, and felt that his own service in exposing Messalina had been so soon forgotten, that he clearly intrigued against Agrippina. Tacitus says that it was he who spread the rumour, which reached the ears of Claudius, that Agrippina was too intimate with Pallas.

We are quite unable to examine the truth or untruth of this charge, and may dismiss it. Agrippina took an early occasion to attack and discredit the Greek. In the centre of the Italian hills was a sheet of water, the Fucine Lake, which had no regular outlet, and often caused disastrous floods. Claudius ordered that a channel should be made to conduct its superfluous water to the river, and celebrated the opening of it, in the year 52, with a naval battle on the lake. Three thrones were erected: one for the nodding, heavy-paunched Emperor, who had somehow been squeezed into glittering armour, one for Agrippina, in her robes of gold cloth, and one for Nero.

The play did not run smoothly, and Agrippina did not spare Narcissus, who controlled it. The great ships drew up before the Emperor, and the men who were about to risk or lose their lives to entertain him rang out the usual salutation. Forgetting that if he returned the salute he absolved them from their dangerous duty, Claudius hailed them, and they claimed the right to abstain. The Emperor is described by

Suetonius as running alongside the lake, angrily urging them to fight. The battle proceeded, but at the close it was found that the water could not be released, and Narcissus was bitterly assailed. The performance was repeated later, when the works were pronounced complete, but a number of people were drowned, and the quarrel was renewed with spirit. Agrippina suggested that the funds for the undertaking had been diverted; Narcissus foiled the attack with a charge of ambition against the Empress.

The Emperor was visibly failing, and there was great excitement at Rome when, at the beginning of the year 54, nature announced once more that some stirring chapter was to run from the reel of the fates. The standards and tents of the soldiers were enveloped in mysterious flames; a rain of blood, in which a modern naturalist would doubtless discover an innocent microbe, spread terror over one part of the Empire, and the birth of a pig with claws like those of a hawk caused equal consternation in another; while Rome heard, with reiterated shocks, that the doors of the temple of Jupiter had been opened by unseen hands, and a horrible comet, followed by the customary pestilence, had appeared in its skies. More significant still to prudent people, perhaps, was the report that Claudius, returning to dine at the palace after presiding at the trial of an adultress, gloomily observed that he had been unfortunate in his marriages; he had punished one unfaithful wife, and would know how to deal with another.

In this observation of Claudius we need see no more than an echo of the whispers of Narcissus, but one can imagine how Rome must have throbbed with expectation and abounded in gossip at the beginning of the year 54.

Nor was this faith in natural oracles disappointed. Two tragedies were added to the sombre chronicle of the city in that year, and in both of them our Empress is accused of having acted criminally.

The first was the condemnation to death of one of the greatest ladies of Rome, Domitia Lepida, sister-in-law of the Empress; and in this case there is every reason to suspect a guilty action on the part of Agrippina. When Agrippina had been exiled by Caligula, her boy had lived for a few years with his father's sister, Domitia Lepida, the mother of Messalina. Lepida was far more indulgent even than Agrippina to the pretty and wayward child, and, when the mother returned to Rome and he was restored to her, there was an acrimonious struggle between the two women for his affection. As it became clear that he would inherit the purple, the struggle became more passionate. Narcissus saw in it an opportunity to escape the ruin which would befall him if Agrippina obtained full power, and, on the ground of his charge of inconstancy against the Empress, he urged Claudius to make Lepida guardian of Nero. It is very probable that this intrigue of Narcissus is the only source of the charge of license brought against the Empress in her mature years.

Angry and anxious, in view of the expected death of Claudius, she took a bold step, and impeached Lepida of criminal conduct. How far Lepida was guilty we cannot say, but as she was charged only with assailing the Emperor's marriage with imprecations, and exercising so little control over her Calabrian slaves as to endanger the public peace, the prudent reader will acquit Agrippina of anything more than an exaggeration of the facts. That exaggeration sufficed, however, to ruin her distinguished rival. Nero, schooled by his mother, gave witness that his aunt had tried to alienate his affection; her very natural comments on the Emperor's marriage were made to assume the dark form of magical imprecations; she was condemned to death.

But those lively convulsions of nature had portended something more momentous than the death of a noble matron, and Rome continued to wait for the great tragedy.

Before long it was announced that Narcissus had retired to Sinuessa for the treatment of his gout.[9] The Emperor was now entirely surrounded by adherents of Agrippina, and we can quite understand the conviction of Rome when Claudius was taken seriously ill at a banquet, and died within twenty-four hours. Tacitus emphatically attributes his death to his wife. Suetonius alone says that, while it was certain that Claudius was poisoned, it was not certain who was guilty; a feeble reserve, since Agrippina was so predominantly interested in his death.

It is not surprising that recent historians have generally followed Tacitus. Roergas de Serviez, who rarely has such ample authority for the crimes he loves to attribute, fastens the murder on Agrippina without the least hesitation.

Merivale sees no ground to question it, though he points out several inconsistencies in the pages of Tacitus.

Mr. Henderson follows the traditional story in his recent and discriminating study of the reign of Nero.[10] But Mr.

Baring-Gould insists that the death of Claudius was quite natural, and any candid student of the evidence must admit that it is inconclusive.

The facts are that on October 12th, A.D. 54, Claudius attended a banquet of the priestly college with Agrippina.

After eating some mushrooms (or figs, according to others) from a dish that was served, he became violently ill and vomited. He was taken back to the palace, attended by his (and Agrippina's) physician, but gradually sank, and died on the morning of the 13th. The theory of the opponents of Agrippina is that she employed a notorious poisoner, Locusta--a Gaulish woman, who was certainly in Rome at the time, and was afterwards employed by Nero--to concoct a slow poison ("a drug that would disturb his mind and inflict a slow death," says Tacitus).

This is supposed to have been inserted in a fine mushroom (or fig), which was taken by Claudius when Agrippina had eaten one from the dish to encourage him. He fell back and began to vomit, and the theory runs that Agrippina, fearing that he might recover and suspect her, called in the physician Xenophon, a dependent of hers, who tickled the Emperor's throat with a poisoned feather and made an end of him.

Mr. Baring-Gould points out that, since Tacitus expressly describes the poison as "slow," Agrippina could hardly be surprised and alarmed when it did not take immediate effect. He concludes that Claudius contracted a violent indigestion from eating too many figs. This is no more convincing than the opposite theory. An attack of vomiting, whether from a natural cause or as an unintended effect of poison, might easily alarm Claudius, who was very suspicious, and so induce Agrippina to act.

An attack of indigestion, on the other hand, would hardly have so violent and immediate an effect. The circumstance of tickling his throat with a feather to cause a vomit, and at the same time introducing poison, is puzzling; but it was an age of skill in poisoning, and the feat may have been possible. The question must remain open. The discrepancies in the narrative are not fatal to it, but the story itself is no more than a retailing of Roman gossip, which was at all times more prurient than scrupulous.

The problem really turns on the character of Agrippina, and this is ambiguous enough to make us hesitate. One may scan the record of her career with the most penetrating charity without discovering any plain indication of high character, while the ruin of Lollia Paulina, Domitia Lepida, and others, may be confidently traced to her. We can only conclude that she was quite capable of accelerating the death of her husband, and would have no light interest in doing so; but the circumstances of his death are quite consistent with the kindlier view that it was due to his own intemperance. We have not yet, however, reached the close of her career, and it may be felt that her conduct after the death of Claudius confirms the darker estimate of her character.

The malcontents of Rome would be sure to agitate in favour of Britannicus unless the succession was secured for Nero before the death of Claudius was known. The art with which Agrippina averted this danger may excite our admiration of her virility and astuteness, but must inevitably lessen our appreciation of her sensibility. She announced that Claudius was dangerously ill, and called an assembly of the Senate. Conscious that the servants of a palace commonly draw their pay from some one without, she put guards at every approach to the chamber of the dead man, and devised and carried out a tragi-comedy of the most extraordinary character. The clothes were drawn over the lifeless body, bandages and poultices were ostentatiously applied to it by her servants, and even the mimes, who had been wont to dance and ring their bells and crack their jokes before the Emperor, were brought in to perpetrate their follies in the chamber of death. In a neighbouring room Agrippina joined her conjugal sobs with the laments of the youthful Britannicus.

We are asked to believe, and we have little difficulty in believing, that while she clung in tears to the weeping youth, she was merely, with cold calculation, preventing him from leaving the palace, lest he should fall in the way of the Guards, or some ambitious partisan, and be proclaimed Emperor.

By noon the preparations of her agents were completed.

The gates of the palace were thrown open, and Nero was sent out, under the care of his military tutor Burrus, the commander of the Guards. A few voices were heard to mutter the name of Britannicus, but the cry was feeble, and the response insignificant. The Guards were long accustomed to see the superiority of Nero over the sickly young prince, and their support was secured by a liberal promise of money. They conducted Nero to the Senate, and bade that helpless body accept him.

The same evening a courier from Agrippina brought word to Sinuessa that Nero was Emperor. Narcissus had lost, and his figure passes from the scene--with the inevitable rumour that he was imprisoned or poisoned by Agrippina.

When the Guards came to Nero that night for the watchword he gave them "The best of mothers," and Agrippina looked confidently from her supreme height into the future. Within five years her son would put her to death with horrible brutality, and jeer at her naked body. No one of the hundreds of thousands who hailed him with the wildest delight, and smiled at his amiable irregularities, can have foreseen so rapid and portentous a degradation. He was then a youth of seventeen, strikingly handsome both in face and figure, with blue-grey eyes and light curly hair and finely proportioned limbs.

His tutor in arms pronounced him "a young Apollo."

But his moral and intellectual trainer had failed as signally as his physical trainer had succeeded. Seneca had vainly endeavoured to implant in his mind the germs of the noble Stoic philosophy. Men have disputed from all time whether it was the teacher or the doctrine that was at fault, while the eugenic school of our time would relieve both from censure, and regard Nero's mind as an incurably corrupt soil. One may venture to differ from both, and wonder if circumstances had not the greater share in his demoralization. However that may be, his accession to irresponsible power at such an age, in such surroundings as we shall discover about him, was a tragedy.

His real advisers were young men, slightly older than himself, and better versed in the ways of luxury and vice; and the first use he made of his Imperial power was to toss aside the treatises of the moralists, and give his whole attention to art, to chariot-racing, and to dissipation.

What sinister use he made of the later hours, or earlier hours, of the day, and in what melancholy condition his girl-wife must have been, we shall see in the next chapter.

Here we have to consider only his relations with his mother.

For a few years after Nero's accession his mother willingly and profitably ruled in his name. It must not be imagined that she had, with the astuteness of a Marie de' Medici, educated him in an indifference to politics so that she might indulge her own ambition. The appointment of Seneca as his tutor is the most creditable, though unhappily the most futile, act of her career. When, however, the young Emperor refused to be interested in any problem graver than the art of driving a chariot or playing the flute, she undertook his Imperial duties, or continued to have that share in the ruling of the Empire which she had had under Claudius. She received embassies, was surrounded by a special German guard when she went abroad, and was associated with Nero on the coinage. It would be difficult to measure with any precision the influence which she had on Roman affairs during this period, since Seneca and Burrus had an equal, if not greater, part in the government; but it may be recalled, with some honour to her, that the first four years of Nero's reign were amongst the happiest and most prosperous that Rome witnessed during the first century.

The first thing to trouble her prosperous and happy use of power was a certain discontent arising from the old prejudice against women in politics. The Senators were annoyed because she injudiciously listened to their debates.

They met at this time in the Imperial library, and the Empress had a door pierced into it from the palace, and sat listening behind a curtain. The Senators are said to have punished her indiscretion by making unflattering remarks in the course of the debates, though it is difficult to believe that they were still capable of so courageous a protest. On one occasion an important embassy came to Rome from Armenia, and Agrippina declared that she would sit by the side of Nero when he received it. This seems to have been a startling innovation, and Seneca had to avert trouble by advising Nero to descend from his throne, when his mother entered, and lead her affectionately from the room.

An incident that shortly occurred gave a nucleus for the crystallization of this diffused annoyance. A distinguished noble, Junius Silanus, died, and the familiar whisper of foul play went once more through all classes of the citizens.

His brother Lucius Silanus was the young noble who had been betrothed to Octavia, and had so cruelly been separated from her by Agrippina. Was it not natural that Junius Silanus should wish to avenge his younger brother, and that Agrippina should detect his plot and have him removed? Tacitus and Dio fully believed this.

As in so many of these cases, however, the only ground for the charge, as far as we know, is the fact that Silanus undoubtedly died, and we will not waste time in discussing it. The Senator had so little of the conspirator in him that even Caligula used to call him "the golden sheep."

But Rome was convinced that the Empress was guilty, and the story spread, and is fully accepted by Tacitus, that she meditated a long series of executions of the men who had opposed her progress, and that Seneca and Burrus had to restrain her bloody vindictiveness.

One may decline to accept this charge on such poor and disputable evidence; but Agrippina now incurred the anger of her son, and descended rapidly from the height of her power. The young Emperor had, as I said, used his Imperial license to ignore his tutors and indulge his low and sensual tastes. He attracted to his side a band of the most dissipated youths in the city, and his nightly exploits were the talk of Rome. One of the less hurtful of his indulgences was his passion for Acte, a beautiful freed slave from the Eastern market, whom Dumas has made familiar. Agrippina resented the liaison--apparently from a sense of justice to Octavia--and rebuked Nero. He turned on her with violence the moment she tried to check his licentious ways, and threatened to discharge her favourite Pallas. Agrippina was alarmed. She saw a powerful party, deeply hostile to herself, growing up about her son, and she felt that the support of Seneca and Burrus was being withdrawn. She ceased to speak of Acte, and regarded with silent distress the coarse ways that her son was exhibiting on the streets every night. A reconciliation at this heavy price could not last. Shortly afterwards Nero sent her some rich jewels and robes from the Imperial treasures. She chose to regard this as a reminder that the Imperial wardrobe was no longer at her disposal, and angrily refused the gifts.

Pallas was at once impeached for treason. The charge was so clumsy, and Seneca defended him so ably, that he had to be acquitted; but Agrippina forgot discretion in her victory. In the course of a quarrel with Nero, she threatened to retire to the camp of the Praetorian Guard with Britannicus and have him proclaimed Emperor. The only effect of this was to open Nero's long career of crime.

The few months--we are still at the beginning of the year 55--of unrestrained license and flattery had destroyed the little moral restraint that Seneca had taught him, and he determined to murder Britannicus. In the Roman prison was the skilled poisoner, Locusta, whom Agrippina was believed to have employed in the murder of her husband. Nero ordered her to prepare a deadly poison, and, when the first preparation failed, he had her brought to the palace. With blows and oaths he forced her to prepare a more deadly drug under his eyes, and it was used the same evening. Britannicus sat with his friends on one of the couches in the dining-hall at the palace, and asked for a drink. It was winter-time, and the wine (not soup, as Serviez says) was heated. He complained that it was too hot, and the poison was administered with the cooling water, so that the taster would not need to take a second sip.

A great horror fell upon the room as Britannicus, writhing with pain, sank to the floor. Octavia sat in silent terror by the side of her husband, who carelessly observed that Britannicus had one of his usual epileptic fits. Agrippina openly betrayed her horror and disgust, and from that date was regarded by her son with bitter hostility. Whether or no it be true that Nero whitened with chalk the spots which broke out on the body, the substance of the story cannot be discredited. It is true that Nero was yet in his eighteenth year only, but his conduct had been vicious and unbridled to a criminal extent. Within a very short time we shall find him sinking to the lowest depths of brutality.

The fact that he is praised in the treatise "On Clemency,"

which Seneca wrote about that time, can only show either that the too indulgent tutor refused to believe the crime, or that, as we have too many reasons to know, the distinguished Stoic came perilously close to that art of casuistry in which moralists of many schools have been apt to excel.

In her abhorrence of the foul deed Agrippina drew closer to the tender and virtuous Octavia, and confronted Nero with a sternness that had been too long delayed.

The breach between them widened. One day Nero ordered that two and a half million denarii should be given to his favourite secretary. Agrippina had the mass of coin brought under the eyes of the Emperor, to make him realize his extravagance. He laughingly observed that he did not think the sum was so small, and ordered it to be doubled.

The more lavishly he squandered, the more carefully Agrippina saved, until the frivolous or malicious companions of his revels suggested that she was gathering funds for the purpose of dethroning him. He at once withdrew the guard he had given her, and ordered her to leave his palace.

Agrippina had enjoyed only for one year the power which she had sought so long. She was yet only in her fortieth year. The envoys of kings had sued humbly at her feet, and her litter and guard had flashed through the streets of Rome with an impression of greatness that no other woman then known had ever possessed. But the reins passed from her hands to her brutal son and his despicable courtiers. From the palace she passed, with a few devoted followers, to the small mansion of her grandmother Antonia, and the sycophantic courtiers deserted her. Graver citizens, watching the rapid degradation of the Imperial house, followed her with sympathy, but few dared to visit her in the lonely mansion. Unfortunately, she quarrelled with one of these few, and came near to losing her life.

Her old friend Julia Silana, a woman of great wealth but very faded beauty, proposed to marry a handsome young Roman knight. Agrippina imprudently advised him not to marry a woman of such advanced years and so adventurous a record. Her words were repeated to Julia, and friendship was exchanged for the most bitter animosity.

Julia Silana was childless, and it is conjectured that Agrippina hoped to inherit her wealth if she died unmarried.

Whether she believed this or no, Julia conceived a deep hatred, and induced two of her clients to accuse Agrippina of high treason. Nero seems to have been in an uncertain mood, and an ingenious plot was devised to win him.

One night when he lay, flushed with wine, after the banquet, his favourite comedian Paris came to amuse him.

Nero noticed that the man was agitated and less merry than usual, and asked the reason. Paris, who was acting in the service of the plotters, confessed with artistic tears that there was a conspiracy afoot to dethrone his noble master; that Agrippina was about to marry Rubellius Plautus, a Senator of Imperial descent, and seize the throne.

The inebriated Emperor at once demanded their heads, but Seneca and Burrus restrained him, and compelled him to hear Agrippina on the morrow. In her speech, which Tacitus has preserved, she refuted and routed her assailants with such vigour that she was, apparently, reconciled to Nero and restored to some authority. Julia Silana was banished, Domitia's chamberlain (who had instructed the actor) was executed, and Agrippina's own followers were rewarded.

The two years that followed this reconciliation are obscure, and we can only dimly conjecture that Agrippina had some peace and prestige, but no longer shared the Imperial rule. Then, in the year 58, another and unexpected woman came into the field, and Agrippina sank rapidly toward an abyss of tragedy.

In an earlier chapter we saw that Messalina drove to death a very wealthy and beautiful Roman lady named Poppaea Sabina. It was her daughter, who had inherited her wealth and her beauty, that now attracted the amorous regard of the Emperor. She had married one of Nero's favourite companions, who babbled in his cups of her dazzling beauty, and inflamed the desire of Nero. In the next chapter we shall read of her natural charms, of the singular art with which she cultivated them and the coquetry with which she employed them, and of the superb and fabulous splendour of her equipage. It is enough to say here that Nero visited her, learned that she was willing to be an Empress, but not the mistress of an Emperor, and resolved to make any sacrifice to secure so unique a treasure.

The first victim to be sacrificed to the new passion was Octavia, and the delicate and timid girl would make little resistance. But Agrippina had espoused her cause with a spirit that redeems much of her irregular conduct, and she now saw that her own interest, as well as that of Octavia, required that she should oppose Poppaea with all her strength. In that resolution she wrote her death-sentence, not ignobly.

Even if we refuse to admit some of the incredible statements that are made regarding it in the chronicles, it is clear that an extraordinary struggle now took place about the person of the Emperor. The antagonists were Poppaea and Agrippina. Octavia was one of those frail, lily-like Roman women who never struggled; Poppaea's husband was easily set aside. Poppaea affected coyness, and refused to have any other than conjugal relations with Nero, while she employed all her charms to inflame him. Agrippina fought so desperately that Roman gossip, and Roman historians, ascribed the most infamous devices to her. In spite of his expression of doubt, it is plain that Tacitus shares the popular belief, which he relates, that Agrippina used to sit with her son in loose robes when he was heated with wine, and to ride in the same litter with him. Against this charge, however, Dio defends her (lxi, 11). He says that one of Nero's courtesans resembled his mother, and that a light remark of his on that circumstance gave birth to the libel. Poppaea would not be indisposed to encourage the story. On the other hand, Mr. Baring-Gould attempts an untenable defence when he speaks of Agrippina as "the poor old lady."

She was only in her forty-second year, and was a woman of great beauty and little scruple.

Whatever arts Agrippina employed in the struggle, she rapidly lost ground before so formidable a rival, and Poppaea incited Nero against her. He harassed her with lawsuits when she was in Rome, and sent men to insult her when she withdrew to her villa in the country. Before long Agrippina became sensible that her struggle for power had passed into the appalling experience of a struggle for life against her own son. Nero made several attempts to poison her, but she was on her guard against this familiar weapon. It is said that she had an antidote compounded of walnuts, figs, rue, and salt. Then a freedman in Nero's suite suggested a more insidious scheme. Her country house was in repair, and Anicetus directed the workmen to saw through the heavy timber over her bed, so that the room would collapse when she went to rest. Agrippina was warned, however, and the plot was defeated.

By the early spring of the year 59 Nero had fallen into a mood of the most sombre and bitter dejection. Poppaea continued to taunt him with his dependence on his mother, and to display her maddening charms just beyond the range of his eager arms. The better citizens of Rome, on the other hand, now perceived his horrible design, and watched the struggle with anxiety. As he sat at the theatre one day in this mood, his attention was caught by one of the elaborate mechanical spectacles which were often put on the stage at the time. A ship sailed into view of the spectators, fell into pieces, and disgorged a number of wild beasts upon the stage. Nero asked Anicetus, who was a skilful mechanic, whether he could build a ship that would thus fall to pieces on the water at a given moment. The man promised to do so, and Nero went down to the coast in more cheerful temper.

It was the month of March, when wealthy Romans were wont to forsake the city for the marble villas which shone in the spring sun on the flowered hills about the northern corner of the Bay of Naples. The season began with the festival of Minerva on March 19th. With some surprise and suspicion, Agrippina, who had gone down to her villa, received an affectionate invitation to join her son at Baiae for the celebration; and she heard from other quarters that he had announced a desire to be reconciled with her. She went on board the Liburnian galley which lay off the gardens of her villa at Antium, and sailed to Baiae. Nero met her in the Imperial galley, kissed her affectionately, and invited her to a banquet which his friend Otho, the husband of Poppaea, would give that night in honour of their reconciliation. She consented, but it is clear that she wavered between her consciousness of the utter unscrupulousness of her son and the bright vision of a return to happiness which he held before her.

When the hour came for going, she was told that her galley had met with an accident, but that a superb gilded galley, with sails of silk and a military guard on board, had been sent as a love-gift from her son in commemoration of their restored affection. She gazed with suspicion on the beautiful object, as it lay mirrored in the waters of the little haven, and decided to go overland, on a litter, to Otho's villa. But the amiable behaviour of Nero at the banquet dispelled the last shade of her suspicion. In the joy which his caresses and his well-feigned affection gave her, she did not notice the passing of the hours until midnight, when she rose to go. The beautiful ship with the gilded flanks and the silken sails awaited her once more, and this time she embarked on it. Nero kissed her eyes and her hands, put his arms about her and pressed her to his bosom, held her while he gave a last long look into her eyes, and then--abandoned her to the murderer Anicetus.

The galley shot out over the smooth scented waters under a canopy of brilliant stars. Agrippina sat in her cabin, in the soft spring air, and talked about the happy future with her one male attendant, Crepereius Gallus, and her one maid, Acerronia Pollia. And suddenly, as they reached the deep water, there was an ugly crack, and the roof of the cabin fell on them. Gallus was killed outright, but the two women were saved, as the stout walls failed to collapse, and there was some misunderstanding among the crew in the dark. The maid rushed to the deck calling for aid for the Empress--others say that she represented herself as the Empress--and was slain. Agrippina listened with terror to the crash of timber and the rush of armed men, and realized the treachery of her son. Still she did not court death. She dropped quietly over the side, and swam toward the distant shore. Her strength gradually failed, and she was about to abandon the awful struggle, when some men who were fishing by night picked her up and took her ashore.

Wounded by the falling timbers, exhausted by the struggle, stricken to the heart by the brutality of her son, she nevertheless rallied at once, and devised a fresh plan.

She calmly sent a message to Nero that, by the favour of the gods, she had survived the wreck of the galley which he had given her, but requested that he would not come to visit her until her wound was healed. Without a word to her attendants about the horrible plot, she ordered the remedies for her condition, and trusted that Nero would repent. Through the remaining hours of the night she lay on her couch, with one maid in attendance, her room feebly lit by a single light. The whole country without was alive with men. The shore was lit up with their torches, and they gathered about the house to express their joy that Agrippina had escaped shipwreck on the very night of so auspicious a reconciliation. As the first light of dawn broke on the encircling hills, Anicetus and his men entered the house with Nero's reply. She read something of its tenor in their faces, and said to their leader: "Hast thou come to visit me? Then tell my son that I have recovered.

Hast thou come to slay me? Then I say it is not my son who sent thee." A sailor struck her over the head with a stick, and she saw that the end had come. Tearing aside her loose robe, and baring her white body to the men, she said sadly: "Strike here, Anicetus, for it was here that Nero was born." She fell dead under a shower of blows.

Nero had heard that his mother had escaped. Dreading that she might stir into flame the resentment of Rome, he called a council of his friends. Seneca is said to have been silent, Burrus indignant. At that moment Agrippina's chamberlain entered with her message. In a flash of cunning Anicetus threw a sword at his feet, and pretended that he had been sent by Agrippina to kill Nero. The Emperor accepted the sordid pretext, and, as Burrus bluntly refused to send his soldiers to execute her, Anicetus gladly charged himself with the task. He was appointed admiral of one of the fleets for his services. It is even recorded, though details like this must always be regarded with reserve, that when the servants bore their mistress's body to the garden, and stripped it for the pile, Nero stood by and said, jeeringly: "I had no idea she was so handsome."

A report was issued, and a formal announcement made to the Senate, that Agrippina had attempted the Emperor's life, and that, when Nero sent men to arrest her, she took her own life. And the Senate licked the feet of Nero, decreed games and festivals in gratitude for his preservation, and led the enthusiasm of the people. So well known was the murder that an actor referred mockingly to it in the theatre. "Farewell, my father," he said, eating a mushroom--"Farewell, mother," he added, imitating the action

of a swimmer. The common folk repeated numbers of these grim jokes. But they enjoyed the games of thanksgiving, and Senators and nobles took part in them on the stage and in the arena, and Rome sank swiftly into the terrible degradation of Nero's later reign, which will occupy us in the next chapter.

It is hardly necessary to add a summary estimate of Agrippina's character. In the view of Stahr and Baring-Gould and a few other recent writers, she was "queenly, honourable, and pure," and had only the doubtful vices of ambition and pride. For Tacitus and the other Latin writers she was capable of any enormity, and guilty of most. It will be seen that I hold an intermediate view.

She was a woman of great distinction, ability, and strength.

Had she lived in an age when virtue was not inexpedient, she would have been an illustrious and virtuous queen.

But she had to struggle to obtain and retain power in an age when a new and more intellectual moral standard was replacing an older and more instinctive standard, and, where it seemed profitable, she availed herself of the moral scepticism which such a change always engenders. She was queenly, but she was not entirely honourable, and she was almost certainly not pure. But she served Rome well, and left it happy and prosperous; and her unselfish passion for the advancement of her son, her chivalrous and fatal defence of his injured wife, and the bravery with which she met his unspeakable brutality, do much to outweigh her evil deeds in the scale of Osiris.

CHAPTER VI

THE WIVES OF NERO

NERO was no longer "the young Apollo" of his boyhood. Unbridled dissipation and precocious crime had made their impress on body no less than on mind. He was a little above the average height, but his prematurely swollen paunch was poorly balanced on his slender and ungraceful limbs, and his skin was blotched and repellent. The dull grey eyes betrayed his unceasing indulgence, and the yellow hair, dressed in stages of short curls, framed a face that was certainly no longer handsome.

His mind was in unmistakable disorder. Our kindly age would invoke this mental trouble in extenuation of the brutal crimes he had committed and the stupendous folly he is about to perpetrate. Were this a biography of the Emperors, we might boldly essay to prove rather that the insanity followed the matricide, but that does not concern us. He was, as yet, only in his twenty-second year.

To this precocious monstrosity of vice and crime was mated one of the gentlest young matrons of the Caesarean house, Octavia, the daughter of Claudius and Messalina.

Married at the very early age of thirteen to Nero, her timid girlish nature was paralyzed by the coarse habits of her husband, and she merely hovers about the stage, like a dimly perceptible shadow, during the earlier part of Nero's reign. It must have been shortly after their marriage that Nero disdained her for the beautiful Greek slave, Acte, to whom he was more constant than to any other living thing, and who, in return, paid the last tribute to his despised remains. At first one of Nero's associates screened the entanglement, but, as we saw, it became known in the palace, and Agrippina made a fruitless effort to press the rights of his girl-wife. The injustice was, however, one that Roman ladies were not unaccustomed to bear. Nero soon fell into more disreputable ways. Octavia would see him leave the palace after supper with his wild companions, and needed little effort of imagination to follow his course when he returned, in the early morning, with torn garments and flushed, if not bruised, features and, occasionally, the painted signs that he had wrenched from shop-doors, or the cups he had stolen in a raid upon some low tavern.

He had gathered about him a band of older youths, who encouraged him in the licentious use of his power, and endeared themselves to him by the fertility of their imaginations.

Chief among them was Salvius Otho, a young noble of Etruscan descent, five years older than Nero--the Emperor Otho of a later date. He had entered the palace in virtue of an amorous relation with one of Agrippina's ladies, and his wide knowledge of adolescent amusements won him the regard of Nero, whom he led into the wildest adventures. They would wander at night through the streets, and revel in the taverns and brothels of the popular quarters of the city, the mysterious dim-lit valleys on which patrician maidens looked down from the mansions on the hills. In those centres of nightly disorder Nero and his companions were the most daring Mohocks, if we may use a phrase that belongs to later history. They violated women and boys, and played the most brutal pranks upon unarmed folk. One night Nero was severely thrashed by a Senator, whose wife he had insulted. The man learned afterwards that it was the Emperor whom he had beaten, and went to the palace to apologize. Nero forced him to atone with his life for the injury he had done to the Imperial dignity. He withdrew the guards from the Circus, in order that he might enjoy the fights of the rival factions, and from the Milvian Bridge, at night, so as to give complete liberty to vice in that nocturnal resort.

The chaste and trembling Octavia, who was still only in her sixteenth year, shrank from his brutal disdain. It was enough for her to have the title of Empress, he said to his mother, when she urged the rights of Octavia.

Presently Nero declared that he would divorce her, and marry the handsome Greek girl, but Seneca and Burrus succeeded in preventing him. To check his disorders entirely they were quite powerless, and they seem to have thought it better to direct, than to resist, his vices. Suddenly, however, in the year 58, Nero transferred his passion to the daughter of Poppaea Sabina, and began the long, tragic struggle to secure her as his Empress.

Poppaea, who will be the next figure in our gallery of Roman Empresses, and therefore may at once be introduced, was one of the prettiest, vainest, and most discussed ladies in Rome. Her mother, with whom we are already acquainted as one of Messalina's victims, had been the daughter of a very wealthy and illustrious provincial governor, Poppaeus Sabinus. Poppaea's father, Titus Ollius, had been a friend of Sejanus, and had been swept away in the flood of Tiberius's anger. She was, therefore, of mature years, but she had protected her charms so industriously that she still had the soft beauty and the fresh complexion of a girl. She had inherited also the wealth, the wit, and--it is said--the easy morals of her mother. The pretence of modesty which she made, by wearing a veil whenever she went abroad, was redeemed by the splendour of her establishment and the elaborate culture of her fair skin and pretty face. The mules which drew the litter of the veiled lady were shod with gold, and the traces of their harness were woven from gold thread. When she moved to her country house, or to Baiae, five hundred she-asses ran in the train of her litter and cars, to provide the milk for her daily bath. If we may trust the busts to which her name is attached, she had a childish grace and delicacy of feature, instead of the tense face of the adventuress; and we know that her amber-coloured hair was so much admired that it set, or revived, a fashion in amber.

She had married a knight, Rufus Crispinus, by whom she had had a son. This marriage was ended by divorce, and she became the wife of Nero's favourite, Salvius Otho.

It is suggested, and not difficult to believe, that she had married Otho on account of his intimacy with the Emperor.

He was by no means handsome, though he covered his baldness with a wig, dressed sumptuously, and had wealth, wit, and taste for art. From him Nero heard, over their cups, the piquant story of Poppaea's beauty and luxury, and it was not long before Imperial messengers were sent to her mansion. They were not admitted, and even Nero, when he sought entrance, was coyly reminded that Poppaea was married, and was devoted to her husband. After a stormy siege she gracefully capitulated so far as to receive innocent visits from Nero, and inflame him to madness with the display of her cultivated beauty. He spoke bitterly of his mother as an obstacle in the way of their marriage. Poppaea twitted him with his dependence on her, and we have seen the outcome.

When Agrippina had been removed, Nero proposed at once to divorce Octavia and wed Poppaea. The silence of Seneca at all these critical points in the degradation of Nero is painful to every admirer of the distinguished moralist. It was the less courtly and less virtuous Burrus who defended the young Empress. If Nero abandoned Octavia, he brusquely said, he must also give up her dowry--the throne--and Burrus was too generally respected to be flouted. Octavia therefore remained in her lonely chamber at the palace, a helpless witness of the vices of her husband.

For a month or two after the murder of Agrippina he behaved as one stricken with a wild and haunting remorse.

He went feverishly from place to place, and gathered about him a band of magicians and charlatans. He feared to go to Rome until he was assured that Rome was rejoicing at his escape from his mother's plot. Few pages in the story of that degenerate city are sadder than that which records the reception, in the month of May, of the Imperial matricide. The Senators and their families, dressed in their gayest robes, hurried out along the Appian Way to meet him, and his route was lined deep with cheering crowds.

He rewarded them royally. Five or six theatres opened their doors, day after day, to the degraded citizens. New things--things that had never before been seen in the whole history of the city--were provided for their entertainment.

Men and women of the highest rank played
the most lascivious parts of the mimes on the public stage, and drove their chariots in the public circus. Nero was a champion of the "green" faction, and pitted his royal skill daily in the circus against the charioteers of the other factions. He sang in the theatre, and organized a band of five thousand handsome youths, in splendid costumes, to lead the applause, and shower upon him his favourite epithet of "Apollo." He even ventured to win praise in the amphitheatre, but the one young lion which he vanquished had been prudently gorged and stupefied before he encountered it. He announced that his skill might be hired for private banquets, and nobles paid him a million sesterces for his services. Apollo, he reflected, had no beard in Greek statuary, so he shaved his beard, and the handful of yellow hair was enclosed in a golden casket studded with pearls, and carried in solemn procession to the Capitol. In the mighty rejoicing over this complete assimilation to Apollo of the tun-bellied, lanky-legged, half-crazy youth, it is recorded that a noble dame in her eightieth year danced on the stage in the theatre.

The descendants of the greatest Roman families voluntarily entered the base ranks of the comedian and the charioteer.

Mr. Henderson is reluctant to admit, in his study of Nero, that he was insane. It would, no doubt, puzzle the most penetrating psychologist to assign the respective portions of guilt and of irresponsible disorder in his conduct; but that there was mental disorder it is at once more natural and more charitable to assume. In any case, a year or so of this delirious life wore out his robust frame, and a serious illness suspended for a time the disgraceful performances. Unfortunately, when he recovered, he lost the one man who had had some power to restrain him, and sufficient honesty to use it. Burrus died in the year 62, and at the same time the slender influence of Seneca was destroyed. This is no place to discuss the difficult and delicate problem of Seneca's conduct in his association with Nero. Enough to say that he was now accused of conspiracy, and, although he successfully defended himself, he ceased to have any power at the palace.

It was now possible for Nero to rid himself of the pale young prude, who shrank in her apartments, and there were men enough to devise the procedure. Salvius Otho had already been sent to a remote part of the Empire, and his place had been taken by a horse-dealer, named Tigellinus, of little culture and even less character. With this new favourite Poppaea entered into alliance, and the young Empress presently found herself accused, with brutal levity, of adultery with Eucer, an Alexandrian slave and musician, and of covering her shame by the crime of abortion. Tigellinus easily obtained witnesses, but most of Octavia's servants refused, even under torture, to belie the virtue of their gentle mistress. The coarseness of Tigellinus had carried him too far, and public feeling was strongly aroused in her favour. Nero fell back upon the ground of her childlessness, of which he could probably have furnished a simple explanation, and divorced her. In deference to the sentiment of Rome, he at first gave her the house of Burrus and the fortune of a noble whom he had executed. A little later, however, probably under pressure from Poppaea, he banished her to Campania. He had married Poppaea a fortnight after the divorce of Octavia.

But the flagrant outrage quickened the better feeling that Rome had not yet entirely lost, and Nero was forced to recall her. To the deep mortification of Poppaea, the crowds invaded the outer court of the palace, crying the name of Octavia. They removed the statues of the new Empress from the temples and public places, and restored to their positions, and crowned with flowers, the discarded statues of Octavia. Poppaea angrily pressed Nero to assert his power, and the resourceful Anicetus, the murderer of Agrippina, was summoned to Rome. Bolder even than Tigellinus, he swore that he himself had had commerce with Octavia, and, after a pretence of trial, she was banished to Sardinia. Poppaea was not yet content, and Nero next announced that Octavia had been detected in an attempt to corrupt the commander of the fleet. She was taken to the rock-island of Pandateria that had already witnessed tragedies.

The good feeling of Rome seems by this time to have been exhausted, and Octavia was lazily surrendered to the brutal band who now surrounded Nero. There is a peculiar melancholy in the closing of that frail and innocent career. Rough soldiers seize the timid form, carry her to the bath, bind her limbs, and open her veins.

Timid and shrinking to the end, the young girl--even now she is only in her twentieth year--starts back with horror from the great darkness, and piteously implores them to spare her life. She faints, and the flow of her blood is arrested. The last pretence of pity is tossed aside, and she is stifled in the vapour-bath.

Poppaea, Tacitus says, sent for her head. It is difficult to decide whether the frequent repetition of this horrible detail in the chronicles increases or lessens its credulity.

But we can have no hesitation in believing Tacitus when he says that the Senate ordered services of thanksgiving in the temples for this fresh preservation of the life of the Emperor.

Another Empress had stepped in blood to the throne, and was in turn to stain it with her blood after a few years of imperial folly. We have seen what type of woman it was whom Nero put in the place of Octavia. Wealthy, coquettish, and beautiful, Poppaea saw in life only a sunny path for the pursuit of butterflies. When she is represented to us as licentious we must remember that no definite scandal attaches to her name, and that she is actually described as "pious" by no less an authority than the Jewish historian Josephus. In fact this circumstance, and a peculiar feature of the disposal of her body, which we will consider, gave birth to a speculation in early times that she had become a Christian. Serviez finds the story of her conversion by St. Paul, and subsequent "return to her abominations," too piquant to admit of doubt. But the conversion is even more disputable than the abominations.

It is now much disputed among our leading divines whether St. Paul ever visited Rome, and there is a simpler explanation of the phrase used by Josephus. The Roman governor of Judaea--the biblical Felix, a brother of Agrippina's favourite, Pallas--had dealt harshly with the Jews, and sent some of their priests in chains to Rome.

Josephus and others went to intercede for them, and luckily met a Jewish comedian who was in the favour of Poppaea and Nero. The historian was received with distinction at the palace, and was so successful in his suit that he might well ascribe piety to Poppaea. We may agree that the incident probably argues some culture on her part. But we shall discover her later in conduct that makes it undesirable to count her as a disciple of St. Paul.

Before the end of the year Poppaea presented Nero with a daughter, and a few weeks of wild rejoicing restored her to general favour, and obliterated the memory of Octavia.

The title of "Augusta" was, in an excess of flattery, bestowed upon both the mother and the infant. Senators raced each other to the Imperial villa at Antium, to express their joy at this substantial promise of a continuance of the Caesarean house which had dragged them in the mire.

The whole of Italy was lit up with rejoicing. Poppaea felt that her position was at last secure. And then, by one of those dread changes which were almost as common in the life of Rome as in the tragedies of Greece, and made men assume that there was a stern and mighty fate behind their puny and indulgent gods, the storm broke over Italy once more. The child withered and died, and Nero's mind fell once more into dark disorder. He glanced round with insane suspicion for possible aspirants to the throne, and Poppaea's remaining son was the first victim. One day he saw her boy (by her former husband) playing at being emperor in his games with the other children. In a few days Poppaea heard that the boy had lost his life while fishing. Many another execution was ordered with the same levity.

OCTAVIA

PORPHYRY BUST IN THE LOUVRE

As before, these terrible deeds were mingled with the most splendid and the most licentious entertainments.

Noble dames of the highest rank wrestled and fought in the amphitheatre before the frivolous crowds; the city abounded in schools where the nobility learned to ape the Emperor's folly, and contribute to the gaiety of Rome with the flute, the zither, or the dance. Nero conceived a new idea, and pursued it with zeal. He would contest the crown with the artists of Greece. Poppaea saw him training in the palace, lying for hours with heavy plates of lead on his chest, restricting himself to a diet of leeks and oil.

She saw him exhibit his skill in the theatre, lifting up his blotched and swollen body, in extraordinary contortions, on his thin legs, as he strained after the high notes. Woe to the man who openly laughed, or who excelled him!

One of his masters was put to death because Nero perceived that he could not equal the man. At last his training was complete, and Rome sighed with relief as the thousand carts, drawn by silver-shod mules, and the five thousand youths of the Augustan band, set out for the coast. They gratified Naples with a show as they passed through. For several days Nero kept the amazed citizens in the theatre, and took his meals in the orchestra, so as to lose no time. Then came the inevitable epilepsy; and it was announced that Nero, perceiving the grief of his subjects at the prospect of his departure, had postponed the Grecian tour.

On his return to comparative health, and to Rome, he once more kept the citizens agog with alternate bursts of frantic dissipation and sanguinary melancholy. From the death of her child until her own violent end, two years later, Poppaea appears very little in the chronicles; but, as we shall see that, willing or unwilling, she supported her husband in his bloody crimes, we may assume that she joined him in his less criminal orgies. One instance will suffice. He ordered that a banquet should be given on a raft, on the large sheet of water known as Lake Agrippa. When the citizens crowded to the shore on the appointed evening, they found the great raft towed by vessels plated with ivory and gold, manned by youths who had won distinction in infamy. Round the shore taverns, brothels, and dining-rooms had been erected.

And when the night fell, and the beautiful scene was lit by the light of innumerable torches, the public found that women of the highest rank were no less accessible to them than prostitutes in the houses by the lake, and the slave was at liberty to embrace his mistress under the eye of her husband. Nero even outdistanced Caligula in the Imperial teaching of vice. In the garb of a bride, he went through the religious ceremony of marriage with a man of base character, named Pythagoras. He had nude children fastened to stakes, and rushed upon them fittingly clad in the skin of a wild beast. And round the frontiers of that vast Empire, which the strength and sobriety of his ancestors had created, the weary soldiers watched the barbarians who prepared to invade it.

It was about this time that the great fire occurred which turned the laughter of Nero's subjects into resentment.

For six days and seven nights the flames ate their way through the blocks of tall tenements, divided only by narrow streets, in the parching heat of July. Nero was in the provinces at the time, and from the conflicting accounts it is impossible to pass an opinion on the rumour that he had ordered the burning of Rome. Dio gives us the familiar picture of Nero twanging his zither, and chanting the "Fall of Troy" from the summit of a high tower on the hill. Others declare, however, that he at once ordered the most expedient methods for checking the conflagration. But it was angrily whispered among the camps of the homeless that men had been seen throwing torches upon their houses, and that they were acting under orders from the palace. Nor were the citizens appeased when he threw the blame on the obscure and unpopular devotees who went by the name of Christians, and afforded them the brutal spectacle of driving round the circus to the light of burning men and women, whose living bodies had been wrapped in tow and soaked in wax and tar. Few believed in their guilt. Even Seneca at length broke his casuistic or diplomatic reserve, and retired in disgust from Rome. Nero went down in great dejection to Baiae, leaving orders that, in the restoration of the city, a new palace should be built for him that should transcend anything within the memory of Rome or of history.

This "golden house," which Nero raised round the more modest palaces of his predecessors, gave a fresh grievance to discontent. The great and unselfish Octavian had been satisfied with a small patrician mansion; Tiberius had built a palace; Caligula had enlarged it; Nero flung out its wings over a vast space. It seemed that Emperors squandered the money of the State in proportion to their uselessness. The colossal edifice and its wonderful park stretched from the Palatine to the Esquiline, across the intervening valley, and was surrounded by a triple colonnade in marble. Citizens huddled in the crowded blocks of the Subura and the Velabrum, while Nero created a miniature world within his marble girdle. There was a great lake, filled with salt water from Ostia, with a small town on its shore; there were vineyards, cornfields, groves in which wild beasts ran loose, fountains, and gardens.

The palace itself was of such proportions that a statue of Nero one hundred and twenty feet high could be conveniently lodged in its porch. Some of the rooms were plated with gold and adorned with precious stones. The supper-room had a ceiling of ivory, with openings through which flowers and costly perfumes might be shed upon the guests. The Egyptian roses whose beauty withered in one banquet in this chamber had a value of PS35,000

in our coinage.

There now dawned on Rome some consciousness of the price that the Empire was paying for the stupendous folly it had so long applauded. While the treasury was being exhausted in entertainments that all could enjoy, the murmuring was confined to the sober few. From the moment when this colossal symbol of Nero's selfishness towered above the city, the murmurs became audible and were multiplied. Nero, alarmed at the sullen looks and the vague reports of plots, went down angrily to the coast.

Then a slave brought a definite accusation of conspiracy against his master, and the stream of blood began to flow.

It is an unhappy fact, and one that confirms the darker view of Poppaea's character, that almost the only detail related of her in the chronicles, after the death of her child, is that she was one of the council of three who directed this horrible series of executions. Nero would not trust the ordinary procedure of Roman justice. With Poppaea and Tigellinus as associate-judges, he himself examined, or endorsed, every charge that cupidity or malignity brought to the palace. Rome was reddened for weeks with torture, murder, and suicide. Students of the decay of Rome have, perhaps, not sufficiently appreciated the effect of this periodic effusion of the best blood in the city. In the earlier wars, both civil and foreign, the good and the base alike had fallen. In these inquisitions for conspiracy, which fill Rome with mourning time after time from the death of Octavian to the accession of Trajan, it is chiefly the men and women of honour who suffer.

They constitute a natural selection of the cowardly and the sycophantic.

The city "teemed with funerals," in the terse phrase of Tacitus, and the gatherings of its citizens were black with mourning. Large numbers of officers and patricians were executed or driven to suicide, and their children were scourged or banished to the provinces. Seneca paid the penalty of his tardy outspokenness, and his admirable end sustains our trust that his character may, in spite of our unconquerable hesitations, have been not inconsistent with his high creed. He and his wife, who nobly asked permission to quit the world with him, had their veins opened, and Seneca passed into the silence with quiet dignity; his wife was, to her regret, recalled to life by the soldiers.

Poppaea did not live to share the punishment which these crimes brought upon Nero. Her end came more swiftly and in more terrible form. The carnage had been interrupted by a fresh outburst of rejoicing. A man declared to Nero that he knew where the fabulous treasures of the Carthaginian queen Dido, which Vergil had so recently sung in the "AEneid," were buried. A fleet was sent to Africa to recover them, and from his sombre brooding Nero passed into a new fit of prodigal entertaining.

He emptied the last depths of his treasury in spectacles and donations. When the fleet returned at length without a single cup or coin, his anger stormed with ungovernable fury, and one day, when Poppaea expostulated with him, he kicked her in the abdomen. The outrage proved fatal, as she was pregnant, and Nero's light mind turned from rage to the most extravagant lamentation. Her body was not burned, as was usual at Rome, but embalmed, and vast quantities of rare perfumes were sacrificed on the funeral pile. This peculiarity of her funeral has been thought to strengthen the interesting legend of her conversion to Christianity. It was more probably due to Nero's frenzied desire to give a unique burial to so unique a goddess, as the Senate declared her to be. It is unthinkable that Nero should make such a concession to Christian ideas, even if she had shared them in any measure, and her life does not dispose us to claim that honour for her. The legend has no foundation in history, and the early Church may easily be relieved of the stain of having counted Poppaea among its adherents.

It is not our place to pursue the insanity of the Emperor through all the forms it assumed after the death of Poppaea, but he took a third wife, whom Mr. Baring-Gould seems to have overlooked, and we must briefly relate the story of her experience. Immediately after the death of Poppaea Nero took a consort whom the pen almost shrinks from describing. It seemed to him that he discovered a resemblance to his beloved Poppaea in one of his freedmen, Sporus. The man was entrusted to the surgeons for a loathsome operation, and then solemnly married to the Emperor.

Dressed in the Empress's robes and jewels, he travelled in Nero's litter, and was publicly kissed and caressed by him.

This abominable comedy soon lost its interest, and Nero decided to marry Octavia's sister, Antonia. Recollecting the recent fate of her sister, she boldly refused, and she was put to death on a charge of aspiring to the throne.

Nero then chose Statilia Messalina, the granddaughter of a distinguished and wealthy Senator who had been driven to take his own life under Agrippina. The last part of the "Annals" of Tacitus, which would cover this date, is missing, and if we are to believe the less reputable chroniclers, Messalina had already been familiar with Nero, and had married, as her third husband, one of his close companions in debauch, Atticus Vestinus. She is described as beautiful, witty, wealthy, and lax; but the description is applied to so large a proportion of the ladies of the time that it gives little aid to the imagination. From some later details we shall conclude that she had more culture, and probably more character, than most of the courtly ladies of Nero's time. One is disposed to think that she married Nero on the maxim, literally interpreted, that it is better to be married than burned. Her husband was one night entertaining his friends when soldiers from the palace entered the room. They took him to his bath, opened his veins, and let him bleed to death; and Statilia Messalina became the tenth Empress of Rome.

POPPAEA

BUST IN THE CAPITOLINE MUSEUM, ROME

There is every reason to believe that she shrank, with prudence, from the executions and entertainments which again proceeded with ghastly alternation. Her five predecessors had been murdered; the preceding lady of Nero's choice had been murdered; and she had herself been divorced by murder. Messalina seems to have concentrated her resources upon remaining alive, until a last and most just murder should release her from her odious connexion.

Men were wearying even of Nero's ridiculous performances, and were stung by his cruelty. He put soldiers amongst his audience, to note the absent and detect the scoffer, so that his festivals became an affliction. Men were driven to the subterfuge of shamming death, and being borne out by their slaves, to avoid the exacting part of admiring spectators. Nero swore that he would exterminate the whole senatorial order; it is the most honourable mention we find of them in the chronicles for many decades. To their relief he now announced that he would proceed with his Greek tour. The silver-shod mules and the gay regiment of the Augustans were set in motion, Nero's hair was permitted to attain an artistic length and negligence, and the comedy was transferred for a time to the land of Aristophanes. How he won every prize for which he competed, how he plundered the temples and the mansions of the Greeks, how his retinue passed like a flight of locusts over the helpless province, must be read elsewhere.

After some eighteen months he was recalled to Italy by grave tidings.

It has been impossible to refrain from speaking in accents of disdain of the way in which Rome had silently witnessed, or joyously acclaimed, the successive follies of Nero, but, as I have previously noticed, it was in a peculiarly difficult situation. The Praetorian Guards were an army of twenty thousand disciplined soldiers, and were paid for personal service to the ruling house, and blind to any other interest than their own. They kept an irresistible check upon every impulse to rebel. That there were such impulses, and probably some attempt to seduce the Guards, the unfailing stream of blood at Rome justifies us in believing.

The hope of the Empire was in the more sober and more industrious provinces, and it was here that the revolt began. The leader of the troops in Gaul, Vindex, entered into correspondence with the troops in Spain. The Spanish commander, Servius Sulpicius Galba, was a Roman of illustrious family, venerable age, and stern character. Nero had heard that the purple had been offered to Galba, and that the legions of Gaul and Spain were preparing to advance on Italy.

On his return to Italy, however, Nero hears that the German legions are advancing against those of Gaul, and that Galba is hesitating. He gaily resumes his follies, and is deaf to political exhortations. At last a manifesto is put into his hands, in which Vindex refers to him as a "miserable player," and the insult to his art cuts deeply.

He writes to the Senate to demand redress, and sets out for Rome. Nothing in the whole of his extraordinary career is so tragi-comic as this penultimate scene. Clothed in a mantle of purple embroidered with gold stars, wearing the Olympian chaplet on his head, he enters Rome as the god of art. Servants bear before him the 1,800 crowns or chaplets he has won in Greece; the five thousand Augustans march behind his chariot. A sacrifice is made to Apollo, and the games resume their familiar course. Then Nero is told that, though Vindex has committed suicide, the German and other legions have joined Galba, and the fire of revolt is spreading round the Empire. He announces that he will advance on Gaul. The ladies of his harem, who form a fair regiment, have their hair cut short, and, with toy shields and other theatrical properties, masquerade as Amazons.

The last scene is brief and inevitable. Galba is marching on Rome, the Praetorian guards have been won for him, the nobles find it safe to desert Nero.

The nerveless brute whimpers and weeps in his helplessness.

He will fly to Alexandria, and earn his living as a musician. The great "golden house" is silent and deserted. Rome is openly deriding him. His servants have fled; one has even stolen the box in which he kept poison for such an emergency. The faithful Acte, Sporus, and a very few of those who fed on his folly, remain with him. Messalina has deserted him, and will appear later as the friend of one of his successors.

In the great silent house, with its walls of gold and its ceilings of ivory, he puts off the purple robes and clothes himself in an old shirt and a ragged cloak. On a miserable horse he rides with them across the vast deserted park, and makes for the house of one of his dependents, a few miles from Rome. There they admit him by a hole they have made in the wall, give him black bread and water, and cover him with a blanket. They discuss the situation, and conclude by offering him a dagger. He shrinks, like Julia, like Messalina, from the horrible darkness, and vainly strains his eyes for a ray of hope. At last they hear the clatter of cavalry on the road, and Nero feebly points the dagger at his breast, for a servant to drive home. And when the customary cremation is over, there are none but Acte and a faithful old nurse to lay the degraded ashes in the tomb.

So the tenth Empress of Rome laid down her brief dignity. Statilia Messalina had had little reason to follow Nero in his humiliation. Whether the charge of laxity that is brought against her be true or no, she was a woman of exceptional intelligence and culture, and had probably only married Nero out of fear. We meet her again, at a later stage, in the chronicles. After Galba's short hour of supremacy we shall find an equally short reign of Salvius Otho, the man who once pillaged taverns with Nero in the Subura. Provincial government had sobered him, and he wrote affectionate letters to Messalina.

He would, no doubt, have made her Empress once more if he had lived, but the throne was wrested from him, and Messalina retired to the calmer world of letters and rhetoric. Our last glimpse of her discovers her delivering orations of great eloquence and learning among the intellectual ladies of Rome.

CHAPTER VII

THE EMPRESSES OF THE TRANSITION

THE house of Caesar had perished with Nero, and few sober folk can have regretted that it had no living representative to win the fancy of the frivolous people or the blind cupidity of the Guards.

There must have been men living in Rome who had witnessed the whole of that appalling degradation, so swift it had been. The Caesars had sunk in little over forty years from the sobriety of Octavian to the insanity of Nero; their consorts had fallen from the strong standard of Livia to the insipidity of Poppaea; the resources of the Empire had been squandered in spectacles that had left its people nerveless and debauched; the old Roman ideal of character had been almost obliterated in the Imperial city.

It was our concern to see what part the Empresses played in this lamentable history of four decades. It is, on the whole, one that their biographer must blush to acknowledge.

We must remember, however, that corrupt rulers would necessarily choose weak or corrupt wives, and we cannot affect surprise or disappointment when we find them floating in the swift current.

We have now to open a new and more attractive gallery of Imperial portraits, to pass in review the wives of those great Emperors who restored the high character of Rome and strengthened anew the fabric of the Empire.

A very brief summary of events will suffice to link the Caesars with the Antonines, and introduce to us one or two curious types of Empresses who dimly figure in the transition.

For a year after the fall of Statilia Messalina the throne of the Empress was vacant, and that of the Emperor had three successive occupants. Galba was a widower at the time of his elevation to the throne. We saw in an earlier chapter that Agrippina had wished to marry him twenty-six years earlier, and he had refused. His wife, Lepida, was a delicate woman, of high character, and he refused to divorce her. She had an energetic champion in her mother, who fought Agrippina sturdily and, if the story be true, laid fair patrician hands on her.

But Lepida died long before her husband was made Emperor, and he refused to marry again. His reign was brief.

Tradition has blamed him for an excessive sternness and parsimony. They were not inopportune vices, but Rome had been too long habituated to indulgence, and Galba was too confident. The discontent at Rome was inflamed by the news of the revolt in the provinces, and within a few weeks the Guards, to whom he had refused the customary donation, set up a new Emperor, and put Galba to death.

The new ruler was no other than the first husband of Poppaea, the companion of Nero's revels, Salvius Otho.

Rome acclaimed the choice, and expected that the circus and theatre were about to reopen their doors. But Otho, who had matured during his years of office in Spain, turned from them in disgust. He did, it is true, restore the statues of Poppaea, and contemplated restoring the discarded statues of Nero, but the alienation of Roman feeling from him is a proof that he intended to rule with sobriety. The same spirit is seen in the fact that he corresponded affectionately with Statilia Messalina, and apparently thought of marrying her. But the legions in the provinces almost immediately rebelled against him, and, in the midst of the struggle, he committed suicide.

There had been no Empress of Rome for twelve months. With the death of Otho, and the accession of Vitellius, we come to the eleventh Empress, Galeria Fundana, a very new and incongruous type in the series of Imperial women.

The name of Vitellius is already familiar to us. His father was the fulsome courtier who had inspired Caligula with the idea that he was a god, and who had worn one of Messalina's little silk shoes under his tunic. His wife, Sextilia, was a woman of strict morality and unambitious temper, but their son, the younger Vitellius, lived in too tainted an atmosphere to prefer the plainness of his mother to the craft and greed of his father. He had learned vice in the band of young men who brought so evil a fame on Tiberius's villa at Capri, and had made his way astutely through the successive reigns of Caligula, Claudius, and Nero. He had made a considerable fortune as proconsul of Africa, and had, on his return to Rome, married Petronia, the daughter of a wealthy consul. She settled her large fortune on her son, and when Vitellius, having consumed his own wealth in luxury and riot, went on to sacrifice his son for the purpose of securing the fortune held in his name, Petronia angrily remonstrated, and was divorced.

He then married Galeria Fundana. She was, says Tacitus, "a pattern of virtue," and since this defect--as Vitellius would find it--was united with plainness of person, modesty of taste, and dull, if not defective, conversation, the match was a singularly unhappy one. Vitellius had so far squandered his money that he was unable to pay his expenses to Lower Germany when Galba gave him the command of the troops there. How he obtained that important appointment is not clear. Some say that Galba selected him because he was not ambitious; others that he secured it through the influence of the "blue" faction at the Circus, of which he was a partisan. He mortgaged his house, and Sextilia sold her jewels, to obtain funds for the journey. Fundana and her child were left in a poor tenement at Rome, little dreaming that they would be summoned from it to Nero's "golden house" in a few weeks.

It is expressly recorded that Sextilia and Fundana had no ambition, and dreaded lest Vitellius should aspire to reach the dizzy heights which some early prophet had promised him. They were, therefore, dismayed to hear, shortly after his arrival on the Rhine, that the troops were offering to secure the throne for him. His genial and indulgent treatment of the soldiers was a betrayal of his trust to the stern Galba, and may have been deliberately effected to win their support. He became very popular, and was hailed as a second "Germanicus." Galba was presently murdered, and, as the German legions had had no part in the choice of Otho, they urged Vitellius to lead them against him. Vitellius wavered for a time between the safe and considerable means of self-indulgence, which he had as commander, and the uncertain, but immeasurably greater, prospect which the throne suggested to his sensual dreams. The officers conquered his hesitation, and he set out for Rome in the rear of the eight legions who had declared for him.

Sextilia and Fundana seemed to be in peril when the news came to Rome that Vitellius was marching upon the city. It is said that Vitellius threatened reprisals if his family were injured, but there is no indication that Otho would stoop to take a revenge on women and children.

They saw him march out at the head of his troops to give battle to Vitellius, and waited anxiously, with all Rome, to hear the issue of the civil war. And while Senate and people were enjoying the mummery of the theatre, a horseman rode in with the news that Otho had taken his own life, and Vitellius was leading his German troops upon Rome. Senate and people united at once to receive him, and sent him the title of Augustus. He politely declined it for the time, and continued his leisurely march upon the city. There had been many a triumphant march over the roads of Italy in the annals of Rome, but never one so singular as that of the new monarch. "The roads from sea to sea groaned with the burden of his luxuries," says Tacitus; and, if we distrust Tacitus, as an admirer of Vitellius's rival and successor, all the Roman writers agree that his first use of supreme power was to command a stupendous ministration to his sensual appetites. He ordered his legions to move slowly southward, while he, in their train, exhausted each successive region of its delicacies, and filled the days and nights with his princely feasting. His example encouraged his wild German troops, and their line of march could be traced across Gaul and Italy by their pillage, cruelty, and debauchery.

The repeated messages from the provinces filled Rome with laughter, in spite of its anxiety. People remembered this princely epicure sheltering, a few months before, in the poorer quarter of the town and evading the duns. The modest and virtuous Sextilia and Fundana shrank in pain from the hollow flattery which was paid them, and followed the march of the Emperor with disgust. He was approaching Rome at the head of sixty thousand men. Legions of tall, fierce, fur-clad Germans, with heavy javelins, were thundering along the Italian roads and terrifying the peasantry. In their rear was a vast army of slaves, cooks, comedians, charioteers, and other ministers to the Imperial appetite. He had sent for the whole of Nero's servants and appointments. It was said that he even intended to outrage one of the most sacred traditions of the city by entering it in full armour, at the head of an army with drawn swords; but the friends who met him at the Milvian Bridge persuaded him to change his costume, and sheathe the swords of his soldiers. He entered, in civil toga, at the head of the terrible Germans, his officers clad in white as they bore the eagles. After visiting the Capitol, and addressing the Senate in terms of pleasant submissiveness to that body and of somewhat nauseating praise of himself, he settled in Nero's magnificent palace with Fundana and her child. His troops, debauched with the license of their march, scattered in disorder through the city; and Rome resigned itself to the inauspicious rule of its eighth Emperor.

We may dismiss the nine months in which Galeria Fundana was Empress of Rome in a phrase: she was a helpless and disgusted spectator of the most imperial debauch that Rome had yet witnessed. Dio strangely accuses her of haughtily complaining of the poverty of the robes she found in Nero's golden house, but the testimony to her modesty is too strong for us to admit this. A more credible statement in the chroniclers is that she begged to be allowed to retire to a humble dwelling of her own, and Vitellius refused. His mother did not long survive her mortification. One rumour preserved in Suetonius is that Vitellius had her starved to death, as it was predicted that she would outlive him; another version says that he sent her poison, at her own request. Fundana was left alone to bewail his colossal gluttony. She saw his chief officers encourage him in his stupefying orgies, while they enriched themselves; and she had to submit in silence while his sister-in-law, Triaria, "a woman of masculine fierceness," goaded him to continued excesses. During the few months of his reign he spent 900,000,000 sesterces (about PS7,000,000) in eating, drinking, and entertainment.

He had three meals during the day, and ended with a costly and drunken supper. His brother one day entertained him at a banquet, at which two thousand choice fishes and seven thousand rare birds were served. Vitellius in return gave a banquet, at which one dish--a compound of the livers of pheasants, the tongues of flamingoes, the brains of peacocks, the entrails of lampreys, and the roes of mullets --cost more than the whole of his brother's dinner.

From this loathsome and stupid dream of Imperial power Vitellius was at length awakened by the echoes of rebellion in the provinces. After a few futile executions, and several relapses into his besetting gluttony, he was forced to set out for the north. He quickly returned, however, and wandered about Rome in hysterical impotence, while the followers of Vespasian closed upon the city. Civil war had broken out, and the Romans gazed with horror on the sacred Capitol besieged by the German troops and bursting into flames. At last Vitellius came out with Fundana and her child, in mourning dress, and announced that he would resign. The consul refused his sword, and the mournful procession directed its steps towards his brother's house. He was persuaded to return to the palace, but the Vespasianists captured Rome, and he was taken to Fundana's house on the Aventine. From this he somehow wandered back to the palace. "The awful silence terrified him; he tried the closed doors, and shuddered at the empty chambers," says Tacitus. Dazed and incapable of flight, he hid in the sordid room where the dogs were kept.

Here the soldiers found him, torn and bleeding, and forced him to walk the streets, while they kept his head erect with the point of a sword, and the people flung filth and epithets at him. They then inflicted on him a slow and painful death, and flung his remains in the Tiber.

Fundana was spared, and her daughter honourably given in marriage, by his magnanimous successor. From the brief and unwelcome splendour of the "golden house"

she passed into private life, and lived only to bemoan the cruel fate that had lifted her husband to the intoxicating height of the Roman throne.

There was no Empress in the reigns of Vespasian and Titus, but a word may be said of the two remarkable women who shared their power to some extent. Vespasian, whose sober and solid administration it would be pleasant to contrast with the orgiastic reigns of his predecessors, was a rough soldier, of humble extraction and homely ways. He had, in the time of Caligula, married the mistress of a knight, Flavia Domitilla, who remains little more than a name in the chronicles. He had won distinction under Narcissus, but the triumph of Agrippina drove him and Domitilla into exile. Nero employed him to crush the rebellion in Judaea, and it was during this campaign that his wife died, leaving him with her two sons--his successors--Titus and Domitian. He was, therefore, a widower when the Eastern troops made him Emperor, but he took into his palace, and treated as Empress, an emancipated slave of the name of Caenis.

The mistress of Vespasian has the distinction of being associated--actively and usefully associated--with him in one of the soundest attempts to restore the decaying Empire. She had been in the service of Antonia, the grandmother of Agrippina, and is said to have been the one who first disclosed to Tiberius the perfidy of Sejanus.

From the first she was a dangerous rival of Domitilla, and, when his wife died, Vespasian entered into the quasi-matrimonial relation with her which is known in Roman

law as *contubernium*. She would probably have been Empress if the law had permitted him to contract a solemn marriage with her. She had considerable ability, but an unhappy reputation for extortion and the sale of offices. It is not clear, however, that the wealth she obtained did not contribute to Vespasian's rehabilitation of the resources of the Empire. They abandoned and destroyed the golden house of Nero, the central site of which is now marked by the Flavian Amphitheatre, or Coliseum. In their quiet gardens in the Quirinal they received any citizen who cared to visit them, and maintained no timorous hedge of soldiers between themselves and their people. They wished to see money spent on public purposes, or hoarded for public emergencies, rather than squandered. "My hand is the base of the statue: give me the money," Caenis is said to have told a wealthy man who proposed to raise a statue to her; but Dio informs us that this and other stories of Caenis's avarice properly belong to Vespasian. She died, however--if the date assigned in Dio is correct--in the second year of Vespasian's reign, and must not be credited with too large a share in that great purification of Rome and reinvigoration of its life with healthy provincial blood which Tacitus regards as the beginning of the recovery of the Empire.

Titus, who succeeded his father in the year 79, and reigned for two years, threatened at one time to give Rome an even more singular and unwelcome type of Empress. He had in early youth married Arricidia Tertulla, who died soon afterwards, and then Marcia Furnilla, a lady of illustrious family. He left his wife in Rome when he took command under his father in Judaea, and became infatuated with a brilliant princess of the Herod family, Berenice. He divorced Furnilla, and brought Berenice to live with him at Rome. But the Romans resented the prospect of a Jewish Empress, and she was forced to return. On his accession to the throne he made no attempt to enforce her on them. He reigned alone for two years, "the love and delight of the human race," and maintained the sober administration of his father.

With the accession of his younger brother, Domitian, Rome received a new Empress, and, by an unhappy coincidence, saw the imperial palace return to the evil ways of the Caesars. Those of our time who attach almost the entire importance to stock or birth, and little to circumstances, in the formation of character, will find a peculiar problem in Domitian and his wife. The Emperor was the second son of the "plain Sabine burgher"

and sturdy soldier, Vespasian, and of the lowly provincial woman, Flavia Domitilla. The Empress, Domitia Longina, was the daughter of Domitius Corbulo, one of the strongest and ablest generals that Rome produced in the first century. Yet of these sound and vigorous stocks came, in one generation, one of the most morbid of the Emperors and an Empress who, in some respects, rivalled Messalina. Rome knew them both, and had no false hope.

Domitia--as she is usually called--makes her first appearance as a young girl of great beauty and promise, caressed and protected by the wealth and prestige of her distinguished father, who, it is interesting to note, was a brother of Caligula's masculine wife Caesonia. She was married to a noble of distinction and character, Lucius AElius Lamia AEmilianus, and she seems to have been an estimable young matron until her father incurred the anger of Nero and was forced to commit suicide. Procopius and Josephus, indeed, represent her as virtuous to the end, but there seems to be little room for doubt that the nearer and less indulgent authorities are correct. Her young mind opened on the sordid scenes of the closing part of Nero's reign and the folly of Vitellius. She then met the fascinating and effeminate Domitian, and very speedily capitulated to his assaults.

DOMITIA

BUST IN UFFIZI GALLERY, FLORENCE

Gibbon speaks of him as "the timid and inhuman Domitian," while Dio opens his biographical sketch of the Emperor with the deliberate epithet, "bold and wrathful."

We shall find a very natural dread of assassination in Domitian's later years, but he was undoubtedly bold and crafty in the service of Venus, and a stranger to moral sentiment. His elder brother Titus had developed the manly qualities of their father on the battlefields of Judaea, and had proved strong enough to crush his irregular feelings on his accession to the throne. Domitian had remained at Rome, discharging only civic duties, and had become one of the most heartless dandies in the group of degenerate young patricians. During the civil strife of the Vitellianists and Vespasianists on the streets of Rome he had made his escape in the fitting disguise of a priest of Isis. Titus knew his vicious and luxurious ways, and endeavoured to check him by offering him his own charming daughter Julia in marriage; but Domitian was engaged in fascinating the pretty and accomplished wife of Lamia AEmilianus, and refused. Titus, on his accession, associated him in the government, and his first act was to separate his mistress from her husband, and marry her.

Domitia's triumph was quickly tempered with mortification.

Julia married her cousin Sabinus, and, out of pique or devilry, Domitian now discovered her charm and seduced her. To such a pair as these the attainment of supreme power meant an occasion of Imperial license, and sober Romans saw their community rapidly lose the ground that had been won in the previous reigns. It was even rumoured that Domitian had hastened his brother's death by putting him in a box of snow during his last illness, though this remains no more than an idle rumour. At all events, Domitia soon discovered the despicable character for whom--or for whose prospects--she had abandoned her saner husband. While the affairs of the Empire needed his most strenuous attention, he would spend hours catching flies and spitting them with a bodkin; and from the spitting of flies he presently passed to the larger sport of murdering men. He conducted his little frontier-wars from safe and luxurious quarters, and came home to enjoy a triumph and erect a colossal bronze memorial of his valour.

He banished eunuchs from Rome, and kept them in his palace; waged war against vice in all forms, and practised it in all forms. In the general relaxation of Roman manners even the Vestal Virgins had been for some decades permitted an alleviation of their onerous vows.

Domitian posed as a moralist, on no other apparent ground than that he was closely acquainted with every shade of immorality, and drastically punished them. He raised fine public buildings, and depleted the public treasury by reckless expenditure and incompetent administration; prosecuted officials for extortion, and put men to death for their wealth; gave brilliant entertainments, and darkened the city and the Empire with his sanguinary brooding.

If we were to accept Josephus's estimate of the virtue of Domitia, we should conceive her as living in melancholy isolation in the gloomy palace, an outraged spectator of her husband's relations with Julia. But there is good evidence that she sought relief with something of the freedom of a Messalina. An authentic occurrence in the third year of Domitian's reign puts her guilt beyond question.

He had the actor Paris murdered in the street, and divorced Domitia. The people boldly sympathized with her, and covered with flowers the spot on which Paris had been killed. The Emperor had a number of them executed, but public feeling seems to have been expressed so strongly that he was forced to recall Domitia to the palace, and the sordid comedy ran on amid the jeers of Rome. A poet was put to death for making it the theme of his verse; Domitia's former husband and others were executed for their freedom of speech. Then the beautiful and captivating Julia perished miserably in an attempt of Domitian's to destroy the too obvious proof of their incest, and he became more sombre than ever.

This is not the place to tell the long and dreary story of the reign of Domitian, of which, for twelve further years, the Empress remains an inconspicuous, and perhaps a sobered, spectator. For a few years he maintained his singular and obscure mixture of good and evil, but the brighter features of his administration gradually faded, and a horrible gloom settled on the palace and the city.

Hosts of spies and informers sprang up; large numbers of nobles, of both sexes, were executed or banished, on the slightest suspicion, and their wealth divided between the informers and the Emperor's shrinking treasury. So great was his dread of assassination that he lined the portico at the palace, in which he used to walk, with white glazed tiles that would reflect the approach of any person behind him. But an extraordinary incident that Dio relates will suffice to give some idea of the reign of terror under which the Empress and all Rome suffered.

A number of the leading citizens of Rome were summoned to a banquet at the palace at a late hour of the night. They were frozen with horror when they found that the entire dining-room--walls, ceiling, and floor--was draped in black, and a miniature tombstone, with his name engraved on it, was placed opposite each guest. As they gazed, a number of nude boys, whose bodies were washed with ink, burst into the room and danced amongst them, and then the dishes of a funeral banquet were served.

The guests sat silent and shivering; the Emperor grimly discoursed to them of deaths and executions. When the banquet was over, they were relieved to find themselves dismissed. They found, however, that their litters had been sent away, and they were put into strange vehicles, with strange servants. The gloomy journey ended at their own houses, and they were beginning to breathe, when they were thrown into fresh alarm by the news that a messenger had come from the palace. The messenger to each guest was one of the dancing boys, now cleaned, perfumed, and clothed with flowers, bearing the gold and silver vessels which the guest had used at the banquet.

The boys and the dishes were presented to them with the Emperor's greeting.

Unhappily, Domitian did not confine himself to intimidation.

The heads of the wealthier nobles fell in quick succession, and, in great secrecy, amid an army of spies, the Empress and a few others came to an understanding.

The story of the actual fall of the tyrant has clearly been embroidered with a good deal of unauthentic detail in popular gossip, but even in its most sober version it does not lack romance.

The version which Dio assures us he "had heard" is one that the conscientious historian must hesitate to accept.

The Emperor, he says, had been informed of the conspiracy, and had drawn up a list of those who were to be executed for taking part in it. He put the list under his pillow, with the sword which he always kept there, and went to sleep. We have previously seen something of the bejewelled boys who used to run with great freedom about the palaces of the Romans of the first century.

Domitian, the great censor of other people's vices, had a number of them, and the legend is that one of them, playing in his bedroom, noticed the parchment under his pillow, and took it out into the palace. Domitia met the boy, and idly glanced at the parchment. She saw her own name at the head of the list of the condemned, and at once summoned the other conspirators. They entered the Emperor's room, snatched the sword from under his pillow, and despatched him.

Pretty as the story is, we must prefer the more prosaic account given us by Suetonius, who lived in the next generation. Domitia felt that the Emperor had at last conceived a design on her life, and she sent her steward to despatch him. He offered Domitian a fictitious report of a plot, and stabbed him while he read it. Other servants rushed in at the signal, and completed the assassination. It is the one action that historians have recorded to the honour of the twelfth Empress of Rome, and we leave her company with little regret. She was an ordinary woman of the patrician world at the time--fair, frail, accomplished, and luxurious. With the death of her husband she merges in the indistinguishable crowd of selfish and wayward ladies on whom Juvenal was then beginning to pour his exaggerated rhetoric.

It remains to describe very briefly how the sceptre passes into the nobler hands of the Stoic Emperors and their wives. The throne was offered to, and accepted by, M. Cocceius Nerva, an aged noble of known moderation and long public service. He at once removed all traces of the hateful reign of his predecessor, and entered upon a sober and useful administration of the Empire. He was in the later sixties of his age, and we find no mention of a wife. But the task of enforcing sobriety on so corrupted a population was too great for his age and moderate ability.

A conspiracy against him was discovered. He disarmed the conspirators by inviting them to sit by him in the theatre, and even putting a sword in their hands and asking them what they thought of its keenness; but he saw that a stronger man was needed, and he chose as his colleague Marcus Ulpius Nerva Trajanus, a Spaniard of great military ability and commanding personality, who was then at the head of the troops in Germany. Nerva died soon afterwards, and, with the accession of Trajan, we come to the thirteenth Empress of Rome and the commencement of a new and more splendid chapter in the

story of the Empire.

CHAPTER VIII

PLOTINA

"IF," says Gibbon, "a man were called to fix the period in the history of the world, during which the condition of the human race was most happy and prosperous, he would, without hesitation, name that which elapsed from the death of Domitian to the accession of Commodus"; and he observes of Antoninus Pius and Marcus Aurelius that "their united reigns are possibly the only period of history in which the happiness of a great people was the sole object of government."

This monumental eulogy of the period which we now approach--a eulogy which the more penetrating study of Renan and the more recent research of M. Boissier and Dr. Dill have not materially lessened--will suffice to warn the inexpert reader against the ancient and popular legend that Rome continued to sink under the burden of its vices until it tottered into the tomb of outworn nations. Under the Empresses whom we have now to consider there was a great improvement of character and recovery of vigour in the Roman Empire, but before we pass to that brighter phase I would enter a brief protest against the general exaggeration of the darkness of the period we have traversed.

Even under its worst rulers Rome was far from being wholly corrupt. The vices of a Messalina, the crimes of an Agrippina, and the follies of a Poppaea, stand out so prominently in that period only because they were perpetrated on the height of the throne. Even they were hardly worse than the crimes and follies of the wives or mistresses of kings in many a less censured period of history; and, if you care to count them, the lilies were as numerous as the poppies in this first series of Empresses, but the lilies drooped earlier, and have been less noticed.

Whenever, in the course of our story, the light has passed from the throne to the less elevated crowd, we have found fine character mingled with the corrupt even in the darkest years of the early Empire. The heads that fell before the Imperial monsters were as many as the heads that bowed.

The truth is that, if we are not misled by the hasty generalizations and plebeian diatribes which Juvenal, in his "Satires," founds upon the dubious bits of gossip that he picked up on the fringe of Roman society, and against which historians now warn us, there was much the same diversity of conduct in the early Empire as in most of the corresponding periods of luxury. The wealthier women of Rome assuredly fell far short of the cloistered virtue of the maid and the matron of Greece; but Greece had only succeeded in maintaining that standard of domestic virtue in its wives and daughters by cultivating a high caste of courtesans for their roaming husbands. It may be admitted, too, that the Roman woman was morally inferior to the wife of the Egyptian noble, and to the wife of the noble or the wealthy merchant of Babylonia. But the patrician women, even of Caesarean Rome, will compare with the women of most of the later civilizations at the same stage of development; at the stage, that is to say, when the nation relaxes from the strain of empire-making, and its veins are flushed with the wealth of its conquests.

I would instance the women of the early Teutonic nations as soon as they settle on southern Europe; the women of Italy in the early Middle Ages; the women of England under the Stuarts and, after a later expansion, under the Georges; the women of France under Louis XIII and Louis XIV; the women of Russia in the nineteenth century.

At Rome, in spite of the positive insistence on vice of Caligula, Messalina, and Nero, in spite of their determined effort to weed out the good, we have found virtue and courage springing up afresh in each generation.

We now come to a period when, three centuries before the fall of Rome, the Empire is purged of its exceptional corruption, and character assumes the normal diversity that it has in any old and wealthy civilization. The city of Rome was assuredly vicious and in decay. But the city was not the Empire, as those rhetoricians forget who talk of its entire demoralization. Rome had been drenched with degrading agencies for half a century; but there was a quite normal amount of stout will and high character in the provinces, and this is now infused more freely into the metropolis. It is only by a similar influx of sounder blood from the provinces that any great city survives the feverish waste of its tissue. The remedy was retarded in Rome because the provincials, even of Italy, but especially of Gaul and Spain, were of alien race. Rome jealously remembered that it was the conqueror; the rest were the conquered. Under Vespasian, however, the provincials were admitted more freely, and with the accession of a Spaniard, Trajan, the process increased.

In the remote and primitive settlement which Agrippina had established on the banks of the Rhine, where the towers of Cologne Cathedral now keep watch over a splendid city, there dwelt, in the year 97, the commander of the forces in Lower Germany, Marcus Ulpius Trajanus, with his wife and a few female relatives. Trajan was of a moderate Spanish family, and had, like his father, cut his own path in the military service of the Empire. He was unambitious, but popular. A large, handsome man, in his forty-fifth year, of singularly graceful bearing and serene features, he charmed everybody by his simplicity and affability of manner, and liked a good carouse and a rough soldierly jest. His wife Plotina was a plain, honest matron of unknown origin. It has been conjectured that she was related to Pompeius Planta, at one time Governor of Egypt, but the only ground for the conjecture seems to be that Planta was a friend of Trajan's. As she had neither beauty of person nor romantic defect of character, the chroniclers have left her largely to our imagination; but she was a type of woman whom it is not difficult to picture--a woman of plain features, level judgment, and of what is euphemistically called grave but agreeable conversation.

She was by no means brilliant, but her close

friendship for Hadrian suggests that she was not too dull and prosy, and had pretensions to culture. Her ways were simple, and her character can be relieved of the one imputation made against it. She compares well with Livia, but as a higher *bourgeoise* compares with a *grande dame.* In a word, she had none of the autumnal colour, the beauty of decay, of the Caesarean women, but she had the less aesthetic and more useful quality that they lacked, conscientiousness. To the courtly Pliny ("Panegyr.," 83) she is the embodiment of all the virtues.

With her at Cologne was Trajan's sister Marciana, a widow of much the same complexion as Plotina, and Marciana's daughter Matidia, who in turn had two daughters, Sabina and Matidia. We can imagine the agitation of this tranquil establishment among the forests of Germany when a courier came from Rome with the news that Trajan was chosen as colleague of the Emperor. They had left Rome six years before, in the middle of Domitian's reign. However, they seem to have received very sedately the prospect of a removal from the camp on the Rhine to the Imperial palace. Although Nerva died in the following January (98),

Trajan remained for the year in Germany, completing his task of strengthening the frontier against the northern barbarians. Then the family set out on the long journey to the capital.

The fame of Trajan's simplicity and geniality of manner had preceded him, but Rome looked with surprise on an Emperor who could wait a year before occupying the palace, enter the city on foot, without guards, and talk so affably with any of his subjects. Nor was Plotina long before she showed that they had received a new type of Empress. As she ascended the steps of the palace, she turned round and said to those below: "As I enter here to-day, I trust I shall leave it when the time comes." The refreshing amiability, simplicity, and moderation of the Imperial couple captivated the Romans, and Trajan responded to their good will with the most judicious and untiring exertions in the public service. He trod out at once the hideous brood of informers, checked corrupt officials, and appointed the best men to public offices.

Indifferent to the splendour and luxury of even the modest palace of Vespasian, he spent most of his reign in frontier-wars or in long journeys for the purpose of bracing the relaxed frame of the Empire; and he enriched and adorned Rome as no Emperor had done since Octavian.

That he was vigorously supported by Plotina is quite certain, and there is evidence that she was much more than a sympathetic witness of his labours. It is related by the Emperor Julian that Trajan often sought the advice of Plotina, and that it was always sound. At the beginning of his reign she had occasion to use her influence. Trajan's dislike of informers was carried so far that, when a case of real extortion occurred in the provinces, the injured were prevented from bringing it to his notice. They appealed to Plotina, and she put the case judiciously to her husband and secured relief. In many other ways she gave useful assistance, so that the Senate offered the title of Augusta to her and Marciana. They declined, as Trajan had refused the special title offered to him, but he relented, and they followed his example.

The reign of Trajan and Plotina was thus one long episode of strenuous and enlightened public service, but before we enter into the particulars of their achievements it is proper to endeavour to obtain a nearer view of their personalities. In this the chroniclers give us little assistance, and the result cannot be very interesting. It is ever the painful reflection of the biographer that the description of a sober life--a life which neither sinks to the lower levels of vice nor soars to some unaccustomed height of virtue--has little interest for the majority of his readers; and this was the life of the Imperial court during the twenty years of Trajan's reign. The Emperor himself was no paragon.

Preferring the easy ways of a camp, he drank somewhat deeply of nights, his jests were apt to be coarse, and he was popularly accused of the vice which so generally infected the men of the Empire. Yet he had this distinction in a long line of Emperors, in the prime of life, that no woman ever shared, or sullied, his affection for Plotina.

Gibbon has remarked, in extenuation of the conduct of his successor, that "of the first fifteen Emperors, Claudius was the only one whose taste in love was entirely correct."

That would be a high compliment to Messalina, but in point of fact, as we saw, Claudius was not entitled to that distinction. The charge against Trajan is vague, and we must rather award the distinction to him. Merivale somewhat harshly speaks of him as only maintaining his self-respect because of the bluntness of his moral sense. If we put his strong sense of public duty and his fidelity in the scale against his one certain indulgence, in drink, we shall hardly agree to that verdict.

The virtue of Plotina, on the other hand, has been more seriously assailed by both ancient and recent writers. In the service of the Emperor was a very handsome and accomplished youth named Hadrian, an orphan, with great taste and skill in art and letters. He had been employed by Trajan at Cologne, both in military service and in filling up the long nights with an occasional carouse, and, after their return to Rome, he was a great favourite of the ladies at the palace. They formed a little circle in which letters were discussed and literary men were patronized. There was something of a literary revival; it was the age of Juvenal, Martial, Quinctilian, Pliny, Suetonius, Celsus, and Dio Chrysostom. Hadrian was a brilliant student, and he appreciated this open and easy way to distinction. Trajan is represented as using the young man for companion, but not regarding him as fitted for promotion, so that it fell to Plotina to urge, and ultimately to make, the fortune of the future Emperor. The magnificent mausoleum which Hadrian raised in memory of her long testified to his ardent and grateful attachment.

There is a good deal of exaggeration in this conception.

We shall see that Trajan promoted Hadrian in such a way as to mark him in the eyes of all as his successor; and his chief advisers in this were the statesmen Sura and Attianus.

In any case, there is no proof that Plotina, who must have been twenty years older than Hadrian, felt more than a very natural fondness for the gifted and charming youth.

Pliny mentions that her friendship for him gave rise to gossip, but insists that she was "a most virtuous woman."

The "Augustan History" leaves her unassailed. Suetonius has no scandal to record. Dio alone describes their attachment as "erotic love"; but on an earlier page Dio has expressly said that her career was stainless. When he has described her standing at the top of the palace steps, to say that she trusted to leave that palace just as she entered it, he adds: "And she so bore herself throughout the whole reign as to incur no blame."[11] The remarkable eulogy of Pliny, the silence of the other authorities, and the conduct of Trajan, must enable us to choose between these contradictory statements of Dio, and indeed compel us to reject this unsubstantial charge against the virtue of Plotina.

The other ladies of the Imperial household were equally without reproach, and life at the palace was harmonious and uneventful. Emperor and Empress moved about Rome without guards, and entertained, or were entertained by, their friends in a simple and unceremonious way. But Trajan had little love for the atmosphere of a palace, and an outbreak in Dacia, two years after his arrival in Rome, gave him an excuse to return to the camp. He took Hadrian with him, and remained in Dacia a year. In the year 103 he rejoined Plotina at Rome, but the war broke out afresh shortly afterwards, and it now took him three years to subdue the province and link it to the Empire by a great bridge over the Danube. He returned in 107, and spent seven years in Rome before he set out on his final journey in the year 114.

PLOTINA

STATUE IN THE LOUVRE

The prolonged absence of the Emperor threw a good deal of responsibility on Plotina, and it would be of great interest, if it were possible, to trace her share in the vast work which was done for the city and the Empire at that time. This, unfortunately, we cannot do. There were able counsellors left at Rome in Trajan's absence, and no doubt most of the work was directly controlled by Trajan during his stay in

Rome from 107 to 114. We know only that he conferred freely with Plotina, and that he left great power to her when he went abroad. We can, therefore, only regard her, in a general way, as contributing to the prosperity and progress that characterize the reign of her husband. She kept Rome tranquil and content, and no doubt followed with close interest the great improvements which Trajan commanded. The neck of hill which linked the Capitoline to the Quirinal, in the heart of Rome, was cut away, and a fine Forum, or broad street with sheltered colonnade on either side, was constructed on the cleared ground between the hills. As previous Emperors had already made slight extensions of the old Forum, the citizens of Rome now had, in the centre of the city, a magnificent *corso* running out toward the great Circus, in the porticoes of which the packed dwellers of the Subura on one side, and Velabrum on the other, could lounge and take the air with comfort. Nor was this a mere meretricious concession to their entertainment. Trajan was equally attentive to their education. A beautiful basilica, two public libraries--one for Greek and one for Roman letters--and other splendid buildings were raised along the sides of the new Forum, and statues of marble and bronze were brought from all parts, even from the palace, to adorn it.

Other cities of the Empire shared in the generosity and public spirit of the new reign. Harbours were constructed for the increase of commerce, fresh roads were flung across the intervening country, and many towns were enriched with stimulating public edifices. Nor were the social needs of the Empire less regarded than the material. Previous Emperors had given a scanty practical expression to the doctrine of the brotherhood of men, which the Stoic philosophy was disseminating. Trajan gave a great extension to this new philanthropy, as we learn from the inscriptions that have been found in the soil of Italy. It is estimated that 300,000 poor and orphaned children were fed by charity or Imperial aid in Italy alone.

The lot of the slave was improved, and the school system of the Empire became better than any that has since appeared in Europe until the second half of the nineteenth century.

Men were returning to the sobriety of their fathers, and were tempering it with the new spirit of peace and mercy, and a regard for culture. Morality improved, and character became a qualification for office. The one open scandal of the long reign--an intrigue of the Vestal Virgins with three young knights--was punished with all the rigour of the old Roman law.

We must be content to know that Plotina had her part in this noble work of restoring the jaded frame of the Empire, and refrain from attempting to measure her particular influence. By the year 114 the administration ran so smoothly, and the Western world was so settled, that Trajan turned his attention to the East. The Parthians had been interfering in the affairs of the Ethiopians, who were vassals of Rome, and Trajan saw in this a pretext of establishing more strongly, if not enlarging, the eastern frontier of the Empire. He had never been in the East, and the deep attraction of its ancient cities and decadent mysticism gave a cultural interest to his expedition. He took with him Plotina and Matidia, his niece. Marciana seems to have died before this time, and Hadrian had married Sabina, the daughter of Matidia. Hadrian, and probably his wife, accompanied them.

The path to the East for the Roman lay through Athens, where Plotina and her companions would survey the decaying splendour of the Greek civilization in which they had long been interested. Envoys from the Parthians met Trajan there, and tried to disarm him, but he dismissed them, and pushed on to the field in which he trusted to win fresh laurels. They reached Antioch at the end of the year, and had, during their stay in that metropolis of Oriental vice and luxury, a novel experience. A great earthquake shook the city, and even the house in which the Emperor lodged. He was forced to make his escape by the window. The accounts of their later movements are meagre, and we can only imagine Plotina passing with wonder through the strange spectacles of western Asia. During the spring and summer an indecisive campaign was waged against the Parthians, and Trajan returned to Antioch for the winter. In the spring of the year 116 the Emperor set out again for Mesopotamia. He passed down the Euphrates, took the Parthian capital, sailed on the Persian Gulf, and even directed a longing eye over the ocean in the direction of India. The spirit of Alexander breathed in him as he trod this theatre of the historic conquerors, but the burden of age and an increasing infirmity put a reluctant limit to his ambition.

He had, in fact, passed the range of his powers, and distended too far the frontier of the Empire. In the following year he became weaker, and the Eastern tribes advanced with spirit. Leaving the task to his generals, the Emperor turned towards Italy.

How far Plotina had accompanied her husband on these remote journeys we are not informed. It would not be surprising, or out of harmony with a general custom of the time, if she covered the whole, or the greater part, of the territory with him. However that may be, we find her with Trajan and Hadrian at Antioch once more in the course of the year 117. Trajan was seriously ill, and had to abandon all hope of settling the Eastern question.

He maintained the troops at the frontier, left Hadrian at Antioch as legate of the East, and slowly and sadly moved towards Europe. His tall frame was bent with age, his hair was white, his limbs made heavy with dropsy and numbed with incipient paralysis. When they arrived at Selinus, a small town on a precipitous rock of the Cilician coast, only a few hundred miles from Edessa, his illness increased, and he died, in the month of August, 117, in the sixty-third year of his age.

The exact truth about Plotina's conduct at the time of Trajan's death will never be known, but an impartial analysis of the statements made by the chroniclers cannot discover any clear ground for dissatisfaction. Dio, whose authority on this point is claimed to be considerable, since his father was then governor of the province of Cilicia, first insinuates a suggestion of poison, in the usual form of an unsubstantial rumour, and then insists that Plotina forged a letter in Trajan's name, nominating Hadrian his successor in the Imperial power. The writer of the sketch of Hadrian in the "Historia Augusta," Spartianus, carries the legend further. He describes how Plotina put a confidant in the bed of the dead Emperor, drew the clothes about him, and directed him to murmur, in a feeble voice, to the assembled officials that he wished Hadrian to succeed him. This second version is wholly negligible. It comes only from an anonymous writer of the fourth century who excites our distrust at all times by his extravagant and unsupported statements. The latest commentators on his work warn us that his aim is prurient and his method devoid of scruple.

The authority of Dio, on the other hand, must not be exaggerated. His father might purvey gossip to him, like any other Greek or Roman, and his story of the forged letter--or forged signature to a letter--might easily be a piece of local gossip. Plotina was evidently anxious to secure the succession for Hadrian, and one may well admit that she concealed her husband's death until Hadrian arrived at Selinus. That concealment would easily give rise to conjectures. Serviez naturally forces on his readers the more romantic version, but more sober writers acquit Plotina of anything more than a formal use of Trajan's name after his death.

The suggestion of poison is frivolous. Trajan had been ailing for months, and his assiduous travelling in a climate so different from that to which he had been accustomed all his life must have worn him out. He arrived in Asia Minor in the sweltering and dangerous month of

August, and a touch of the enteric fever which so commonly overcame the European in the insanitary East of the time put an end to his life. Plotina had for some time urged him to nominate Hadrian as his successor. We must not hastily infer from his reluctance that he thought Hadrian unfit to succeed him. He had just left him in a position of the gravest responsibility, and must have appreciated what a great historian calls Hadrian's "vast and active genius."

But he may not have deemed it proper for him to dictate to the Senate how they should exercise their power of choice. What actually occurred is certainly obscure. A letter was dispatched to the Senate, after Trajan's death, in which Hadrian was nominated, and Dio says that the signature was put to this letter by Plotina. One would imagine that such a deception, as Dio represents it to be, would easily be detected and resented by Hadrian's powerful enemies in the Senate. It is probable that, as Merivale supposes, the letter was really dictated by Trajan, and the signing of it by Plotina was only formal. We may admit Dio's narrative of facts, yet believe that the Empress was merely carrying out Trajan's will.

On the other hand, there is no reason to quarrel with, or put a base interpretation on, her zeal for the succession of Hadrian. We shall see how well he maintained the sound work of Trajan. He was at once summoned to Selinus, to consult with Plotina and with the elderly Senator Attianus, who had been his guardian together with Trajan, and had been as zealous as the Empress in urging his advancement. They decided that Hadrian must return to his post at Antioch, and Plotina set out for Rome with the ashes of her husband in a golden urn.

The last resting-place of Trajan was under the magnificent column which still bears witness in Rome to his many victories, and for centuries afterwards the most flattering compliment that the Senators could pay to an Emperor was to cry that he was "more fortunate than Augustus, and better than Trajan."

Plotina lived at Rome for four years after the death of her husband. The first year was, as we shall see, one of great anxiety and trial. There was much discontent at Hadrian's accession, and before long his reign was stained by the execution of four of the most distinguished nobles.

Matidia died in the following year, and it was known to all Rome that Sabina lived unhappily with Hadrian. It is said that Plotina continued to have an active share in the administration of the Empire, though she must now have been in, or near, her seventh decade of life. Dio places her death in the year 121. Hadrian was in Gaul at the time, and the luxuriance of his mourning gave encouragement to the libellers. He went into deep mourning, breathed a passionate grief in a beautiful poem, and ordered the building of a temple for the cult of the divinity which he conferred on her. In Nimes, where he was staying at the time when her death was announced, he raised the superb mausoleum which kept her name for ages in the mind of Europe.

It is both pleasant and legitimate to believe that there was neither rhetorical display nor the memory of an irregular love in the princely mourning of Hadrian over the death of his patroness. Apart from his own indebtedness to her, the world owed her much. She had been at least a most worthy and helpful companion of a great Emperor, a type of womanhood to which the eyes of Roman matrons might happily be directed. On the day when her inanimate frame was borne from the palace to the funeral pile, men could repeat that she had in truth left that home of temptation as she had entered it. The saner and sunnier life of the vast Empire was, in part, her monument.[12]

CHAPTER IX

SABINA, THE WIFE OF HADRIAN

WE are already familiar with the extraction and the training of the next Empress of Rome. Sabina was the elder daughter of Trajan's niece Matidia, and came of the sound and sober stock of the Spanish provincials. We first meet her in the little settlement on the Rhine, where she lived with her widowed mother and grandmother, in Trajan's house, during the reign of Galba and Nerva. She was in her early teens, a grave and modest child, easily directed by the three sedate ladies of the house. Very shortly after the accession of Trajan, a charming young officer burst into the camp to offer his congratulations. He had a romantic story to tell, how a jealous brother-in-law had bribed his servants to break down the chariot on the way, and he had crossed the great forests on foot to greet his guardian and cousin. It was the future Emperor, and her future husband, Hadrian.

The wicked brother-in-law, Ursus Servianus, presently arrived, and put before Trajan a proof of his ward's enormities in the shape of a list of his debts. But Trajan was charmed with the handsome and brilliant young officer, kept him in his suite, and took him to Rome when he went up to occupy the throne; and we saw that he became a great favourite of the Imperial ladies. His father had been a first cousin of Trajan, but Hadrian lost him at the age of ten, and was committed to the guardianship of Trajan and Attianus. The finest masters of Rome directed his studies in letters, art, rhetoric, and philosophy, and he became a most accomplished and learned, as well as, by hunting and exercise, a graceful and energetic youth.

The "Historia Augusta" expressly says that Trajan "loved him," and he advanced quickly, and enjoyed the brilliant literary society of the palace and the capital. About two years after their coming to Rome he married

Sabina. One chronicler represents him as spending large sums of money to win her, and so incurring the annoyance of Trajan; another states that he turned with disdain from her plain propriety, and had to be persuaded by Plotina that the marriage was to his interest. It was, at all events, clearly a *mariage de convenance*, and was destined to have the customary sequel.

Sabina would be in her twelfth or thirteenth year at the time, and we can imagine the mating of the prim little maiden with the brilliant scholar and promising officer of twenty-four. For many years she is no more than the silent shadow of her husband, and we can only dimly follow her movements as she accompanies him about the Empire. Whether she accompanied him on the Dacian wars between 101 and 106, or, as seems more probable, remained at Rome to develop a taste for letters in the palace of Plotina, we cannot confidently say, but it is recorded that she did lean to culture. Hadrian was back in 106, high in the favour of Trajan, who gave him the diamond ring he had received from Nerva. He could both fight and carouse to the Emperor's satisfaction. He was made praetor on his return, and gave brilliant games--at Trajan's expense--in which 11,000 beasts were slain. In quick succession he became legate in Lower Pannonia and consul. The aged statesman Sura told him that he was destined for the throne; the rumour went about Rome, and the nobles, at first disdainful of his provincial accent and jealous of his progress, began to respect him. He, and most probably Sabina, accompanied Trajan on his fatal journey to the East, and we have seen what happened.

In the year 117, in about the thirtieth year of her age, Sabina found herself Empress of Rome, but the elevation seems to have brought her little happiness and impelled her to no exertion. There is little room for doubt that, either in the camp or in the tainted atmosphere of Rome or Antioch, Hadrian had contracted the vice which prevailed among Roman men. There is another reason, however, why Sabina remains in obscurity in the chronicles.

Hadrian's biographer, Gregorovius, has relieved him of the common charge that he relinquished the conquests of Trajan, and neglected Imperial interests, in a less enlightened zeal for art and letters. Hadrian had a clear, commendable, and vast policy. He believed that the Empire would only be weakened by extension, and that it was a saner ambition to enrich and uplift the life within its frontiers than to enlarge them. His life was spent in a magnificent realization of this design; and it was a design so far beyond the modest range of Sabina's political intelligence that she was forced to remain a spectator of his work. She seems, very naturally, to have carped at his one frailty, which so nearly concerned her, and Hadrian replied peevishly, and merely conveyed her as an uninterested encumbrance in the remarkable voyages which fill the twenty years of his reign.

Hadrian was then in his fortieth year, a tall, very handsome and athletic man, of brilliant conversation, untiring energy, and great public spirit. The most artistic of all Roman Emperors, one of the most artistic and cultured of monarchs, indeed, he could nevertheless endure the plain bread-and-cheese of the soldier for weeks together; and he so much discarded his horse and his

chariot, for their encouragement, that a chronicler describes him as having covered the entire Empire on foot.

By diplomacy and by bribes, which we may or may not admire, he secured an almost unbroken peace for the Empire during two decades; and the works of use or adornment with which he enriched every province of the Empire during those twenty years make up an almost fabulous achievement. Much as we must sympathize with the Empress in her resentment of the practice into which his Greek-Oriental tastes betrayed him, we cannot deny that Hadrian was a great and beneficent ruler. The sketch of his life in that prurient work, the "Historia Augusta"--the *chronique scandaleuse* of the middle Empire--is a monumental, if unconscious, panegyric.

The biographer of the Empresses cannot escape the conclusion that Sabina was not a fitting mate for so versatile and constructive a genius. Her superiority in decency is enormously outweighed by Hadrian's magnificent work for the Empire. The natural alienation of the two in sentiment would not encourage her to co-operate in his work, in the fashion set by Livia and Plotina, but one feels that this is not the sole explanation, and that her mediocre faculty was entirely absorbed in a small pursuit of culture. It is not impossible that, if there had been cordial co-operation between them, she would have saved Hadrian from the only serious stains on the record of his reign.

The first of these occurred in the year following his accession. Bringing to the Imperial task a fresh and vigorous mind, untainted by mere military ambition--though he was an excellent soldier--Hadrian glanced round the Empire, and saw that peace must first be established on its frontiers. The East was aflame with revolt, the African and German boundaries were disturbed, and trouble was announced from Britain. He at once sacrificed the conquests beyond the Tigris and Euphrates, appeased the Jews and the other peoples of the East, and passed to Lower Germany to still the restlessness of the northern frontier. There had been some discontent among the older soldiers and statesmen of Rome at his being forced on them. From Judaea he had imprudently sent one of Trajan's most fiery commanders, the Moorish prince Lusius Quietus, back in some disgrace to the capital, and this man and others formed a party of opposition. When they saw that he was sacrificing Trajan's conquests and reversing his policy, and especially when he proposed to evacuate Dacia also, they entered, it is said, into something of the nature of a conspiracy.

How far Hadrian was really responsible for the execution of the leaders of this party we cannot say, and his emphatic denial of responsibility is entitled to consideration.

We know that, when the aged statesman

Attianus wrote to urge him that the Roman prefect and other distinguished malcontents ought to be removed, he refused to take any action. The Senate now announced that a plot to assassinate Hadrian had been detected, and it put to death, without trial, four men of consular rank, Nigrinus, Palma, Celsus, and Lusius Quietus. A sullen murmur passed through the city, and Hadrian hastily composed his affairs on the Danube and went to Rome.

He resolutely denied that he had consented to the executions, and the question remains open.

With this public resentment in view, Hadrian at once lavished the most princely favours on Rome, and swore that he would never execute a Senator without the consent of his order. He remitted debts to the treasury to the extent of PS9,000,000, extended the existing charities to orphans and widows, provided magnificent spectacles for the people, and made a sacrifice of Attianus, by deposing him, to the anger of the malcontents. When the Senate offered him the triumph which had been due to Trajan for the Eastern victories, he refused it, and placed a wax image of the dead Emperor in the triumphal chariot. The citizens of Rome may have been less impressed when he showed a zeal for public morals, and forbade the mixed bathing that had hitherto been permitted; but he succeeded, by two years of untiring public service, in removing the earlier resentment. That he wished to kill Attianus, and did actually execute the architect Apollodorus, are idle legends. Serviez seriously reproduces the story that the architect had snubbed him--telling him to "go and paint his pumpkins"--when he had made a suggestion to him in earlier years, and that Hadrian avenged himself when he came to the throne. The truth is that the "Historia Augusta" describes him in consultation with Apollodorus on some building project ten years later.

The details of this vast activity of Hadrian's do not concern us, as Sabina seems to have taken no part in it.

The busts we have of her seem to show a cold and irresponsive temper, as if the Empress were contemplating disdainfully the figure of the beautiful Oriental youth on whom Hadrian's affection became concentrated. There is distinction in the smooth lines of the face and in the lofty forehead, and there is a proud strength that might very well make her "morose and harsh," as Hadrian described her, when he gave her such palpable cause for resentment.

Her mother died in 119. In a florid oration Hadrian praised her beauty of person and character, but the death would not be likely to improve the relations of the Imperial spouses.

In the year 120 or 121 Hadrian set out on the first of the long journeys which fill the rest of his career, and Sabina made the tour of the world with him. Had their intercourse been more pleasant, the lot of Sabina during the next fifteen years would have been one of great fortune.

They passed together over the whole Roman world from Eboracum (York) to Arabia and Egypt, surveying the ruined Empires of the past and the young nations of the future in the light of whatever culture the age afforded; and so beneficent was their passage that myriads of inscriptions and coins, bearing such legends as "Golden

Age" and "Restorer of the Earth," handed on to posterity the memory of the great works which Hadrian everywhere inaugurated. Through Gaul--probably through the flourishing Greek colony of Massilia (Marseilles), the solid and cultured city of Lugdunum (Lyons), and the little trading centre, Lutetia, that would one day be brilliant Paris--they passed on to Germany, and traversed the boundless forests that hid the soil of a great modern nation. No glittering pomp of guards surrounded the Emperor. Bareheaded alike in the snows of Germany and under the sun of Syria, marching commonly on foot in the dress of a soldier, and living on soldier's fare, he restored the rigid discipline of the legions wherever he went. Bridges, aqueducts, roads, temples, and colonnaded squares sprang up in the rear of his march. His staff was a band of engineers and architects.

SABINA

BUST IN THE BRITISH MUSEUM

In this novel and admirable company Sabina made the round of Gaul and Germany, and crossed over to Britain in the Imperial galleys. From the little colony of Londinium (London), which had been destroyed sixty years before, and was now restored by Hadrian, they passed along the solid Roman road to Eboracum (York), the last great station from which civilization looked out on the turbulent waves of Scottish barbarism. It was then that Hadrian ordered the building of the great wall, to keep off the Caledonian marauders, of which the traces still exist. Sabina may have remained in York while Hadrian surveyed the rough territory to the north, and it seems to have been on the Emperor's return that an episode occurred which must have greatly embittered her.

One of Hadrian's secretaries was the historian Suetonius, whose work on the Emperors has provided us with much material. With him and the cultivated commander of the Praetorian Guards Sabina maintained a close friendship, and Hadrian made a grievance of it. So closely did he pry into the affairs of his friends that the rumour was set about that he had many mistresses among their wives.

It was reported to him that Suetonius and Septicius Clarus "were behaving with more familiarity than the dignity of the Imperial house permitted," as Spartianus puts it, and they were dismissed. There is no suggestion of grave irregularity on her part. The idea of divorcing Sabina, which Hadrian is said to have discussed, is expressly connected with what he called her "moroseness and asperity"; and we can well believe that her asperity took the form of bitter complaints about his own conduct.

Nothing further was done, and, though we may regard with reserve the statement that Sabina deliberately prevented herself from having a child, lest she should put a new monster on the throne, the Imperial couple continued their uncongenial companionship.[13] Some of the coins which were struck in commemoration of their passage ventured to bear the legend, "Concordia Augusta"--struck in honour of the harmony of the Imperial household.

From Britain they returned to Gaul, where Hadrian excited comment by the opulence of his mourning over the death of Plotina. They then passed to Spain, where Roman civilization had taken deep root, and on to the land of the Moors. The colonies which Rome had planted along the strip of territory descending from the mountains to the sea had been devastated by the barbarians, and the frontier had been obliterated. Hadrian drove back the tribes, restored the towns, and returned, after an absence of more than a year, to Rome. The city was tranquil, and the building of the great villa which still, in its ruins, excites the amazement of the visitor at Tivoli, was proceeding.

After a year or two of peaceful administration, seeing that the west, north, and south of the Empire were secure and prospering, Hadrian turned his face towards the east.

We need not follow him in this journey to Greece and Asia Minor, since it is not clear whether Sabina accompanied him, but it had a sequel of melancholy interest to the Empress. From the cities of Greece he made his way along the coast of the Black Sea to the region of the Parthians, where he again restored peace, and back through Asia Minor and the islands to Rome. Two or three years had been occupied in this journey, and Hadrian had become less Roman in taste than ever.

He came home surrounded by Greeks, and with a great zeal for Greek and Eastern institutions. In particular he brought in his train a beautiful Bithynian youth whose name is from that time inseparably connected with his.

Hadrian's passion for Antinous is the chief stain on his character, and was probably the chief ground of Sabina's resentment. The Emperor had visited Bithynia, and presumably met the youth there. Every traveller among rude and healthy nations is aware that such practices are by no means confined to decadent civilizations, nor does the student of contemporary morals see in them anything distinctive of the life of ancient Syria, Greece, or Rome.

Nevertheless, the remarkable beauty of Antinous, which is familiar to us in many a statue, and the wanton openness of his association with the Emperor, attracted general attention and greatly embittered Sabina.

When, therefore, she set out with Hadrian, at the end of 128 or the beginning of 129, for a fresh and more extensive tour in the East, her enjoyment must have been heavily clouded by the daily and hourly presence of the Emperor's companions. The young Adonis was not the only source of offence in Hadrian's suite. Closer still to Hadrian was a young Roman noble of the most effeminate charm and the most dissolute life. Lucius Ceionius Commodus was later taken into Imperial partnership by Hadrian, and, although he did not live to attain supreme power, his descendants will more than once enter and disturb our story of the Empresses. Spartianus ascribes to him a "regal beauty" of face and person, a manner of great charm, a witty and sparkling conversation, and an utter depravity of morals. He had won the regard of Hadrian, not so much by the famous new dish which he had invented for the epicures of Rome--a boar, ham, pheasant, and peacock pie--as by the sensuous charm of his person and the exotic sensuality of his life. He would lie, washed in exquisite Persian ointments, on a couch strewn with roses, with a coverlet of lilies drawn over himself and his companion. Such ways were entirely foreign to the nature of Hadrian, but his robust vigour was singularly united with a fine artistic sensibility and a love of the softer east, which led him into many inconsistencies.

Sabina had for companion a Greek poetess, Julia Fadilla, of such virtue and attainments that a statue was somewhere raised to honour her as a pattern of integrity.

The incongruous party, with its conflicting groups of virtue and vice--a fitting symbol of the unhappy union of West and East--crossed the sea to Athens, and then visited Corinth, Eleusis, and the other surviving cities of Greece.

The frame of that superb civilization still gleamed, almost intact, on the soil of Hellas, though the soul of Greece had departed. It was as if one gazed on the smooth white corpse of a beautiful woman. Groups of sophists still disputed in the gardens or under the shady colonnades; but they were puny mimics of Socrates, Zeno, and Epicurus. Politicians still babbled in the Agora; but they blessed the hand of Rome that had closed brutally on the throat of their fair country. The Acropolis still shone in its panoply of Parian marble, and Hadrian had restored the harbour and repaired many of the ravages of time and violence. He regretted the greed of his forerunners, and sought to restore the ancient spirit. But the poor revival of art and letters and religion, which he succeeded in effecting, was only the last flicker of the vitality of Greece.

They crossed the sea to Ephesus, which at that time rivalled Antioch and Alexandria as a metropolis of the decaying civilizations of the East. Its great Temple of Diana, a teeming store of art and treasure, drew men from all parts, while priests of all religions mingled in its streets with panders to all vices and ministers to every form of art and luxury. Smyrna, another flourishing city of Asia Minor, attracted them next, with its magnificent assemblage of temples, colonnades, baths, and theatres, and they passed on to Sardis and the other cities of that fascinating and repellent Greek-Oriental region, where new mysticism ran like veins of gold in the old volcanic deposits. The winter was spent in the luxury of Ephesus and Smyrna, and with the spring they traversed the successive provinces of Asia Minor, admiring and restoring the remains of Greek and Persian grandeur. Through Syria, where famous Antioch detained them for a time, they went on, probably, to the ruined cities of Tyre and Sidon, and returned to Heliopolis, Damascus, and Palmyra.

In Palestine they found the survivors of the scattered Jewish nation living in great poverty and dejection among the ruins of their cities, or still scrutinizing the prophets and looking for the Messiah in the larger communities on the coast. On the site of Jerusalem, where a few broken towers gave a melancholy reminder of their former prosperity, Hadrian ordered that a new Roman colony should be established.

From Judaea they moved to Arabia, and then to Egypt.

Alexandria was then the second city of the world in importance, the first in interest. All the exhausted streams of the older civilizations had poured into it. Never before or since was there so cosmopolitan a population, such a gathering of old vices and new moralities, dead religions and fresh religions, cults six thousand years old and the latest gospels of Judaea and Persia. Its harbour still held the ships of every port in the Mediterranean, its Serapeum, Museum, and Caesareum sheltered the art and culture of the world, and its deafening streets rang with the tongues of the world. But the soul of Egypt, too, was dead, and the Imperial party moved up the Nile to admire the surviving relics of its past. No doubt priests and learned men from Alexandria would attend as interpreters. They wandered in Memphis, which the sand of the desert was beginning to bury, passed through Heliopolis, and reached Besa, where they experienced the great sensation of the tour. The beautiful Bithynian youth was drowned in the Nile, and Sabina had to regard with disdain the womanly tears and the extravagant mourning of the Emperor. It is not clear to this day whether the death was accidental or voluntary. Hadrian, of course, said that it was accidental; but a rumour lingers in the chronicles that the Emperor, in his new zeal for Oriental superstition, had learned that his life was doomed unless some loved being was sacrificed for him, and Antinous offered himself. Hadrian has taken the secret with him, but the temples and statues he raised all over the Empire kept the memory of the pretty youth fresh for centuries.

This occurred about the month of October. The dates of these journeys of Hadrian are much disputed, but a trivial detail has determined this part of the tour. They went on to Thebes, and, in accordance with custom, cut their names and the date in the great statue of Memnon.

They probably pushed on as far as Philae, to see the temple of Isis, but we find them back in Syria at the end of the year, or the beginning of 132, and soon afterwards in Rome. The great villa had now been completed at Tivoli, and we must assume that Sabina lived there during the three or four years that remained for her.

They were years of continued melancholy. Hadrian was sobered, but soured. The Jews had disturbed his cherished peace by rebelling, on account of his design to cover the site of their holy city with a Roman colony, and he had ruthlessly destroyed what remained of their cities, and erased the name of Jerusalem by calling the new town AElia

Capitolina. Illness began to enfeeble his frame, and he brooded darkly over the question of a successor, which men were discussing. He passed in heavy dejection through the lovely gardens and marble temples of his villa, still mourning the loss of Antinous. An obelisk has been found there with the inscription that it was raised to the youth by Hadrian and Sabina--a fiction that must have angered the Empress, if it were done before her death. But she did not live to see the darker gloom of his closing years. She died in, or about, the year 136, "not without a rumour of poison," says Spartianus; the rumour is not worth considering. She had been entitled "Augusta" by the Senate in 127, but Hadrian refused her the divine honours which were usually bestowed on dead Empresses. They were awarded by his successor.

The busts of Sabina which we have suggest just such a personality as we have gathered from the meagre references to her in the chronicles. She was a woman of smooth and regular features and fine person, without beauty or charm.

Her face gives an impression of intellect, virtue, and silent suffering. She is the kind of woman who would neither overlook the vice of her husband nor actively resent it, or assert herself in any way; the kind of woman to retreat in disdain to her books. That she was "treated as a slave" by Hadrian, as Aurelius Victor says, we may decline to believe, and regard the statement as a popular exaggeration; nor, on the other hand, can we agree with Gregorovius that a letter in which Hadrian invites his mother to dine with him on his birthday, and says that Sabina has gone into the country, shows their "mutual dislike." Duruy quotes this very letter in disproof of the belief that they were estranged, and points out that it goes on to say that Sabina had "sent her share for the family dinner." The French historian believes that the legend, "Concordia Augusta," on some of the medals of the time expressed a fact. We cannot, however, imagine Sabina resigning herself to her husband's passion for youths, and the few authentic details left us about her relations with Hadrian generally indicate a mutual aversion.

As an Empress, she was a nonentity; as a woman, an admirable blend of old-world sobriety and new-world culture.

Hadrian survived her for two unhappy years. The whole Empire was covered with monuments of his public service, the coinage of every province proclaimed his beneficence, the slave, the widow, and the orphan gratefully told of his magnanimity. But the illness and depression of his last year permitted him to commit a crime, and, so accustomed was the new generation to good conduct in its rulers, the recollection of his great deeds was almost obliterated. To the astonishment of all, and the indignation of the thoughtful, Hadrian announced that he had chosen as Caesar his dissolute and decadent companion, Lucius Verus. His brother-in-law Servianus, now an old man of ninety, and the grandson of Servianus, a youth of nineteen, seem to have been among the murmurers, and, on trivial pretexts, they were put to death. These cruel murders brought a deep shadow over Hadrian's last year, but a last opportunity was given him to repair his action.

Lucius Verus, worn and consumptive from debauch, died, and Hadrian now made choice of the most worthy man in the Senate, Titus Antoninus; adding, however, in his quaint way of mingling good and evil, that he must in turn adopt the son of Lucius Verus and young Marcus Aurelius, a Sybarite and a Stoic, two antithetic types of Roman life.

He went down to Baiae, suffering acutely from dropsy.

The pain and weariness were so great that he tried to secure poison or a sword, but Antoninus prudently guarded and nursed him. He died in the year 138, "done to death by physicians," he ironically said. In his last days he composed some slight verses, which I may translate:

Little soul, so tired and still,
Guest of this decaying flesh,
Whither, now, will thy flight be?
Pale and cold and reft of speech,
Never more to utter joke.

It was the note of the time-spirit, which was so strangely incarnated in Hadrian. He united in his person all the contradictions that were at strife in his era of change--asceticism and sensuality, public spirit and selfish sensibility, Stoicism and Cyrenaicism. He needed a stronger Empress. But the better spirit prevailed in him at the end, and the Stoics came to the throne.

CHAPTER X

THE WIVES OF THE STOICS

ON the twenty-fifth of February, in the year 138, Hadrian had summoned the Senators to the palace.

Verus was dead, and the whole world wondered on whom the erratic fancy of the ailing Emperor would rest next. Among the Senators was a distinguished, able, and amiable statesman and commander, Titus Aurelius Fulvus Boionius Arrius Antoninus, whose great merit had--as the long series of names implies--been richly rewarded by older relatives. He had been much consulted by Hadrian in his last years, and was respected by all. To the great relief of the Senate the wavering finger of the Emperor fell on this man, and he was acclaimed Caesar. He attended Hadrian devotedly, prolonged the useless life which lingered between him and the throne, and--it was rumoured--saved many a noble head from execution in the last frenzies of Hadrian. Early in July that great traveller set out on his last journey, and Aurelius Antoninus--a name to which the Senate soon added the appellation of Pius--ascended the throne.

The new Empress of Rome was Annia Galeria Faustina, a matron in her thirty-fourth year, of an ancient and distinguished Italian family. It is of some interest to regard the extraction of Faustina. Through her the Imperial throne is about to pass once more to one of its most ignoble occupants, and Rome will sink rapidly from the reign of Marcus Aurelius to the riot of Commodus. The two opposing tendencies of Roman life meet in her family, and the Stoic succumbs to the Epicurean--or, rather, to the Sybaritic or Cyrenaic, for the gospel of Epicurus was one of dignity and sobriety. Rome might have said, in the later language of Goethe, as he depicted himself passing through a similar phase:

Zwei Seelen wohnen, ach, in meiner Brust.

One soul leaned to sloth, sensual and selfish indulgence: one, with larger horizon, was for temperance, vigour, and Imperial duty. The curious feature of this critical stage in the fortunes of Rome is that the two tendencies are developed within the same family, and the Stoic yields to the Sybarite. Annia Galeria Faustina was born of the same parents as the father of Marcus Aurelius, and was reared in the same atmosphere of old Roman virtue, or manliness, as the word signifies. The great-grandfather of Marcus Aurelius was Annius Verus, a Senator of great merit and of Spanish extraction. His son Annius Verus was twice consul, and both his sons in turn--the father and uncle of Marcus Aurelius--were promoted to the consulate. Everything we know of the family suggests a fine and sober patrician type, and confirms the beautiful picture of it given us by Marcus Aurelius in his "Meditations."

The one element of possible weakness in the ancestry of the Faustinas and of Commodus is in the mother of Annia Galeria Faustina. Annius Verus had married Rupilia Faustina. Her family is obscure, and, though one must hesitate to trace to her this strain of weakness and vice on such slender grounds, one is disposed to believe that she was married for her beauty, and brought into that strong family the tainted germ which ripened in more than one of her descendants. It may, however, very well be that the strength of the stock was decaying--Marcus Aurelius himself was delicate--and its later descendants succumbed to the evil influences about them. A genealogical table will show how the fate of Rome hung on this family for more than a generation:--

FAUSTINA THE ELDER

BUST IN THE LOUVRE

* * * * *

Annius Verus (twice consul)
and Rupilia Faustina
|
+--------------------+----------------------------+
| | |

Annius Libo Annius Verus (consul) Annia Galeria Faustina
(consul) (marries Domitia Calvilla) (marries Antoninus Pius)
| |
+-----------------+ ------+-------
| |
Annia Cornificia Marcus Aurelius Annia Faustina
(marries Annia Faustina) |
| |
+--------------+---------------+
|
Commodus

Faustina had inherited her mother's beauty, and was reared in a very conscientious home. It was the home in which Marcus Aurelius learned his first lessons in virtue, as his father died early, and all the chroniclers speak of it with great respect. We know very little about her, however, until she becomes Empress, and, as she died three years afterwards, we have not much concern with her.

She is believed to have married somewhat late for a Roman girl, in or about her sixteenth year (120). Titus Aurelius Antoninus was then in his thirty-fourth year, a tall, graceful, and handsome man, of quiet and captivating manners, good cultivation, fine character, and a face of great dignity and sweetness. He was of good family, and was advancing rapidly in the public service. Shortly after the marriage he became consul, and he remained in Rome in one or other civic capacity until 128 or 129. He was very wealthy and greatly esteemed.

One of the chroniclers has charged her with light behaviour, and, as this is the only period in which we can plausibly entertain it, we may regard the charge for a moment. The book of Dio's history for the reign of Antoninus Pius is lost, so that neither he nor his commentators throw any light on Faustina. Aurelius Victor and Eutropius say nothing of her character. The one hostile witness is "Julius Capitolinus," the anonymous writer of the fourth century who provides the sketch of the life of Antoninus Pius in the "Historia Augusta." He says (c. 3): "Many things are said of his wife's excessive freedom and looseness of life, which he had painfully to overlook." Serviez enlarges on this with his usual license.

But as he makes Faustina the sister of AElius Verus, and says that she neglected the education of her children, which is also untrue, we may ignore him.

It is now more customary to reject this charge against the elder Faustina, on the ground that the single witness is a light anecdotist of the fourth century. Moreover, when the tutor Fronto wrote a glowing panegyric of Faustina after her death, Antoninus Pius answered that it was even more true than eloquent, and swore that he "would rather live with her at Gyaros [a barren island, to which criminals were deported] than in a palace without her." Nevertheless, we must leave the question open. Antoninus Pius was not a puritan. When the Emperor Julian introduces him before the gods, in his charming contest of the Emperors for the highest praise ("The Caesars"), he calls him "a moderate man, not indeed in love-affairs, but in the administration of the Empire." Faustina was probably charming enough to merit his sincere lament. But as Capitolinus mingles truth and untruth with a very light hand, and the relevant book of Dio is wanting, we cannot decide the issue.

In the year 128 or 129 Antoninus was appointed Proconsul of Asia, and he and Faustina went to Smyrna. The elder of their two daughters died about the same time. An amusing incident in connexion with their arrival is narrated by Philostratus in his "Lives of the Sophists." The Proconsul at once occupied the finest house in Smyrna, the home of the teacher Polemo, who was absent. Polemo was the idol of Smyrna, and was proportionately conceited.

He drew youths from all parts to his school, and had won much favour from Hadrian for the city. He travelled in a superb Phrygian chariot, and his mules had silver trappings; and when some grumblers had hinted that he had diverted to his own pocket some of Hadrian's subsidies, he had pompously written to the Emperor: "Polemo has given me an account of money given by you to him." This conceited sophist reached his house in the middle of the night, and found the Proconsul and Faustina abed there.

He promptly turned them out, and roundly abused them.

Years afterwards, when the genial Antoninus was Emperor, and Polemo came to the palace, he said laughingly to an attendant: "See that Polemo has a chamber in the palace, and that no one turns him out." Later an actor came from Smyrna to complain that Polemo, the autocrat, had turned him out of the theatre. "At what hour?"

asked the Emperor gravely. It was at midday. "That is nothing; he turned me out at midnight," said the Emperor.

The amiability and solid work of Antoninus must have won Polemo, as Hadrian is reported to have said in his will that it was he who advised the adoption of Antoninus. But the East generally so much appreciated the Proconsul that, when he returned to Rome, he stood very high in the favour of Hadrian. We again lose sight of Faustina until he becomes Emperor, and then there are one or two brief references to her before she dies in 141. At his accession he refused the greater part of the money (*aurum coronarium*) which was due to him, by custom, from the provinces, and drew very liberally on his private fortune for paying the great expenses entailed. Faustina naturally demurred.

"Foolish woman," he is said to have answered, "when we obtained the Empire we lost what we previously possessed."

The only other reference is contained in a letter of the younger Faustina to Marcus Aurelius: "In the defection of Celsus my mother exhorted Antoninus to be concerned first about his own family." We know nothing of this revolt. Apparently Antoninus, like Marcus Aurelius, was disposed to be dangerously lenient. The final reference to Faustina is that she died in the third year of his reign (141), and was deeply mourned by him. Nominated "Augusta" in life, she was deified at death, and Antoninus built in her honour the beautiful temple of which traces are still seen in Rome. He also instituted in her honour a fresh charity for orphans, the "Puellae Faustinianae," and ordered that gold and silver statues of her should be borne in the processions.

This sincere tribute of the Emperor tells at least of a great affection and esteem, but the literary references to Faustina are too meagre and disputable to bring her clearly before us. The busts that are believed to represent her do not, unfortunately, assist us much. In the Capitoline Museum at Rome is one that may depict her in her twenties or earlier. It has a round and tranquil face, not devoid of strength, but more directly suggesting an even and sober character. Another bust, in the Vatican Museum, shows the same features at a later age; but a third, in the same Museum, has not so pleasant an expression.

The oval face is hard and querulous. The loose lips droop at the ends; the large eyes, prominent cheekbones, and strong chin have an expression that is very far from tender or spiritual. The bust that is attributed to her in the British Museum is between the two. The elder Faustina remains in obscurity, and we pass to her more notorious daughter and successor.

For twenty years after the death of Faustina there was no Empress of Rome. Antoninus, who was in his fifty-fifth year, refused to marry again, and took a concubine--an arrangement recognized in Roman law and

practice, in which marriage had several degrees. It was an era of general peace and great prosperity. The group of Stoic lawyers that the

Emperor gathered about him humanely moderated the rigour of the laws, medical service was supplied to the poor in the towns, the school-system was further endowed, and works of mercy continued to multiply. The armies usually rested--and, it is to be feared, rusted--the treasury was again filled, the Empire was happy and prosperous. In the year 161 the cheerful, benevolent Antoninus passed away, and the two men whom Hadrian had compelled him to adopt came to their joint reign. With them are introduced two new Empresses of no little interest.

The two boys whom Hadrian had lightly designated as the heirs to the throne after Antoninus were Annius Verus, or Verissimus, as Hadrian genially called him on account of his precocious gravity and piety, and Lucius Verus, son of Hadrian's dissolute companion. Annius was a great favourite of the Emperor. He received office in his sixth year, and donned the philosopher's cloak in his twelfth.

He was the pet of his grandfather's palace, but so serious in his Stoicism that his mother had difficulty in persuading him to sleep in a bed instead of on the floor. In his sixteenth year Hadrian gave him the manly toga, and betrothed him to the daughter of Lucius Verus. In his eighteenth year he was "terrified" to hear that he had been chosen for the succession, and must go to live in the palace. Then Hadrian died, and Antoninus adopted him.

Gibbon has greatly praised Antoninus for preferring the welfare of the State to the interest of his family in this adoption. It is true that, as we know from coins, Antoninus and Faustina had had two sons, as well as two daughters, but they must have died before the year 138. Dio expressly says that Hadrian ordered Antoninus to adopt the two youths "because he had no male children at the time."

His boys, like his elder daughter, must have died before that time; and indeed we have no further mention of them.

But if this particular grace cannot be allowed to Antoninus, we must admire his careful control of their education and his discriminating guidance of their fortunes. The best masters in Rome instructed each of them, and it was only the deep-rooted difference in their constitutions--the moral strength of the one and weakness of the other--that led them to diverge so widely. The vigilant eye of the Emperor observed the dissimilarity of promise. He left Lucius Verus out of the way of promotion, and destined Marcus for the great advancement.

No sooner was Antoninus on the throne than he approached Marcus, through Faustina, with a proposal of marriage with his daughter. She had been promised by Hadrian to young Lucius Verus, and Marcus was to marry Ceionia. The Emperor proposed to cancel these contracts, and marry the younger Faustina to the young Stoic. It would be extremely interesting if we could penetrate the feelings of the young princess at the time.

The later busts of her suggest a pretty, round-faced girl, probably in her early teens, with small eyes and a lively temperament. The grim and austere young scholar would not attract her, and one can imagine her feelings when he asked time to consider whether he would accept the hand of the Emperor's charming daughter. Marcus philosophically weighed the proposal in his mind until the time he asked had expired, and then he consented to betrothal.

He was appointed Caesar and consul designate, and given the palace of Tiberius for a dwelling. A bust that we have of him, in the Capitol Museum, represents him about this time--a face of singular beauty and refinement framed in a mass of short curly hair.

Their marriage--a superb ceremony--did not take place until about seven years later (145), a circumstance which we may regard as a further philosophic error. During the years of waiting, and during most of the reign of Antoninus, Marcus was absorbed in study. He was penetrated with the aphorism of Plato, that the State would be happy whose prince was a philosopher. What the effect was on Faustina we may be in a better position to say later. Her mother had died in 141, her womanhood was fully born, and the eye of her father had an Empire to survey. At the death of Antoninus the throne was at once offered to Marcus. In his last moments Antoninus had ordered the golden statue of Fortune, which he kept in his chamber, to be conveyed to Marcus. From a sense of duty he, unluckily for Rome, associated Lucius Verus with him in the Empire. Somewhat delicate himself, he relied on Verus for such work abroad as was immediately necessary, and continued to frequent the schools.

His peaceful studies were quickly interrupted. Fatal floods and scarcity of food disturbed the capital; the eastern frontier was again aflame, and the German frontier was threatened. Marcus sent Verus to take command in the East, after betrothing him to his daughter Lucilla, held off the northern barbarians with bribes and diplomacy, and worked hard for the relief of Rome. For a time his policy seemed to triumph. The Germans were pacified, and the eastern peoples repressed. Verus, indeed, advanced no farther than the voluptuous palaces of Antioch and the licentious groves of Daphne. Once only during the campaign did he quit the luxury of Antioch. He heard that Marcus was coming East with his daughter Lucilla, and hastened to meet him otherwhere than in garrulous Antioch.

Marcus did not leave Italy, however, and Verus wedded Lucilla, and returned to his perfumed vices. Happily, there was in the East a Roman general of the old stamp, Avidius Cassius, a strong and blunt man, disdainful of luxury. He lashed the debauched troops into a state of discipline, pacified the East, and let Verus return to Rome to enjoy his triumph.

Here begin the stories that have gathered about the memory of the younger Faustina, and have persuaded many a writer that, as one of the authorities says, she became a second Messalina. If we are to believe the "Augustan History," she behaved with the most abominable license throughout her whole married life. Four Roman nobles are specifically named as notorious lovers of the Empress, and she is charged with general license. One of the four was named Tertullus, and it is said that one day, when Marcus was in the theatre, an actor made flagrant reference to this liaison. Asked for the name of a certain lover, he said three times (*ter*), "Tullus, Tullus, Tullus."

It is added that Marcus--who might very well miss a point in the theatre, as he read and wrote letters there--was quite aware of the liaison, because he one day surprised Faustina at breakfast with Tertullus. The Empress is further charged with adultery with the voluptuous colleague of her husband, and with wantoning among actors, gladiators, sailors, and others of the baser sort.

The more sober writers on Faustina have generally been unwilling to admit this debauchery. Duruy rejects the stories altogether, Merivale recommends reserve, and Renan thinks that "careful research has reduced to very small proportions the accusations which scandal was pleased to bring against the wife of Marcus Aurelius." It seems to me that we can only come to the same conclusion as we did in regard to Messalina; we must regard particular legends with reserve, but must conclude that the general opinion of Faustina at the time, which the stories embody, must have had a serious basis. Some of the stories put on record by Capitolinus in the "Augustan History" are palpably false. One runs that she confessed to Marcus her passion for a certain gladiator, and that Marcus was directed by the Chaldaean sages, whom he consulted, to kill the man and bathe the Empress in his blood. Her passion was cured, but her next child was the brutal Commodus. This story is so gross--I do not reproduce all the details--that the writer does not insist on it, but he continues: "Still, as her conduct with the gladiators is well known, Commodus probably was the son of a gladiator." Now the tutor of the princes, Fronto, remarks in one of his letters, and the surviving busts bear him out, that Commodus had a striking likeness to Marcus Aurelius.

I may add that Commodus was born in the year of the Emperor's accession, when such conduct is incredible.

FAUSTINA THE YOUNGER

BUST (REPUTED) IN THE BRITISH MUSEUM

Other parts of the legend are just as vulnerable. Thus it is said that Faustina poisoned Verus when he boasted to his wife of his relations with her. He died a very natural death, as we shall see later. On the other hand, Dio, who lived shortly afterwards, and had no dislike for scandal, knows nothing whatever about this looseness on the part of the Empress, and there is nothing in Eutropius or Aurelius Victor. The only other writer who, in a general way, accuses Faustina of dissoluteness is the Emperor Julian ("Caesars," c. 28). We are therefore in a dilemma, and must not too readily speak of Faustina as a second Messalina. The quiet assumption of her guilt in Julian, and the fact that the stories in the "Augustan History" are professedly taken from Marius Maximus, an historical writer not far removed from her time, imply a very general belief in her guilt. In one place Capitolinus says (c. 23) that the Emperor "cleared her by his letters"

of the charge of loose behaviour with actors, and in another represents him as saying, when he is urged to divorce her on account of her vices: "If we send away the wife, we must give up her dowry," though the Empire could hardly be called Faustina's dowry. In a third place, however, Capitolinus leaves it open whether Marcus "was ignorant of, or ignored," his wife's misconduct. For many writers, in fact, the attitude of Marcus is decisive. If such things had been done he must have known, and, with such knowledge, he could not have spoken so highly of his wife in his "Meditations," and would not have dared to set up, in her memory, an altar on which the maidens of Rome should offer sacrifice before marriage.

The scale, in truth, is somewhat evenly balanced, yet one cannot easily conceive that the heavy charges of Marius Maximus and the deliberate verdict of Julian had no foundation. Whether from weakness, or from an excess of casuistry, Marcus Aurelius lacked decision or penetration in such matters. He married his daughter to a profligate, whom he afterwards deified, and he committed the Empire to a son who had given early promise of vice.

His grave and ascetic ways probably repelled the gay and beautiful woman whom he had diplomatically married, and she seems to have sought relief. None of the busts, medallions, or coins, which more or less convey an image of her to us, suggest character or culture, but rather a weak control and a sensuous temper. From her Commodus derived the enfeebled will that put him at the mercy of his more dissolute courtiers, and the sensuality that made his short reign an indescribable debauch. Much as we should like to relieve Marcus Aurelius of the shame of having begotten such a monster, we must admit his parentage, and cast what blame there is on the mother.

In this unsatisfactory haze we must leave the conduct of the Empress during the years in which her husband wrought for the safety of the Empire, bequeathed his austere reflections to later ages, or contemplated the golden images of his teachers in his *lararium*. The triumphant return of Verus was quickly followed by years of gravest anxiety. In the pestilential East the legions had absorbed the germs of plague, had strewn them along their route, and had now disseminated them throughout Rome. Thousands of victims, rich and poor, succumbed to the subtle malady. Marcus vainly summoned the ministers of every religion and the medical men of all schools, and sacrificed those obscure Christians on whom popular anger was ever ready to visit a calamity. His trouble increased when it was announced that the fierce Marcomanni of the north had burst into the Empire, and were driving the Romans before them. With great energy he mustered the demoralized legions in the north, and set out with Verus against the enemy. In the middle of the war (168) Verus, who had repeatedly tried to return to the comfort of the capital, died. He had an apoplectic fit on the journey, and we may ignore the various suggestions that either Lucilla, or Faustina, or Marcus put an end to his useless career.

Marcus continued for several years the task of settling the frontier tribes. It seems that Faustina went with him on these arduous campaigns, though whether we may see in the circumstance any merit on her part, or a device of the Emperor to control her conduct, it is impossible to say. She at least earned a title--"Mother of the Camps" and "Mother of the Legions"--which is found on few coins of the Empresses. It is probable that her disorders belonged to an earlier date, before and in the early part of the Emperor's reign. It is chiefly at Gaeta, the pretty bay on the coast where many Romans had villas, that Capitolinus places her familiarity with gladiators and sailors. Possibly the sobriety of her later years was accepted by her husband as an expiation, and held to justify his eulogy of her.

Those later years were full of trouble and anxiety.

Not only did two of their children die, and their daughter Lucilla become the widow of a notorious profligate, but the gods seemed to have entered upon a contest with the virtue of Marcus Aurelius. A great earthquake shook the East, the plague left a blackened trail over the Empire and infested the camps, and other disasters were crowded into a few years. The treasury ran short, and Marcus was obliged to put up the

Imperial treasures at auction to obtain funds for carrying on the war. His one consolation was that the Eastern frontier was tranquil, yet in the year 175 a messenger came to announce that his great general, Avidius Cassius, was in revolt, and claimed the Empire.

Verus, who must have felt the scorn of the stronger man, had warned Marcus years before that Cassius was dangerous, but the actual revolt is persistently connected in the chronicles with Faustina. Cassius had ambition, and had only been prevented by his father in earlier years from rising against Antoninus Pius. In 174 or 175, it is said by Dio, he received a message from Faustina, proposing that, in the event of Marcus dying, he should marry her, and occupy the throne. Shortly after this a false message reached him that Marcus was dead, and he at once announced to the legions that he assumed the Empire. The message was quickly contradicted, but Cassius thought it too late to retire, and he prepared for a struggle. Marcus sadly moved towards the East.

Before he had gone far, however, he learned that the soldiers, who hated Cassius for his rigour, had put him to death.

The position of Faustina is once more in grave ambiguity. The writer on Cassius in the "Historia Augusta" gives the rumour implicating her, but rejects it. Unfortunately, his rejection is in this case no more weighty than his acceptance in others. He admits that his source, Marius Maximus, believes Faustina guilty, and ascribes it to "a wish to defame" the Empress. Except that the hatred of Commodus at Rome may have for some time been extended to the woman who had borne him, there is no clear reason why Maximus should calumniate Faustina. Dio, who lives very close to the time, gives it as a positive fact that Faustina secretly urged Cassius to marry her, and occupy the throne, if Marcus died. We may concur in the verdict of most of the writers on the matter. Marcus was ailing, delicate, and overburdened with work. It seemed to Faustina that he would not live long, and, as Commodus was a callow and unpromising youth, and by no means sure of succession, she sought an arrangement by which she should remain on the throne if her husband died.

It is not generally felt that there was anything gravely reprehensible in this, but a secret negotiation of such a character does not present her to us in an attractive light.

Her subsequent zeal for the punishment of Cassius and his friends is equally unpleasant, even if we recall that she had no intention of raising him against the Emperor while he lived. Several letters which passed between Marcus and Faustina have been preserved in the "Historia

Augusta," from Marius Maximus, and there seems to be little ground to doubt their genuineness. They suggest that Marcus was in the habit of consulting with Faustina on matters of grave importance. "Come up to the Alban Mount," he writes her, after telling of the sedition, "and by the favour of the gods, we will discuss the affair in safety." Faustina replies:

"I will set out to-morrow for the Alban Mount, as you command, but I at once implore you, if you love your children, to visit these rebels with the utmost severity.

The soldiers and their leaders have fallen into evil ways, and they will crush us if we do not coerce them."

In another letter she presses him again:

"My mother Faustina urged your father [by adoption]

Pius, at the time of the secession of Celsus, to feel first for his own family.... You see how young Commodus is, and our son-in-law Pompeianus is older and is abroad.

Do not spare men who have not spared you, and would not spare me and the children if they won."

A later letter of Marcus tells that he has read her exhortation in his villa at Formiae (on the Gulf of Gaeta).

By that time he has heard that Cassius is dead, and he will hear of no further revenge on his family. He will spare his wife and children, and beg the Senate to be moderate in punishing the accomplices, because "there is nothing that so much commends the Emperor of Rome to the nations as clemency." We know, in fact, that he treated the family of Cassius with great generosity.

The Emperor and Empress then went to the East to complete the work of pacification. In the course of the voyage, in a little village at the foot of

Mount Taurus, Faustina met her end in the year 175. As a matter of course she was placed among the gods, but Marcus was not content with the customary honouring of her memory.

He gave the village the name of Faustinopolis, founded a fresh charity with the title of "Puellae Faustinianae," and built a beautiful temple at Rome, which, when he died a few years later, was dedicated in their joint names by the Senate. As if to obliterate all the rumours about her infidelity, he went on to ask extraordinary honours for her of the Senate. He set up a special altar, with a silver statue of her, in the temple of Venus, and directed that maidens about to marry should offer sacrifice on it; and he had a golden statue of her placed on her seat in the theatre whenever he attended its performances.

Dio gives two versions of the death of Faustina which were current in his time. Some said that she died of gout, from which she suffered; others held that she put an end to her life in fear lest her complicity with Cassius should be discovered by Marcus in the East. The second theory is superfluous. The natural cause of death seems adequate enough, nor would she be in any serious danger if Marcus heard that Cassius had made her the pretext of his rebellion. Her chief misdeeds were to live after her.

Frivolous, and probably licentious, in her early married life, she seems to have settled in sober ways when she became Empress, but we find no influence of hers in the ordering of affairs. Had she only reared healthy children to succeed her husband, she might have contributed worthily to the mighty task of supporting the shaken Empire. Instead, she gave to the Empire Lucilla and Commodus, her two surviving children, and it fell into a fresh degradation.

CHAPTER XI

THE WIVES OF THE SYBARITES

AS Marcus Aurelius and Lucius Verus had been equal in Imperial power, and both were married, we have one more Empress to regard before we pass on to the wives of Commodus; and the account we have already given of Verus will justify us in relegating her to this distinct chapter. Verus had married Lucilla, the eldest daughter of Marcus and Faustina; but the ambiguous repute of her mother will warn us not to expect a painful spectacle of vice in alliance with lofty virtue. Lucilla carries a step further the unhappy disposition which we have suspected in her grandmother, and more palpably detected in her mother. By her union with Lucius Verus vice was once more decked with the Imperial purple and justified in the eyes of Rome. We may briefly consider Lucilla as Empress before we follow her lamentable career under the reign of her brother.

Lucilla was born in the first year of the married life of Marcus and Faustina. Marcus was then a pale and thin-blooded scholar, Faustina in the full warmth and sensuousness of young womanhood, and it was not unnatural that the child should inherit the temper of her mother without the spiritual restraint of her sire. She was educated with the greatest care, and was betrothed to Verus in her sixteenth year. Presumably by the will of her father, and certainly with the full assent of Verus, she remained two further years in the palace, while Verus wore out his strength in the dissipations of Antioch. Marcus heard of his conduct, and sent out Lucilla to marry him; as if a union with a young woman of seventeen or eighteen would be apt to have a sobering influence on a man of Verus's habits and parentage. Verus met her at Ephesus, married her there with great pomp, and returned with her to his pleasures at Antioch.

They came to Rome at the peace of 166, and Marcus could not fail to learn in full the character of the man to whom he had entrusted his daughter and half his power.

The villa which Verus occupied in the Clodian Way was the most notorious house of debauch in Rome. It swarmed with the dancing-girls, boys, Eastern slaves, musicians, conjurors, etc., that Verus had brought from the East.

One room was fitted up as a popular tavern, and we must leave under the veil of a dead language the abominations that were perpetrated there. One can only repeat such comparatively decent details as that Verus would have gladiators to fight in his house during dinner, and prolong the carouse until his slaves had to bear away his stupefied form on his couch; or that, on other occasions, he would emulate the early feats of Nero, and revel at nights in the wine-shops and brothels of the popular quarter. One night he gave a superbly furnished banquet, and at the close, in a drunken fit, presented to his guests the costly plate, and even the litters, with silver-harnessed mules, in which they were taken home.

Marcus made several futile attempts to brace him by a campaign in the north, and must have been sincerely relieved when he at last paid, by a premature death, the price of his excesses. Lucilla had then been Empress for eleven years. As she is barely noticed in the chronicles, we are left to imagine the effect on her of living through her early womanhood in such a palace as that of Verus. Probably disgust saved her very largely from the taint. Verus's sister Fabia lived with them, and was generally believed to be intimate with her brother. She at least usurped the place of Lucilla in authority, and the Empress must have been as much relieved as her father when Verus died. He was rumoured to have been poisoned by Lucilla because of his relations with Fabia; by Faustina, for betraying his relations with her; and by Marcus, to rid the Empire of his sottishness. But an apoplectic fit would be so natural a crown to such a career that we can dispense with so much poison.

Lucilla was then married by Marcus to an elderly and worthy Senator, Claudius Pompeianus. She and her mother strongly resented the marriage, and demanded a younger and more attractive husband; but the Emperor was unusually firm. Unhappily, his firmness was misplaced, for the austerity or age of Pompeianus effected what the profligacy of Verus had failed to do, and Lucilla fell into vicious ways. We may conjecture that this did not happen until after her father's death. Marcus had returned to the war against the Marcomanni, and, after three years of great exertion and sacrifice, was within sight of victory when death carried him off. He had not married again, in spite of Fabia's efforts to win him. In the fashion approved even by philosophers, he took a concubine to his bed, and virtuously refused to put a stepmother over his children. At his death a new Empress comes upon the scene, and, as Lucilla still retained her Imperial dignities and privileges, we shall have to consider them in an unamiable conjunction.

The last and most fatal blunder of Marcus Aurelius was to leave the Empire in the very uncertain hands of his son Commodus. War had drained the treasury; plague, famine, and sloth had thinned and weakened the population; vice had again been enthroned for all to admire and imitate; the lusty barbarians were thundering at its gates. A new Vespasian or Trajan was needed to restore its vigour, if such a restoration were possible. Yet Marcus persuaded himself that the pretty youth, with bright eyes and curly golden hair, who played at soldiering in his suite in Germany, could bear this enormous burden. Herodian, whose history of the Emperors now opens for us, tells us that Marcus was really concerned on the matter as he lay in his last illness. There were disquieting stories about the character of Commodus. It was said that in his twelfth year he had, at Centumcellae (Civita Vecchia), ordered the bath-attendant to be thrown into the furnace because the water was not hot enough. On another occasion Marcus had driven away certain corrupting attendants, but had recalled them at the petulant tears of his son. They were with him in Pannonia. We may at least assume that even the fond eye of a father must have discerned the weakness of character which, in the course of a year or two, would let Commodus sink to indescribable depths. Marcus, however, trustful to the end in the sublime truths of his philosophy, was content to summon Commodus to his tent, make a pretty speech to him in the presence of his counsellors, and hand over to him the reins of government.

For a time Commodus remained in the camp, and let the elders govern. Before long the lighter courtiers hint that it is more comfortable in Rome, and he talks of going.

The elders frown, and Pompeianus lectures him. He bows submissively, but it is not long before he decides to go.

Numbers of officers discover a similar call to the capital, and a gay cavalcade sets out. Rome is enchanted, and goes out miles along the road to meet Commodus, and strews flowers and laurel in his path, and enthuses over his handsome face and the curly hair that shines like gold in the sun. It was the coming of Caligula and Nero over again. The

Roman people--*quantum mutatus ab illo!*--had come to appreciate a pretty face, and a prospect of endless games, immeasurably more than the security of the frontier.

When Commodus had set out with his father for Germany, he had been married--"hastily married," the chronicle says--to a lady as young and thoughtless as himself. Crispina was a very beautiful girl, and of distinguished family. Her father, Bruttius Praesens, was a Senator of great merit. It seems that she accompanied Commodus to the camp, and returned with him to Rome. In his train were the evil counsellors whom Marcus had banished and recalled. Their hour had come.

For three years Commodus enjoyed the pleasures which they provided or invented for him, and left the administration in the capable hands of his father's servants. Possibly this was the highest virtue Marcus had expected of him.

But the ambition of his confidants steadily grew, and a bitter feud in the palace now came to a head and gave them an opportunity. Crispina and Lucilla were violently opposed to each other. The Imperial title of Lucilla paled beside that of the wife of the ruling Emperor. The fire which had been borne before her when she went abroad now passed to Crispina, and she had to yield precedence in the palace and the theatre. Crispina, on the other hand, resented the familiarity of Commodus with his sister, and would hardly be ignorant of the interpretation that was generally put on it. The adherents of the palace were thus divided into two parties, and the Empresses fought for the monopoly of Commodus's favour. At last Lucilla despaired of gaining her end through Commodus, and resolved to have him murdered.

There is no room for doubt that the daughter of Faustina and Marcus Aurelius was an abandoned woman.

Dio declares that she was "no better than Commodus."

We may trust that this is an exaggeration, but the other authorities speak of the looseness of her conduct, and are emphatically agreed that she inspired the plot to murder her brother. No one doubts that her purpose was to recover supreme power. The inferences and impressions we draw from Imperial portraits are not very substantial, but it is interesting that the statue of Lucilla, which we have, suggests just the type of woman that the historians represent her to have been. It is the figure of a full-bodied woman, of strong and imperious temper, sensual to the limit of grossness. In her the beauty of her mother, instead of being enhanced by the purity of her father, is blighted by a general expression of coarseness and self-assertion.

Her criminal design was gradually imparted to her lovers. Among these was a young noble named Quadratus, whom she soon fired with a sense of her grievances, and a conspiracy was framed. The actual assassination was undertaken by her stepson, Claudius Pompeianus.

Herodian says that his name was Quintianus, and he may have had this name in addition. Dio gives a confused and contradictory account--he describes Pompeianus as married to Lucilla's daughter, whereas Lucilla was married to his father, and he says that she was intimate with him, yet hated him and wished to destroy him--but, as he lived in Rome at the time, we must accept the substance of his story. The young Senator Pompeianus was an intimate friend of Commodus, and only an infatuation for Lucilla could have drawn him into the plot. He spoiled it, and ruined the conspirators, by his melodramatic display. As Commodus entered the amphitheatre, he rushed upon him with a drawn sword. But he announced his purpose by crying out: "The Senate sends thee this sword," and the guards arrested him.

The plot gave Commodus an opportunity to make a bloody clearance of those who hampered his plans, and caused him to regard the Senate with dark suspicion.

The male conspirators were executed, and Lucilla was banished to Capreae. But Crispina had no triumph by the removal of her rival. She had herself been tainted in that atmosphere of vice, and was detected in one of her liaisons by Commodus. She was banished to Capreae, and there both she and Lucilla were put to death.

LUCILLA

BUST IN THE NATIONAL MUSEUM, ROME

The conspiracy took place in the year 182, the third year of Commodus's reign. The remaining ten years of his life it would be more agreeable to leave in the untranslatable language of the chroniclers, but he virtually shared his throne with a woman of a singular and interesting type, and we must include her in the gallery of wives of the Emperors. Among the property of the wealthy young conspirator,

Quadratus, which was at once confiscated, was a very handsome and engaging concubine of the name of Marcia. The *concubinatus* was, as I have said, a legal and recognized union in Rome, and we must not regard these women, who enter our chronicle in that capacity, in quite the same light as the mistresses of later Christian princes. They were sometimes of moderately good family, though they seem generally to have belonged to the class of emancipated slaves, and were included in the man's property. Marcia was of the latter class. Probably an orphan at an early age, she was brought up by a eunuch, and sold by him to Quadratus. At the dispersal of his property, or even during his life, she attracted the notice of Commodus, and was transferred to the populous harem of his three hundred concubines.

A few years later (185) an event occurred that greatly increased her growing power over the Emperor. The chief favourite of Commodus was a low-born and despicable courtier named Perennis, who encouraged the Emperor to pursue his morbid sensual impulses, while he himself accumulated wealth and power. He flattered and indulged every fancy of his besotted master, and controlled all the resources of the State in his own interest. He was commander of the guards, and seems to have at length conceived an ambition to displace Commodus. One day, when Commodus presided at the games, which he very liberally provided, before an immense crowd, a mild-looking man--said to be a philosopher--rushed into the centre of the stage and roared out a warning to the Emperor that Perennis was acquiring wealth and aiming at the throne.

The prefect had him burned alive, and escaped the Emperor's suspicion; but the end was nearer than he expected.

A regiment of fifteen hundred men from the legions of Britain marched into Rome, demanded the head of Perennis, and forced Commodus to recognize and punish the faults of his minister.

From that time Marcia occupies the place of *prima inter pares* in the harem of Commodus. A good deal of research has been expended on this leading concubine of the Emperor, because there was a tradition in early Christian literature that she favoured and protected, if she did not herself belong to, the new religion.[14] It was said that she sent the eunuch, who had reared her, to liberate the repressed Christians of Sardinia, and the peace which they enjoyed at Rome during the reign of Commodus is attributed to her influence. But if Marcia had ever belonged to the austere sect of the early Christians, we must, for its credit, entirely dissociate her from it in her Imperial days.

She seems to have been to the brutal Commodus what Caesonia had been to the equally licentious Caligula. She dressed willingly as an Amazon, and is actually represented on the coins, with Commodus, in the helmet of a female warrior. If we may put any trust in that meagre portrait of her, she seems to have been of much the same type as Caesonia: a handsome, strong, vulgar woman, owing her influence to her masculine robustness.

For seven years she occupied, without a quarrel, the chief place in a palace in which all the orgies of Caligula, Nero, and Verus were concentrated. At her persuasion Commodus changed the name of Rome to "the Colony of Commodus." One might almost suspect her of genial irony in thus removing the venerable name from the Imperial city during the years when it was degraded by Commodus. Evil as the practices of Caligula and Nero had been, they were surpassed by the insanities and obscenities of the son of Marcus Aurelius. We must leave the veil over the life that was witnessed in the palace during those ten years; but the crimes of Commodus were not confined to the wild indulgence of his unbridled appetites. The company of gladiators and the daily pleasure of killing degraded him to the character of a mere butcher. He forced the priests of orgiastic Eastern cults to perform on themselves the mutilations which their ritual described; he beat them with the emblem of Anubis which he carried in their processions. On one occasion he had all the citizens of Rome with some infirmity of the feet gathered in one place, and more or less dressed as dragons. Then the Roman Hercules--as Commodus loved to be called--fell upon them with a club, and killed numbers of them.

This and other stories of his indescribable lust and cruelty are told by an historian who saw Commodus daily.

In the year 189 Marcia obtained even greater power over her insane lover. The place of Perennis had been at once occupied by another of the Emperor's despicable courtiers, Cleander, a Phrygian slave who had risen, by base means, to be the first minister of the Empire. Like his predecessor, he encouraged Commodus to wallow in his vices, while he took advantage of his insanity to enrich himself. The highest positions in the State were sold by him, and men could even purchase from him the right to take vengeance on their enemies, or the privilege not to be executed for their wealth. The treasury was again diminishing, and noble blood poured out freely to refresh it. A great pestilence swept over Italy, exacting thousands of victims daily in Rome alone. A terrible famine succeeded it. The people, observing that the avaricious minister was endeavouring to make a corner in corn, now broke into rebellion and pressed to the palace of the Emperor.

Commodus was enjoying himself at the beautiful palace of the Quintilians in the suburbs, which he had obtained by murder, when the crowd surged up to the gates.

Cleander turned the cavalry upon the people, but the infantry sided with them, and they returned in a storm of anger to the palace. None of his ministers dare approach the room in which Commodus wantoned with his companions, but his sister Fadilla and Marcia broke in with the news that his life was in danger. Some writers say that it was Fadilla who informed him, some that it was Marcia. We may suppose that both of them endeavoured to awake him. The voluptuous coward at once sacrificed Cleander to the crowd, and returned to his vices.

Marcia had now the leading influence over Commodus, and Rome sank lower and lower. The butcheries of the amphitheatre were his chief concern. He consorted daily with the gladiators, killed vast numbers of beasts in the arena, and even fought with men who had meekly to submit to be slain by him. Numbers of distinguished or wealthy Romans were put to death on the most frivolous pretexts, yet the Senators were compelled to view and applaud his daily slaughters with such cries as: "Thou conquerest the world, O brave Amazonian." Dio, who sat among the Senators, tells us that one day Commodus made a grotesque attempt to intimidate them. He had just killed an ostrich, and came toward them with the head in one hand and the bloody sword in the other.

He grinned and wagged his head, without saying a word, as he approached them, as if intimating that it would be their turn next. Dio says that his appearance was so ludicrous that he had hastily to pluck a leaf of laurel, and chew it, to prevent him from laughing. We nearly missed the writing of one of the most valuable histories of the period.

The "Golden Age," as the Senate was compelled to describe this appalling decade, came to a close through a fresh excess on the part of Commodus Pius, as he was now styled. They had reached the last day of the year 192, and were preparing for the great festivities of the morrow. Commodus informed Marcia that he would spend the night in the house of the gladiators, and issue from it on the morrow at their head. He ordered his chamberlain Eclectus and his commander of the guard Laetus to make the necessary preparation. Marcia and the officers were horrified at his proposal, and besought him to abandon it. After reading the disgusting details of his career in the "Historia Augusta"--even if we make allowance for exaggeration--one has some difficulty in realizing their indignation. Apparently, however, this proposal to identify himself so intimately with the degraded caste of public gladiators was regarded by them as something of an entirely different nature from the filth and obscenity of his practices in the palace, and they boldly opposed him. He angrily shook them off, and put their names on his condemned list. The "Augustan History," recalling a story we have heard before, introduces an element of romance into the adventure. It makes Commodus tie the tablet to his bed, and go to sleep, when the tablet is playfully removed by one of his jewel-decked boys, and delivered accidentally into the hands of Marcia.

It is better to follow the version of Dio, who was in Rome at the time. The two officers and Marcia, realizing that they had incurred his anger, discussed the matter, and decided to assassinate him. Marcia was directed to poison him. She put the poison in the meat he ate, but its effect was spoiled by the quantity of wine he had drunk, and it caused him to vomit. He became suspicious and threatening, and went to the bath. They then hastily took into their confidence his powerful and athletic bath-attendant, Narcissus, and he entered and strangled the Emperor.

One reads with something like amazement that the successful conspirators, instead of gladly announcing that they had rid Rome of such a brute and tyrant, deliberated anxiously how they should proceed. So blind was the attachment of the troops to their paymaster, and of the common citizens to any generous provider of games, that they concealed the deed. Commodus had himself fought 735 times in the public amphitheatre, and on those performances alone had spent 200,000,000 drachmas. The

temper of the demoralized people and soldiers was uncertain, and they decided to put the Empire at once in the hands of a strong soldier.

In the romantic story of the accession of the various Empresses of Rome there are few cases so dramatic as that which introduces the next Empress in the series.

There was living in Rome at the time an experienced commander, in his sixtieth year, of the name of Pertinax.

His father had kept a kind of tavern in a village of Liguria. The son had obtained some education, and rapidly climbed the ladder of promotion. He had married Flavia Titiana, the accomplished daughter of a very wealthy and distinguished Senator. Himself enamoured of Cornificia, the sister of Marcus Aurelius, he had overlooked the vivacity of his wife, and she had at one time attracted comment by her open regard for a musician. At the time of the murder of Commodus, Pertinax was Prefect of Rome. He retired to bed on that last night of the year 192 with no suspicion of the great events that were happening in the Domus Vectiliana, to which, it seems, Commodus had gone.

In the middle of the night he was awakened with the message that the captain of the Praetorian Guards wished to see him. He calmly said that he had for some time expected to be executed by Commodus, and he continued to lie, in quiet dignity, when Laetus entered to tell him that they offered him the Empire. He begged Laetus to abandon his unseemly joke, and carry out his orders. He was at last convinced that Commodus was dead, and, through the darkness of the stormy winter night, they made their way to the camp. They announced to the guards that Commodus had died of apoplexy, and that Pertinax was submitted to be chosen by them as Emperor.

The soldiers listened with no enthusiasm. Under the license of the reign of Commodus they had been permitted to take the most extraordinary liberties, and they dreaded the accession of a commander. The news had, however, spread by this time through the city. People crowded into the torch-lit streets, and poured out toward the camp, hailing the name of Pertinax and execrating that of Commodus. A promise of 3,000 denarii to each man overcame the last opposition of the Guards, and they coldly consented to the choice. In the Senate, too, there was hesitation. "We see behind you," said the consul Falco, "the ministers of Commodus's crimes, Laetus and Marcia." Pertinax himself, indeed, was still very reluctant; but the Senate urged the Imperial power upon him, and the new year dawned at Rome upon a people angrily scattering the statues and memorials of Commodus, and expressing a wild rejoicing over the advent of its new ruler.

Titiana never bore the title of Augusta, and we may dismiss very briefly her few months of residence in the palace. The Senate offered the title of Augusta to Titiana, and that of Caesar to their son, but Pertinax refused both.

"Let the boy earn it," he said of his son; and Dio says that he kept the title from his wife, either because of the insecurity of his position, or "because he would not let his lascivious consort stain the name of Augusta." Titiana was evidently not the kind of woman to co-operate with Pertinax in his reforms, and she probably shared the disdain with which her friends regarded his ways. Although he at once began to undo the evil wrought by Commodus--to banish the informers, regulate the taxes, and purify the administration of justice--he alienated the Romans by passing to an extreme of sobriety. The palace he purified in very summary fashion. He had the whole apparatus of Commodus's luxury sold by auction, and Rome looked on with delight as the three hundred pretty boys and three hundred choice concubines, the gold and silver plate, the precious vases and silks and chariots and wonderful machines of the Sybarite were exposed to their view.

But Pertinax carried his economy too far. Patricians told with contempt that he would put half a lettuce on the Imperial board, and would make a hare last three days; the people missed the unceasing stimulation of the amphitheatre; the soldiers chafed at the discipline he sought to enforce. Within three months of his remarkable accession to power Pertinax was assassinated by the Guards, and Titiana fell back into the obscurity from which she had momentarily emerged.

Another Empress of a day, and one that came to the throne under no less romantic circumstances, claims our attention for a moment before we pass on to a more imposing figure.

It was on the 28th of March, 193, that the soldiers brutally assassinated Pertinax. On the rumour of trouble Pertinax had sent his father-in-law, Sulpicianus, to secure tranquillity in the camp. As he lingered there the soldiers returned with the dripping head of the Emperor, and he recognized that the throne was vacant. With a callousness that is almost incredible, but is fully attested, he at once made an offer of money to the soldiers for the Imperial power. It occurred to some of the soldiers that a higher bid might be secured, and they announced from the rampart of their camp, in which they had enclosed themselves, that the throne was, virtually, on sale. In particular, they sent word to one of the wealthiest citizens, Didius Julianus, and invited him to make an offer. Whether or no it be true that he yielded to the vanity of his wife and daughter--he does not seem to have needed pressure--Julianus went to the camp, and made a higher offer

than that of Sulpicianus.

It was the early evening, and a crowd had gathered to witness the appalling spectacle of the sale of the Empire.

Julianus pointed out that his rival was the father-in-law of the man they had killed, and might be expected to have some design of revenge. The soldiers admitted Julianus by a ladder, and the two Senators made bids against each other, the soldiers on the wall announcing their offers. At length Julianus made an offer equal to more than PS200 to each soldier, and he was greeted as Emperor. Under the close guard of the soldiers he was conducted, amid an angry people, to the Senate, and forced upon the Senators. They then concluded their bargain by conducting him to the palace, and the vain old man had time to reflect on the extraordinary situation he had suddenly reached. His wife, Manlia Scantilla, and daughter, Didia Clara, joined him "in fear and concern" (the "Historia Augusta" says), and he finished the day with a prolonged entertainment.

His wife and daughter were decorated with the title of Augusta on the morrow, but they soon found that Julianus had squandered his comfortable wealth on a dangerous bauble. Not only did the Roman people jeer at him whenever he appeared, but the news soon came that the distant legions were aflame with anger, and were about to march on Rome to wrest the Empire from him. Presently he heard that the commander of the troops in Pannonia had begun his march at the head of a formidable army. Julianus first had him declared a public enemy, and sent men to assassinate him; then he offered to share the Empire with him. Severus and his hardened troops passed relentlessly over the Alps, and proceeded along the plains of Italy. Julianus stung the demoralized soldiers who had sold him the Empire into some pretence of resistance, threw up earthworks in the suburbs, endeavoured to train his elephants for the fight, and, as a last resort, fortified the palace. But his effeminate troops quailed before the seasoned legions from Germany, and, when Severus reached Rome, Julianus found himself deserted. The Senate decreed his death, and he was beheaded in the palace which he had enjoyed, at the price of his fortune and his life, for sixty-six days. And the two broken-hearted Augustae laid down their dignity, and bore the body of Didius Julianus to the tomb of his ancestors.

Marcia, too, had ended her semi-imperial career with a violent death. After the assassination of Commodus she had married the chamberlain Eclectus, with whom she had long been intimate. Eclectus became the chamberlain of Pertinax, and perished, not ignobly, with his master.

Marcia did not long survive her husband, however.

Julianus had promised the soldiers that he would avenge the murder of Commodus, and he sought the remaining members of the conspiracy, Laetus, Narcissus, and Marcia, and put them to death.

CHAPTER XII

JULIA DOMNA

WITH the accession of Septimius Severus to the throne, we find ourselves confronting one of the most dominant personalities in the long line of Roman Empresses--a woman of the standard of Livia, Agrippina, and Plotina--and passing again into one of the brighter periods of the life of the Empire. The degradation of Commodus's reign will disappear like a mist on a summer morn; the jaded frame of the Empire will seem to recover all its vigour in a few years. These periods of rapid recovery are not sufficiently appreciated by the rhetorical censors of the morals of Rome, whose investigations are almost entirely confined to the reigns of Caligula, Nero, Commodus, Caracalla, and Elagabalus; as if it were just to define the climate of a region by its worst days only. Let a strong man rise to power, let an imperial encouragement be given to virtue and manliness, and even the city of Rome takes on a normal moral aspect. The throne is but an electric point, and, according as it is positive or negative, it draws into the light of history either the good or the bad elements of Rome. Both are there all the time. And if the good rulers had made as drastic a purge of evil types, as evil rulers made of good types, when they came to power, the Empire might not have provided so much material to the censors of extinct civilizations.

The Empresses whom we have hitherto considered were, with a few exceptions, the daughters of Roman patricians, or of distinguished provincials who had lived in Rome for a generation or two. In Julia Domna, the wife of Severus, we have for the first time a woman of the East on the throne; and, as her family will for some time deeply influence the fortunes of the Empire, it will be interesting to glance at her origin.

On the bank of the Orontes in Syria, at the large village or small town of Emesa (now Hems), there was in the second century a very ancient and prosperous religious centre. At some early date in the history of the land a mysterious stone had been cast on the country from the home of the gods--a meteorite, modern science would call it--and it had been set up as a symbol of the Regenerating God (Elagabal, which the Greeks improperly turned into Heliogabalus, or Sun-god). A fine temple was in time built to shelter it, pilgrims sought it from the whole country, and the richest gifts were made to the god and his living representatives. About the middle of the second century the priest in charge was a certain Bassianus, who had two handsome and very clever daughters. The planets which presided at the birth of the elder promised her, according to the astrologers, a throne; and, as there was a camp of Roman soldiers near Emesa, and the temple was a great attraction to the soldiers in their exile, the pretty Syrian girl and her horoscope came to be known very far away. In the year 186 or 187 an offer of marriage came to the priest's daughter from one of the highest officials, the *legatus*, of the rich province of Lower Gaul, and she crossed sea and land to accept it. Within six years this officer, Septimius Severus, was Emperor of Rome, and Julia Domna was Empress.

Some doubt has been thrown on this pretty story, and Serviez, whose chapter on Julia Domna is a piece of irresponsible fiction, describes her as coming to Rome, on her own account, in search of adventure. But we have abundant evidence that Severus was a most enthusiastic astrologer, and there is nothing improbable in the story.

Severus was of the province of Roman Africa, of humble family, and, like so many energetic men in the days of Antoninus and Marcus, had earned promotion from office to office. He had first married a certain Paccia Marciana at Rome. He was then made Praetor, had a military command in Spain and Gaul, spent some years in study at Athens, and became Legate of the Lugdunian province.

At Lyons he lost his first wife, and sought a second. Hearing that there was a maid in Syria with a royal horoscope, he sent for her, and married her at Lyons. A child was born the first year, and, although Bassianus (more popularly, Caracalla) is described by Eutropius and Aurelius Victor as her stepson, he was undoubtedly her first child. Geta, his brother and co-Emperor, was born two years later.

By that time they were living in Rome, where Severus was Consul. Commodus, whose follies excited his ambition no less than his disdain, gave him the command in Lower Germany. Immediately afterwards

Commodus was assassinated, and about three months later came the news of the murder of Pertinax. It was easy to inflame the troops with anger on this occasion, and, as Severus offered a more than usually heavy bribe, he was acclaimed Emperor, and, as we saw, led the legions upon Rome. We do not know whether Julia had remained at Rome, or accompanied him, but she would be present when Rome greeted its new ruler. He rode in full armour, in the centre of a picked body of six hundred men. When, however, he saw that Rome had entirely deserted Julianus, he entered the city in civic costume, on foot. Flowers and laurel and gay hangings decorated all the houses, and the early summer sun shone on the white-robed masses of the citizens. Another splendid, but less joyous, spectacle was offered on the morrow, when a wax image of Pertinax was honoured with an Imperial funeral. Then he set about the stern business of securing his Empire. He had no title to it but his sword, and there were two other able generals--Albinus in Britain and Niger in Syria--urging the same title on their own behalf.

We do not know whether Julia accompanied Severus during the long civil war that followed. Some of the authorities represent her as egging on her husband to the destruction of his rivals. The advice would not be unnatural, but it would be so superfluous that we disregard the statement. With a craft that has not won him the regard of historians, Severus held Albinus in Britain with the empty title of Caesar, while he proceeded to crush Niger in the East. As there are coins of the year 196 which entitle Julia "Mother of the Camps,"[15] she probably accompanied Severus to the East, but we need not pursue the long campaign. Severus committed the work to his generals, and kept watch over Rome and the West. Several years were absorbed in pacifying the East, and he then turned toward Britain. Acting under the strain of African barbarism which undoubtedly existed in the nature of Severus, he sent men with a treacherous commission to murder Albinus, and the discovery of the plot brought the British legions thundering over Gaul. The rivals met decisively at Lyons, and a titanic conflict ended with the triumph of Severus.

Rome had followed the even struggle with suspense, and some had ventured to take sides. The omens were ambiguous. A strange light--the aurora--flickered in the northern sky, and a rain mixed with silver--Dio soberly assures us that he plated several bronze coins with it--fell upon the city. Human judgment had been as uncertain as that of the gods, and many of the Romans had espoused the "white" (Albinus) or the "black"

(Niger) cause, instead of that of the "grey," to put it in the language of the hour. For Severus to have abstained entirely from punishing those who had supported his rivals, after the years of anxiety they had caused him, is too much to expect; but it must be admitted that his vengeance was cruel, and that his plea of the security of the State was little more than a cloak for a very human resentment, The "Historia Augusta" gives a ghastly list of forty-one Senators whom he put to death, and crowds of lesser folk suffered from his vindictiveness. From Syria to Gaul he marked the progress of his triumph with a trail of human blood.

Of the attitude of Julia in regard to these executions we have no knowledge. Severus was a cruel and passionate African, and we have no reason to think that any one impelled him to commit these deeds. His whole behaviour in the hour of triumph was injudicious and unworthy. He made a most unpleasant speech to the Senate in praise of Commodus, and directed that the highest honours should be paid to his memory. It may be that the consciousness of his lowly origin--which his sister tactlessly irritated by coming to Rome, and displaying her rural innocence to the amusement of the nobles--made him more suspicious of the patrician order than he need have been. Albinus, however, had come of a most ancient and honourable, if somewhat decayed, stock, and his finer blood may have influenced the Senate.

Leaving Rome under a painful impression of his harsh use of power, he set out for the East, where the Parthians were again in arms. Julia accompanied him on this campaign, but it is of little interest. The Parthians retired before his advance, and he pursued them down the Euphrates, and for a time held Babylon and several of the ancient cities of the East. Foiled, and incurring heavy losses, in the siege of Hatra, he retired sullenly from Mesopotamia, and sought consolation in a pleasant tour through Palestine and Egypt. They returned to Rome, about the beginning of the third century, for their first long stay in the capital.

The remarkable number of inscriptions that still survive in the most distant parts of the Empire bear witness that Julia was already regarded as an active Empress, not merely as the companion of Severus. Probably she comes next to Livia--some would place her before Livia--in the general recognition of her political existence. But on her return to Rome she found a bitter opponent in the person of Severus's chief minister, and for a time she confined herself to personal concerns. This minister, Plautianus, was a fellow-townsman, possibly a relative, of the Emperor, and enjoyed and abused his entire confidence. He was promoted to the command of the Praetorian Guards, whom Severus, after punishing them for the murder of Pertinax, had reorganized and enormously increased. Finding himself at the head of fifty thousand picked men, and entrusted, during the long absence of the Emperor, with the supreme affairs of State, Plautianus indulged his vanity in the strangest excesses. When his superb chariot drove through Rome, runners were sent ahead to warn the common folk that they must turn away, and not gaze on his august person; and there were more statues of him in Rome than of the Emperor. He even had a hundred Romans, of all ages, including many of noble birth, emasculated, in order that his daughter might be attended with all the splendour and security of an Oriental harem. Severus begged the hand of this privileged maiden for his elder son. Bassianus was then (203) in his sixteenth year, and had just been nominated Caesar by his father. Plautianus consented, and a princely wedding took place. People remarked, as the rich gifts were borne through the Forum to the palace, that the Prefect of the Guards had been able to give his daughter a dowry that would have sufficed for the daughters of fifty kings.

Two circumstances conspired to wreck this auspicious marriage. Bassianus disliked Plautilla, Julia hated her conceited and overbearing father. A third circumstance, in the opinion of Rome, was that Bassianus was already too intimate with a fiery little Syrian cousin, then living at the palace, of whom we shall see much in the next chapter.

At length Plautianus brought a formal charge against the Empress, and there was agitation in the palace. The charge seems to have been one of adultery, and, though it was not established, some of the later historians declare that she owed her escape only to the fondness of Severus. Aurelius Victor ("De Caesaribus," xx) says that "his wife's infamies robbed Severus of the height of his glory"; and he charges her with, to the Emperor's knowledge, loose ways and treason. Lampridius ("Historia Augusta," "Severus,"

c. 18) affirms that she was "notorious for her adulteries and guilty of conspiracy." Eutropius and Herodian join with them in bringing an even graver charge against her later. Dio, however, who was on the spot, brings no charge against her character, and many hold that his silence is more instructive than the chatter of later compilers. We may add that Severus was very eager to stamp out adultery, and, although his efforts were frustrated by the unwillingness of the citizens to use his law--Dio, when he was consul, found three thousand charges lying unheeded in the offices--his known temper must be taken into account. On the other hand, Dio wrote his history in the reign of a member of Julia's family, and may have omitted much out of discretion.

The evidence is, as usual, perplexing, and there is no need to press for a verdict. The Oriental religion, to which Julia adhered, was not one to lay bonds upon the passion of love, and the removal from the guarded seclusion of the East to the free life of the West would not engender scruples. The charge, in fact, was not admitted by Severus to be proved, though noble dames were tortured to wring evidence from them. After this scorching ordeal, however, Julia moderated her open hostility to Plautianus, and sought consolation in a close application to letters and philosophy. Her sister, Julia Maesa, had by this time come from Emesa to join her in the palace, and had brought two married daughters, of whom we shall hear more.[16] With these, and the literary men of Rome, she formed an intellectual circle, and withdrew from politics.

But there can be little doubt that Julia encouraged her son's dislike of Plautilla. Herodian declares that the young wife was "a most shameless creature." We may refuse to accept this description of the unhappy young princess, and see in it only an echo of the attack upon her. Bullied and threatened by Bassianus, she at last returned in tears to her father's mansion, and the Prefect renewed his attacks with great warmth. Severus refused to hear complaints against him, until his brother Geta suggested to him, on his death-bed, that Plautianus was acquiring his enormous wealth with a view to seizing the throne. From that hour Severus behaved more coldly to his minister, and Julia's party took courage. At length Bassianus persuaded his father that the minister was plotting. If we may believe the romantic version, Plautianus sent a man to assassinate Severus and his sons.

The man betrayed him at the palace, and was directed by Bassianus to return and pretend to bring the Prefect to see the dead bodies. At all events, Plautianus came in haste to the palace, was alarmed to see the gates close behind him, and was led to the presence of the Emperor and Bassianus. Shortly afterwards, the head of Plautianus was tossed on to the street from the roof of the palace.

Dio adds that a man plucked a handful of hair from the bleeding head, and rushed with it to Julia and Plautilla, crying: "Behold your Plautianus!" The unhappy girl was banished to Lipara, and was executed there by Bassianus after the death of his father.

It was perhaps inevitable that a series of executions should follow the fall of the favourite, but in a short time the life of the palace fell into a quiet routine. Severus, a big, powerful man, with a crown of grey hair above his venerable features, set an example of sobriety and industry. He was generally at work before dawn, and would return to work after a frugal midday-meal with his boys. They were years of peace and prosperity, and he made admirable use of the opportunity to restore the decaying buildings and institutions of the Empire, and to replenish the treasury. He regretted his lack of culture, and listened with deference to the learned discussions in which his wife and her relatives engaged. His one accomplishment in the way of science was a thorough command of the mysteries of astrology, as the golden stars with which he decorated the ceilings of his palace informed the visitor.

Julia joined with him in the work of restoration. We know that at Rome she rebuilt the temple of Vesta, and the numerous provincial inscriptions suggest a much wider interest. Under her lead the women of Rome were encouraged to look beyond their homes. Sabina had erected, or dedicated, a meeting-hall for women in the Forum of Trajan, but it had fallen into decay. Julia restored this early "women's club," and no doubt introduced into it the enthusiasm for letters and philosophy which she still had. Her "circle," as Philostratus calls it, probably included the historian Dio, who was still at Rome, and the poet Appian, who had some years before described her as "the great Domna." Philostratus himself, a Greek writer and rhetorician, one of the most learned men of the time, was closely associated with her. It was at her request that he wrote his famous "Life of Apollonius of Tyana."

In his "Lives of the Sophists" (Philiscus) he speaks of her as "Julia the Philosopher," and in one of his letters (lxxiii) he refers with high appreciation to her learning.

Julia was then in the prime of her life, and in her happiest days. The bust of her that quickly catches the eye in the Vatican Museum--the largest surviving portrait-bust of the period--will hardly be deemed to possess the beauty with which the historians invest her. The thick lips and large nose, which betray her ancestry, do not compare well with the features of other Empresses. But the grave, strong, thoughtful face and large eyes, which we may imagine instinct with Syrian fire, are undeniably handsome. Her sister, Julia Maesa, was with her--a woman of similar strength, moderation, and judgment.

But the younger generation in the palace gave them concern.

The young men, Bassianus and Geta, were loose and luxurious in their ways; and one of the daughters of Maesa, Julia Soaemias, was a fit companion for Bassianus.

Severus, noting the advance of his gout, looked with grave eyes on the soft habits and the constant quarrels of the sons whom he wished to leave partners in the Empire.

JULIA DOMNA

BUST IN THE VATICAN MUSEUM

An irruption of the Caledonians in the north of Britain led him to think that a campaign under his eyes would alter the evil ways of his sons, and he set out for the West. Julia accompanied them, but we can hardly suppose that she ventured further north than Eboracum (York).

The mist-wrapped hills and watery lowlands beyond were to the Roman a shuddering wilderness, fit only for the breeding of savages who were as amphibious as rats.

Dio unflatteringly describes the north Britons and Scots of the time as "inhabiting wild, waterless mountains and desolate, swampy plains," and "dwelling in tents, without coats or shoes, possessing their wives and rearing their offspring in common." We may find some consolation in the assurance of Lampridius that Britain (south of this region) was "the greatest glory of the Empire." Even the Scots, however, had their glories. When Severus returned to York, after having pushed to the extreme north of Caledonia, and lost 50,000 men without bringing the elusive enemy to battle, he brought with him envoys of the Caledonians to discuss the terms of peace. Among them was the wife of the chief "Argentocoxus"--should it be Macdermott?--with whom the philosophic Empress held converse through an interpreter. Julia insinuated that their matrimonial arrangements were not all that could be desired. "We satisfy the needs of nature in a much better way than you Roman women," said the hardy Scot. "We have dealings openly with the best of our men, whereas you let yourselves be debauched in secret by the vilest."

Eugenics is an ancient practice, if a modern theory.

Severus was borne back, weary and dispirited, on his litter to York. Bassianus, impatient to reach the throne that he would soon disgrace, had attempted his father's life, and fully exhibited the brutality of his character. Yet Severus, who had often censured Marcus Aurelius for entrusting the Empire to Commodus, listened in turn to the fond pleading of his parental feeling, and designated his sons as his successors. He died at York in February, 211, and a hasty settlement was made of affairs in Britain that they might return at once to the capital. They placed the ashes of the Emperor in an alabaster urn, and set out with it for Rome.

From that day the life of Julia Domna was one of anxiety, and we may trust that it was one of pain. Even on the journey homeward her sons were ostentatiously armed against each other's designs. Bassianus--or Antoninus, as he had now been named--was a strong, brutal, and imperious youth, as eager to murder his brother as he had been to shorten his father's life. Geta was brighter, gentler, and more cultivated, and the affection of the legions for him kept Antoninus in check while they were with the army. When they arrived in Rome, their first business was the funeral of Severus. His pale wax image was laid on a lofty ivory couch, and the black-robed Senators and white-clad matrons watched it for seven days.

Then it was borne to the old Forum, where the chorus of sons and women of the nobility sang the old funeral chants, and on to the great wooden tower, stuffed with spices and inflammable matter, in the Field of Mars; where, from the midst of the flaming pile, the released eagle symbolized the passage of the soul of Severus to the home of the gods.

The quarrel between Antoninus and Geta at once broke out with greater menace than ever. They kept their separate apartments rigidly guarded in the palace, and a troop of soldiers and athletes watched day and night over the person of the younger Emperor. Some one suggested that the Empire should be divided, as it was later, and that Geta should take the Asiatic half. Herodian says--though one reads with suspicion his full reports of speeches that were made a century before--that Julia opposed this plan passionately. They must divide their mother, she declared, before they should divide the Empire.

The gloom grew deeper over the palace, and the inevitable end did not tarry long. Antoninus one day professed that he wished to be reconciled, and invited Geta to meet him in his mother's room. As soon as Geta entered, the officers whom Antoninus had at hand drew their swords.

Geta flew to his mother's bosom, and she put her arms about him; but they killed him in her embrace, and even cut the arm in which she clasped him. Once more the channels ran with the best blood of Rome, as Antoninus turned vindictively upon the supporters of his brother.

Even ancient nobles who had survived several of these massacres, such as Claudius Pompeianus, the second husband of Marcus Aurelius's daughter, now came to a violent end. The aged sister of Marcus Aurelius, Cornificia, was put to death for weeping at the news of the brutal crime.

Dio assures us that no less than 20,000 men and women, including some of the finest of the time, were put to death in that awful carnage. Surely one of the chief causes of the deterioration of Rome--these repeated purges of its best elements--has been overlooked in the endless speculations about its fall!

The "Historia Augusta" tells us that Julia herself was discovered in tears by Antoninus, and only escaped death because the Emperor feared a rebellion if he killed her.

Curiously enough, the same historian, and several others, go on to give us a far different and less honourable account of her conduct after the death of Geta. In the general horror with which his abominable deeds were contemplated, Antoninus had the astuteness to purchase the favour of the army. He bestowed an extraordinary donation on the Guards, and entered upon a systematic policy of enriching and indulging the troops. From the pale faces of the citizens of Rome he retired to the military quarters on the Danube, and endeavoured by a year of hard hunting and carousing to banish the ghosts which, he confessed, haunted him. Inscriptions have been found in Germany which suggest that his mother was with him. However that may be, she joined him when he crossed the Hellespont to Asia--and was nearly drowned in the passage--and began to take a most important part in the administration. With the Senate, over whom he had set in authority a Spanish juggler, he was too disdainful to deal, except on the most important subjects. His chief aim was to wring money out of Rome and the provinces, and spend it on the troops. He "plundered the whole earth," says Dio. He wore the long rough cloak of a Goth--from which he was given the nickname of "Caracalla"

(the name of the garment)--and ate the rough food of a soldier on campaign; though he gave himself wildly to the luxurious life of the cities of Asia Minor.

Julia settled in Nicomedia, where she spent a good part of 214 and 215, and then in Antioch. Caracalla never married again; indeed, there can be little doubt that venereal disease was the chief cause of his madness and brutality during these years. As a boy, "reared by a Christian nurse," says Tertullian, he had been most gentle and humane. Julia, therefore, was still Empress, and she undertook the greater part of Caracalla's work. All letters from Rome were forwarded to her, and she dealt with them all, except a few that had to be submitted to the Emperor. The inscriptions cut in honour of her during these years were remarkably numerous, and from them and the coins we learn how great were her authority and influence. Her official title grew until it at length became: "Julia Pia Felix Augusta, Mater Augusti et Castrorum et Senatus et Patriae." All the several epithets that were ever bestowed on other Empresses were gathered together in her name.

This intimate association with so foul an Emperor as Caracalla lent colour to the current belief that she was linked with him in another capacity than that of mother.

Herodian (iiii), Eutropius (viii), and Aurelius Victor ("Epitome," xxi), give the charge as an undoubted fact.

Spartianus ("Historia Augusta," "Caracalla," x) gives a circumstantial story of the mother leading the son astray, and Aurelius Victor gives the same anecdote in his "De Caesaribus," xxi. She is said to have presented herself to Caracalla in what Serviez calls "an exceedingly magnificent and becoming dress"--*se maxima corporis parte denudasset*, is the text--and yielded with ease. The anecdote is too common a sample of the salacious gossip of the time to be taken seriously, but the substantial charge is not so easily set aside. Dio, it is true, does not give it. When he speaks (c. 10) of Caracalla having "possessed the rascality [panourgon] of his mother," he does not indeed pay a tribute to her character, but the word he employs seems to indicate craft, perhaps unscrupulous craft, rather than lasciviousness.

But even Dio relates an adventure which fairly shows that this grave charge against Julia was widely credited in his day. In the year 216, during his tour in the East, Caracalla announced that he would honour Alexandria with a visit. Unsparing as the Alexandrians had been in their witticisms on the ugly, bald, and prematurely old young man, with all his brutality and folly, they had no suspicion of his real intention, and they prepared to receive him with great honour. Once inside their gates, however, he savagely precipitated his troops on the unarmed citizens and for several days directed the carnage and pillage from the temple of Serapis. This savage onslaught is said by Dio to have been a punishment for the jibes of the Alexandrians, and we know from Herodian that one of their

most deadly shafts was to speak of him and his mother as OEdipus and Jocaste.

It cannot therefore be said that Dio is unaware of the current belief, nor can we follow Miss Wilkins when she suggests that the "elderly Empress" was incapable of such conduct. Julia had been married only twenty-nine years before, and may very well be presumed to have been in her early forties in the year 216. She was in "the full flush of life," as Dio expressly says, and is not known to have embraced any system of ethics or religion which would lay a stigma on incest. But the general moderation of her career and the repellent character of Caracalla, unrelieved by a single grace of person or disposition, must weigh heavily in the scale against the gossip of Rome.

We know, at least, that she endeavoured to curb the wild excesses that were bringing a doom on her son and endangering the stability of the Empire. When he debased the coinage, and despoiled his subjects, she remonstrated, but he laughingly drew his sword and said: "Courage, mother, while we have this, money will not fail us." "In such things," says Dio, "he paid no heed to his mother, who gave him much excellent advice." She continued to act as the first minister of her son, while he wandered from region to region in search of adventure. One of his exploits will suffice to illustrate his peculiar method of winning glory. From Egypt he advanced against the Parthians. He sent a flattering letter to the Parthian king, submitting that the two great Empires ought amicably to divide the world, and asking for the hand of his daughter. His persistent lying disarmed even the crafty Parthians, and he was admitted into their kingdom with a body of troops. He at once flung his troops upon the vast unarmed multitude that came out to greet him, mingled their blood with the flowers they had strewn in his path, and sacked a large part of Medea and Parthia.

But the end of his infamous life was rapidly approaching.

He had written to Rome, some time previously, to direct that the Chaldaeans should be consulted as to the name of his successor, so that he might slay the man named. The minister to whom he wrote had some grievance against one of the officials in the East, Opilius Macrinus, and he wrote to inform Caracalla that Macrinus was designated by an African soothsayer. The more romantic historians say that this letter reached Caracalla just as he was engaged in directing a race, and that he gave it, unopened, to Macrinus himself to deal with. More plausible is the story related by Dio. The letter went, as all letters went, to the Empress at Antioch, and a delay was caused. Macrinus had, in the meantime, learned from Rome the danger that threatened him, and he set energetically to work. A discontented soldier in Caracalla's body-guard was secured, and on the 8th of March, 217, he ended that Emperor's infamies with the thrust of a dagger. It was a timely release for Rome. It was discovered after his death that he had bought great quantities of poison in Asia.

Julia indulged in an unusual display of violence when the news reached her at Antioch. She mourned little over the removal of her son, says Dio, as she "had hated him when he was alive"; but the prospect of laying down her Imperial power, and retiring into private life, in the prime of her womanhood, filled her with anger. She learned that, after a brief hesitation, Macrinus had promised the usual bribe to the troops, and obtained the Empire.

Rumour quickly recognized in him the assassin of Caracalla, and Julia made the most violent attacks on him.

Meantime, he had written to assure her that he would recognize her Imperial status, and not remove her guard of honour. He feared the attachment of the soldiers to Caracalla, and disavowed his share in the assassination.

Julia perceived his weakness, and, abandoning her first resolve to take her life by refusing food, she entertained a hope of unseating the upstart. But the soldiers, however much attached to Caracalla, had little idea of putting a Semiramis on the throne of Rome. Her plan miscarried, and Macrinus heard of her invectives. He ordered her to leave Antioch, and go where she willed.

Her sister and nieces returned to the paternal temple at Emesa, where we shall soon rejoin them, but Julia, failing entirely to foresee the extraordinary adventure by which they would shortly return to power, racked with the pain of a cancer, which she had aggravated by a blow on the breast in her first anger, decided to leave the world. She refused food, and died in May or June, 217.

Her remains were afterwards buried with great pomp at Rome, and her name was added to the quaint list of the Imperial gods and goddesses.

CHAPTER XIII

IN THE DAYS OF ELAGABALUS

THE fates were now preparing as strange a revolution, and bringing upon the Imperial stage as grotesque a figure, as any that have yet come under our notice. Three women--the sister and the nieces of Julia Domna--are the engineers of this revolution, and, clothed with the Imperial dignity, control the fortunes of Rome in the extraordinary period that followed it. But before we introduce the tragi-comic figure of Elagabalus, we must clear the stage of the temporary Emperor and his faint shadow of an Empress.

Opilius Macrinus was a weak, vain, and unimpressive old man. Accident had put the Empire within his reach.

He timidly grasped it because no other offered to do so, and held it until another desired it. He was in his fifty-third year, a man of obscure African origin, an adventurer in the public service. He was married to Nonia Celsa, of whom we know only that her qualities were not generally believed to include the possession of virtue.

Their son Diadumenianus was a tall and handsome youth, with black eyes and curly yellow hair. When his father made him Caesar, and he donned a purple robe, the spectators are said to have melted with affection. He lived long enough to show, by urging his parents to deal more drastically with rebels, that his heart was not so tender as his pretty looks had suggested.

"How happy and fortunate we are," Macrinus wrote to his family, when his accession was secured. In little more than a year he would be flying over the hills of Asia Minor, and he and his handsome boy would be cruelly put to death. He set out at once, with great display, against the unruly Parthians. But he soon purchased an ignoble peace from them, and repaired to the banquets and pleasures of Antioch. Anxious as he was about his position, he made the fatal error of keeping the troops in camp, and there soon passed from legion to legion an ominous murmur. The soldiers contrasted his luxury with Caracalla's sharing of their march and their cheese, and chafed under the discipline he rightly sought to enforce.

The rumour spread, too, that Macrinus had given offence to the Senate; and that a mule had borne a mule at Rome, and a sow had given birth to a little pig with two heads and eight feet. The apparition of a comet and an eclipse of the sun made it yet more certain that something was going to happen, and confirmed those who were preparing the event. In the month of May Macrinus heard that a boy of fourteen, supported by three women and a eunuch, had claimed the throne, and seduced some troops. He sent a general, with a moderate force, to bring him the boy's head.

In a week or two a messenger returned with a head--his general's head. He roused himself from the drowsy luxury of Antioch, and set out with his army.

The three women were, as I have said, Julia Maesa, sister of Julia Domna, and her daughters, Soaemias and Mamaea. At the death of Julia Domna they had retired to the ancestral home at Emesa, in Syria, but with a very considerable fortune, which Maesa had gathered at the court of Severus and Caracalla. The two daughters seem to have lost their husbands, though each had a son.

Soaemias had a child of fourteen years, named Varius Avitus Bassianus, a strikingly pretty boy.[17] His cousin Alexianus was three or four years younger. Avitus was therefore clothed with the dignity of priest of the temple, which seems to have been hereditary, and the little group resumed the life they had quitted, twenty years before, to dwell in the Imperial court. Maesa, and probably Soaemias, found this rustic tranquillity unendurable, and followed political events with interest. The one retained dreams of Imperial power, the other of Imperial indulgence. Their chief servant was a clever eunuch, Gannys by name, who is strangely described by Dio as "practically living with Soaemias." A geographical accident brought their vague dreams to a practical issue.

Near the little town of Emesa was a camp of the Roman soldiers. Cosmopolitan as they now were in race and religion, and fretting at their detention in the dull countryside, the soldiers took a close interest in the temple of the strange god. The great wealth and fame of the shrine, the peculiar nature of its deity and its ritual, often attracted them, and the knowledge that these rich and handsome women of the priestly family had been so closely connected with their popular Caracalla increased the interest. But the chief feature that drew their attention was the beauty of the young high-priest. The soft and feminine delicacy of his form and features was enhanced by a long robe of Imperial purple, fringed with gold, and a crown that flashed back the rays of the Syrian sun from its precious gems.

The romance was not lessened when they reflected that the great Severus had often fondled this boy in his arms, and that he might have inherited the throne. The women, or their servants, now doubled the interest of the soldiers by insinuating a whisper that he was the son of their Caracalla, and when Maesa's gold began to pass freely into their purses, they contrived to see a resemblance to the dark and repellent features of the late Emperor in the girlish beauty of the boy. Soaemias had no difficulty in paying the poor price of her reputation for a return to court. Lampridius bluntly calls her a *meretrix*.

On the night of May 15th, 218, the three women and the two boys were transferred to the camp. Maesa's fortune went with them, as the price of Empire, and on the following day the soldiers announced that Bassianus, as he was now called, was Emperor. The camp was fortified, and in a few days Macrinus's general, Julianus, appeared before it with his troops. Their companions in the camp exhibited the young son of Caracalla on the rampart, and, as they exhibited also the bags of Maesa's gold, they convinced and seduced the assailants. Julianus's head was cut off, and sent to Antioch. Macrinus now marched against them, and the two armies met in the intervening country on June 8th. The softened troops wavered on both sides, and it looked as if Macrinus might win, when Maesa and Soaemias sprang from their chariots in the rear of the army, rushed into the ranks, and spurred their flagging followers on to victory. Macrinus fled, in an ignominious disguise, across the hills and valleys of Asia Minor, and within a few weeks Nonia Celsa learned that she had lost her throne, her husband, and her boy. The Emperor of Rome was the pretty boy-priest of Elagabalus.

Imperial power, however, meant to the Syrian youth an unrestrained indulgence of his sensual dreams, not a grave concern with the affairs of a mighty people. He dallied in the East, and willingly left his duties to his grandmother, while he devoted himself entirely to his rights. He gathered about him the ignoble company of ministers to lust which the cities of Asia Minor were at all times ready to supply, and there was no depth or eccentricity of vice in Antioch or Nicomedia which he did not explore. Before the end of that year the boy's nature was completely perverted, and the last trace of masculinity eliminated from it. Maesa was alarmed, for the cities of the East were wont to talk freely of the vices they implanted or cultivated in their visitors, and the sentiment of Rome could not be ignored. But Bassianus laughed at her timidity, and lingered throughout the following winter in the voluptuous chambers of Nicomedia.

As to this Roman Senate, of which she spoke, he sent the grey-beards a painting of himself in his flowing sacerdotal robes and womanly jewels, to be placed over the altar of Victory in their meeting-place.

In the following spring he condescended to visit the capital of his Empire. Rome had received many a strange procession during the centuries of its Imperial expansion, but no spectacle had aroused so much curiosity as the arrival of the young monarch on whose picture the Senators had gazed with bewilderment. The original was even more extraordinary than the portrayal. For the entry into Rome the young priest-Emperor stained his cheeks with vermilion, and artfully enhanced the brilliance of his eyes, like a Syrian courtesan or an actress. He wore his loose robes of purple silk trimmed with gold, his delicate arms were encircled with costly bracelets and his white neck with a string of pearls, and a tiara of successive crowns, flashing with jewels, surmounted his strange figure.

And, as the alternative and real power in administration, the Romans regarded with anxiety the two women who rode with him--the grave and dignified Maesa, and the richly sensuous and evil-famed Soaemias. There is in the Vatican Museum a statue of the mother of Elagabalus as she appeared at this time. She has chosen to be portrayed in the costume, or lack of costume, of Venus; and the voluptuous body and soft round limbs, the low forehead, thick lips, and large nose, combined with the hard and shameless expression, reconcile us to the coarsest epithets the historians have attached to her memory.

JULIA MAESA

BUST IN THE CAPITOLINE MUSEUM, ROME

To the horror of the Senate this woman was at once associated with him in a character that no Empress, or no woman, had ever assumed in the long history of Rome.

At his first visit to the Senate the Emperor demanded that she should be invited to sit by his side and listen to their deliberations. Even Livia had been content to listen behind the decent shade of a curtain.

Soaemias, however, had not the wit or seriousness to interfere in any way.

She was appointed president of the Senaculum, or "Little Senate," of women, which Sabina had founded, and Julia restored, in the Forum of Trajan; and she found an easier and more congenial occupation in controlling the grave deliberations of the matrons of Rome on questions of etiquette, precedence, costume, and jewellery. It was left to Maesa to wield the political power, and she did so with sobriety and judgment. Unhappily, the Emperor was more willing to listen to the easier counsels of his mother than to Maesa, and he began at once to entertain or disgust Rome with the appalling license which makes his short reign an indescribable nightmare.

He had brought from Emesa the celestial stone, the emblem of Elagabal, to which all his prosperity was due, and his first care was to provide the god with a worthy home. A magnificent temple was raised to it, and the stone, encrusted with gems, was borne to it on a chariot drawn by six white horses, the Emperor walking backwards before it in an ecstasy of adoration. In the temple a number of altars were set up, and rivers of blood--even the blood of children--were poured out on them; while the Emperor and his family croned the barbaric chants of primitive Syria, and the highest dignitaries of Rome stood in silent respect. As the earlier officials were soon replaced by men of infamy, chosen, very frequently, on a qualification that one may not describe, we need pay little attention to their feelings. If we suppose that the Emperor, or Elagabalus, as he now called himself, was aware that the conical stone was really a phallic emblem, we may find a clue to some of the stranger vagaries of his erotomania.

Rome had long been accustomed to the barbarism of the more ancient Oriental cults, and had indeed taken a willing part in the orgiastic processions of the mysterious Mother of the Gods, whenever their rulers permitted them. But the security of the Empire seemed to them in danger when Elagabalus went on to place every other idol in a position of subordinate respect in the temple of his fetich. Jupiter, Juno, Venus, and Mars, were not at that time favoured very widely with a literal belief; nor were the Romans concerned when he stole the Astarte of the Carthaginians, and married her, in a magnificent festival, to his lonely deity. The temples and cults of Rome were like the temples and cults of modern Japan.

They contributed to the gaiety of life. But if there was little sincere polytheism at Rome--the educated world was divided between an

Epicurean Agnosticism and an eclectic Monotheism--there was much superstition, and few could regard without concern a desecration of the ancient Palladium, or statue in the temple of Vesta, to which the fortune of the city was peculiarly attached, and other ancient emblems. Elagabalus despotically overrode their feelings. He broke forcibly into the home of the Vestal Virgins, and bore away the sacred Palladium; since we may regard the later boast of the Virgins, that they cheated him with a substituted statue, as insincere.

Of the Empresses whom he made by marriage we

have little knowledge. In less than three years he married, and unmarried, either four or five women. The first was Julia Cornelia Paula, a woman of very distinguished family and, if we may trust the bust in the Louvre, a woman of dignity, refinement, and some strength of character. We may see the action of Maesa in the choice.

A few months later he divorced her and, to the horror of Rome, married one of the Vestal Virgins. Possibly the beauty of Julia Aquilia Severa had caught his fancy when he broke into their sacred enclosure. The Senators were deeply concerned at this sacrilege, for the fate of Rome was still closely connected with the integrity of the noble virgins who tended the undying fire before the altar of Vesta. Elagabalus, who, it was generally known, had no hope of progeny, brazenly argued with the Senate that he was consulting the future of the State, since a union of priest and priestess gave promise of a family of divine children. In any case, he said, he was a maker, not an observer, of laws; and he established Severa in his palace.

The coins give her the title of Augusta.

His roving eye soon afterwards was attracted by the charms of Annia Faustina, the great-granddaughter of Marcus Aurelius. The portrait-bust of her in the Capitol Museum has a round full face of great beauty and an expression of sweetness and modesty. She seems to have escaped the taint of the Faustinae. She was married to Pomponius Bassus, and Elagabalus released her by the familiar device of executing her husband, and transferred her, leaving no time for mourning, to the palace. Her beauty seems to have been too tempered with refinement to engage his affections long. She was dismissed, and replaced by some unknown victim. Then Elagabalus returned to his priestess of Vesta. In all, he seems to have married four women in three years, not counting Severa, whose marriage Dio does not seem to regard as valid.

Severa was the chief associate of his life in the palace, and it is quite impossible to convey an impression of the sordid scenes into which she had passed from the austere sanctuary of Vesta. Twelve condensed pages of the "Historia Augusta" are occupied with his enormities, and at the close of what is probably the most appalling picture of unrestrained license in any literature--even if we admit exaggeration--Lampridius assures us that he has, from a feeling of modesty, omitted the worst details. It would seem that the human imagination, in its most diseased condition, could devise nothing lower. We do not know whether Severa was an Octavia or a Poppaea, but the circumstance that she consented to live is grave enough. In that vast colony of vice, to which a system of pandars, spread over the Empire, dispatched every man who had some special physical or moral feature to fit him for the orgies, no decent woman would have clung to mortality.

A Caesonia or a Marcia might laugh when Elagabalus returned at night, dressed as a common female tavern-keeper, from the low wine-shops in which he had been

rioting--might even smile when she saw Elagabalus's "husband," a burly slave, beating and bruising him for his infidelity, or when she heard at night the rattle of the golden rings and the shameful appeal of the new Messalina behind his curtain--but Severa was of noble birth, the daughter of a man who had twice been consul.

One of the unpardonable sins of Rome was that it hesitated so long to assassinate some of its rulers. The very excesses of Elagabalus protected him for a long time, as he urged the people to share or imitate his pleasures. No screen was drawn about his vices. He would discuss them with the Senate, or collect all the *meretrices* of Rome in a hall, and address them on those various schemes of vice which we find to-day depicted on the walls of the *lupanar* in Pompeii. He would invite the common folk to come and drink with him at the palace, where they might see the furniture of solid silver, the beds loaded with roses and hyacinths, the swimming-baths of perfume, the gold dust strewn in the colonnades, the paths paved with porphyry. He provided for them the spectacle of naval battles in lakes of wine, and a mountain of snow, brought from the remote mountains, in the middle of summer. But his chief device for cajoling the citizens was to distribute tickets, as for a lottery, and see them press for the sight of the gifts corresponding to their numbers. You might get ten eggs or ten ostriches, ten flies or ten camels, ten toy balloons or ten pounds of gold; and the mania grew until your chance lay between a dead dog, a slave, a richly caparisoned horse, a chariot, or a hundred pounds of gold. At times he would invite a crowd to dinner, and smother them, with fatal effect to some, under a thick shower of flowers; or seat them on inflated bags, which slaves would deflate in the middle of the banquet; or have them borne away intoxicated at the end, to find themselves in the morning sleeping with bears or lions.

The frivolous Romans were so much entertained by these vagaries that they overlooked his personal luxury, and made no inquiry into the state of the treasury. No dinner could be placed before him that had not cost thirty pounds of silver. Robed in a tunic of pure gold or pure Chinese silk, sitting under perfumed lamps, amid masses of the choicest blooms, he picked delicately at the tongues of larks and peacocks, the brains of thrushes, the eggs of pheasants, the heads of parrots, or the heels of camels.

He fed his horses with choice grapes and his lions with pheasants. His chariots were of gold only, studded with gems, and they were drawn through the streets by strings of nude women, or by stags. Delicate in every detail, he had cords of silk and swords of gold prepared for inflicting death on himself in case of need. He little knew that he would die in the latrine of the soldiers' camp.

Soaemias seems to have enjoyed this orgiastic life, but the more prudent Maesa was concerned. Finding that remonstrances were quite useless, she cunningly persuaded Elagabalus to associate his cousin with him in the government.

Alexander--as Alexianus had now been named--was three or four years younger than the Emperor, and did not share his disease. His mother, Mamaea, inherited the prudence and sobriety of Maesa, and guarded her boy from the contamination with the utmost care. His excellent disposition ensured the success of their plan, and Elagabalus began to perceive that the younger boy was winning a dangerous popularity. It is said that a judicious distribution of money by Mamaea fostered the growing esteem for him, especially among the soldiers.

From suspicion Elagabalus passed to hatred, and from hatred to a design on his cousin's life. Mamaea secured the favour of the guards with great adroitness, and watched the actions of Elagabalus. He first, in order to test public feeling, sent word to the Senate and the camp that he had withdrawn the title of Caesar from his cousin; and he directed that the boy should be put to death if this announcement created no disorder. In the anxious hour that followed, Alexander waited in a room of the palace with his trembling mother and Maesa; Elagabalus went down to the gardens to supervise the preparations for a chariot-race, and await impatiently the news that his cousin was dead. Presently a tumultuous crowd of the guards rushed across the city, and burst into the gardens of the palace. Elagabalus fled to his room, and covered himself with a curtain; and the soldiers conveyed the two women and the boy in triumph to the camp, many of them remaining in the garden to threaten Elagabalus.

Soaemias, seeing the Empire slip from her, awoke to energetic action. She hastened on foot to the camp, and pleaded passionately for her son. They did not wish to take his life, the guards said, but must have a security for the life of Alexander and a promise of reform. They returned to the gardens, and the young autocrat, in his purple silks and jewelled shoes, had to plead with the rough soldiers to spare the favourite ministers of his vices. He had filled the highest posts with men whose only qualifications were such that we cannot describe them, and his army of attendants were the scum of the Empire. The guards forced him to dismiss the most obnoxious, preached him an inglorious sermon on his infamies, and directed their officers to watch over the life of Alexander.

The swords of gold and the cords of variegated silk were not employed, but Elagabalus could never forgive the degradation he had experienced. He made several attempts to remove the obstacles to his design: sent the Senate from Rome, and removed or executed several of the soldiers. Mamaea watched him assiduously, and Maesa easily penetrated his secrets. Not a particle of food or drink from the Imperial kitchen was allowed to pass the lips of Alexander. Rome knew that the end was near. It was only a few years since Bassianus and Geta had disgraced the palace with a similar quarrel. Maesa attempted in vain to conciliate them. On January 1st, 222, they were both to receive the consular dignity from the Senate.

She had to threaten Elagabalus with a fresh mutiny of the guards before he would go.

Some ten weeks later the feud came to a crisis. Elagabalus, to test the soldiers, sets afoot a rumour that Alexander is dead. The guards, believing the rumour, withdraw their contingent from the palace, and shut themselves in the camp. Elagabalus takes his cousin in his golden chariot to the camp, to show that the rumour is false, and loses control of himself when the guards burst into exclamations of joy at the sight of Alexander. Mamaea and Soaemias come upon the scene, and an angry altercation follows, each mother making a wild appeal to the soldiers. Either there is a division of feeling among the soldiers, or some of Elagabalus's ministers are present, for swords are drawn and are soon at work. Elagabalus and Soaemias, the Sybarites, rush into the latrine of the camp for safety, and are slain there by the guards. Their bodies are disdainfully thrown out to the mob, who have gathered outside. The effeminate frame of the young Emperor, with its soft limbs and large pendent breasts, and the voluptuous body of his mother, are dragged through the streets, and, as the opening of the sewer is too narrow to receive them, they are thrown into the Tiber. And the cry of "Ave, Imperator!" rings in the ears of Mamaea and her boy.

CHAPTER XIV

ANOTHER SYRIAN EMPRESS

TO the thoughtful Roman the name of Syria must have suggested an abyss of corruption, and the extension of the Empire over that swarm of Asiatic peoples to whom the name was vaguely applied must have seemed an infelicitous triumph. From the cities of nearer Asia, in which the senile energies of the older civilizations seemed incapable of rising above the ministry to vice, luxury, and folly, had come the larger part of the taint that had infected the blood of Rome. It is therefore singular to observe that, of the five women whom Syria placed on, or above, the Roman throne in the third century, four were distinguished for sobriety of judgment and concern for the common weal. The family from which the first four of these women sprang is variously described as "humble" and "noble." We may reconcile the epithets by a conjecture that the family which controlled the wealthy shrine of Emesa descended from some branch of the fallen nobility of the East. Both Soaemias and Mamaea had married Syrians, and we may assume that Mamaea had done the same. In those circumstances, the public spirit with which Julia Domna, Julia Maesa, and Julia Mamaea used the great influence they had is not a little remarkable.

Of the three--to whom we must presently add a fourth remarkable woman of the East--Mamaea had the greatest power, and made the best use of it. She is not blameless, as we shall see; but even if it be true, as is commonly said, that she was unduly covetous of money and power, we must at least admit that she employed them solely to restore peace and prosperity to the Empire, and prolong the reign of a high-principled ruler.

Mamaea entered upon her work with all the shrewdness which we have already recognized in her. Instead of claiming the right, which Soaemias had enjoyed, to sit in the Senate and sign its decrees, she preserved a discreet silence when the Senate abolished the innovation, and poured out their long-repressed annoyance on the memory of its author. The Senators ostentatiously enjoyed their shadow of power: Mamaea quietly possessed the substance.

She provided the finest preceptors for the education of her son Alexander, who was in his fourteenth year, and selected sixteen of the most distinguished Senators and lawyers as a Council of State. With these she worked energetically and harmoniously for the renovation of the Empire. The palace was purged of the quaint and the loathsome officers that she found in it, Rome was relieved of Elagabal and his ghastly ritual, competent officials were substituted for the ministers to the lust of the late Emperor, and the heavier taxes of the previous two reigns were remitted or lessened. In this work, which extends over the thirteen years of the reign of Alexander Severus, Maesa had little part. She died soon after the beginning of this happier era, and Mamaea alone guided the willing hands of her son. It is remarked by all the authorities that Alexander was singularly subservient to his mother.

Troops and Senate had been happily united in the elevation of Alexander, and all the epithets of Imperial dignity were at once conferred on him. The title of Severus he accepted from the soldiers, but he declined the name of Antoninus, which the Senate pressed on him, since that revered name had been so impiously disgraced by his predecessors. He spontaneously discarded the womanly silks and jewels of his cousin, covered the rough shirts of Severus with the Roman toga, and gave equal attention to manly exercises, the lessons of his tutors, and the wise counsels of his mother. He thus grew into a handsome and virile youth, with the piercing black eyes of his race, but with a moderation of temper that delighted his Stoic teachers. When we read the account of his career in the "Historia Augusta"--an account that might have been written by a Xenophon or a Fenelon for the edification of a young prince--we are tempted to feel that, either the gossipy Lampridius had for the moment a more serious object than the entertainment of Rome, or Alexander Severus was more virtuous than the circumstances required.

Mamaea is described by the same writer as "holy, but avaricious." Avarice was a not inopportune vice. Elagabalus had squandered the treasury on his follies; the troops, encouraged by him and by Caracalla, were becoming more and more exacting; while Mamaea had, by lightening the taxes, spared the Empire a substantial share of its contribution. In these circumstances it was prudent to cultivate a close concern about money, and no single writer ventures to say that the Empress--the Senate had at once entitled her Augusta--spent much on her personal service or pleasure. It is said that her zeal for the accumulation of money was carried to a stage of offensiveness. But it was necessary for her murderers to detect or invent some vice in extenuation of their foul deed, and the position in which the charge is found in the historians reveals that it came from that tainted source. "Avarice" means little more than that she would not yield to the improper demands of a demoralized army.

When we reflect that both her parents were Syrians, we notice with some surprise that the portrait-bust of Mamaea has a singularly Roman face; and in her strength, solidity, and sobriety she recalls the old Roman type rather than accords with the general conception of a Syrian woman. She had the defect of her type, and an incident that occurred early in her reign is regarded as a grave betrayal of it. It is not at all clear, however, that Mamaea acted with the "jealous cruelty" which Gibbon sees in her conduct. For the wife of her son she had chosen Sallustia Barbia Orbiana--we find the name on coins, though the historians do not give it--daughter of the Senator Sallustius Macrinus. Alexander, not an exacting husband, seems to have lived happily with his bride, and her father was promoted to the rank of Caesar. Before long, however, we find Macrinus executed on a charge of treason, and his daughter banished to Africa.

Gibbon believes, on the authority of Dio, that this was entirely due to Mamaea's unwillingness to share the power and the affection of her son with another woman. The word of an historian and a member of the Senate, whom we may almost describe as an eye-witness, must assuredly have weight, yet we cannot ignore the assertion of the other authorities that Macrinus was betrayed into acts which easily bore the construction of treason. We may recall Merivale's just warning, on another occasion, that a contemporary Roman writer is particularly apt to reproduce the unsubstantial gossip of his day. Herodian, who nevertheless believes that Macrinus had no treasonable intention, says that Mamaea was so cruel to Orbiana that the girl went in tears to her father, and he repaired to the Praetorian camp with bitter complaints against Mamaea.

Such a course very strongly suggests a treasonable design.

The troops, chafing under the rule of Mamaea and her son, whom they eventually murdered, were notoriously discontented; and flying to the camp was commonly the first

overt act in a plot to displace the ruling Emperor. When we further find that Lampridius ("Historia Augusta") says, on the authority of Dexippus, an Athenian writer of the succeeding generation, that Macrinus was expressly attempting to replace Alexander, we must at least suspend our censures. We know nothing of the character of Macrinus and his daughter, and are therefore unable to say how far Mamaea's interpretation of their conduct may have been influenced by her feelings, and how far her harsh treatment of Orbiana may have been justified.

The charge against her is further weakened by a circumstance that Gibbon has overlooked. Lampridius says that Alexander married Memnia, the daughter of the ex-consul Sulpicius, and speaks incidentally of "his boys."

It seems, then, that the jealousy of Mamaea did not prevent Alexander from marrying again, and that Memnia must have shared the palace with the Empress-mother for a number of years. Of her character we know nothing, except that, together with Mamaea, she remonstrated with Alexander on account of his excessive affability with his subjects. No guards, it seems, barred the entrance of the palace against them. The austere character of the life which adorned it was the only test of the integrity of those who approached him. After a day of exertion he would spend the evening in the refining enjoyment of letters or the exercise of his musical skill. He sang and played well, but guarded his Imperial dignity by admitting none to hear him except his young sons. Actors and gladiators he avoided, nor would he spend much in exhibiting their skill to the public. His one luxury was a remarkable collection of birds, which included 20,000 doves; his one weakness a delight in the puny and almost bloodless combats of partridges, kittens, or pups. His baths were of cold water, and his table was regulated by the most minute directions, admitting even the slight luxury of a goose only on festive occasions. When a string of costly pearls was presented to Memnia, he ordered that they should be sold, and, when no purchaser could be found in Rome, he hung them upon the statue of Venus in the temple.

JULIA MAMAEA

BUST IN THE BRITISH MUSEUM

From such details as these we may construct a picture of the quiet and temperate life of Alexander's palace, and we shall be disposed to think lightly of the quarrels which are said to have disturbed the relations of mother and son.

We can hardly believe that one so frugal as Alexander would profess much indignation at his mother's assiduous nursing of the treasury, nor can we suppose that Mamaea greatly resented the young monarch's accessibility to his subjects. Their frugality, indeed, must not be exaggerated, as they were generous in gifts. Instead of sending men to extort their incomes from the provinces in which they took office, Alexander provided them, when they left Rome, with an outfit so complete as to include a concubine. His deference to his mother may, in fact, be said to be the only consistent charge against him. The Emperor Julian ("The Caesars") insinuates that he showed a mediocrity of intelligence in allowing his mother to accumulate money, instead of prudently spending it. In a sense Julian was right; though it was not weakness of intelligence, but severity of principle, that restrained Alexander and Mamaea from this prudent expenditure. Had they lavished their funds upon the troops, the history of Rome during the next ten years might have run differently.

From an early period in the reign of Alexander the attitude of the troops cast a shadow over the palace and the Empire. Five successive Emperors, besides earlier ones, had received the purple from the hands of the troops, and had been compelled either to refrain from pressing the necessary discipline upon them, or to compensate the rigours of discipline with excessive rewards. The soldiers became conscious of their power, and sufficiently demoralized to abuse it. Less exercise and more pay led to a lamentable enervation; and the filling of the ranks from the more distant peoples, who had not contributed to the making of the Empire and were insensible to its prestige, dissolved in the legions the old spirit of nationality. From the lonely forests, the frozen hills, or the blistering deserts of the frontiers, they sought ever to be withdrawn to the comforts and pleasures of the cities. And when they found that a fresh effort was being made to restrict their indulgences and restore the earlier discipline, when they reflected that it was only the feeble hands of a woman and a youth that would enforce this austerity, they broke into sullen murmurs of discontent.

The most dangerous part of the army was the extensive regiment of Praetorian Guards, which, from its camp at the walls, overshadowed Rome with its power. Over these men Mamaea had placed a civilian, the distinguished jurist Domitius Ulpianus. It was natural that Ulpian should wish to extend to the guards the valuable reforms which he was introducing into every department of the State; equally natural that the soldiers should chafe under his discipline. The citizens took the part of Ulpian and Mamaea, who protected him, and the irritation at last erupted in a bloody struggle, in which the populace fought for three days against the soldiers in the streets of Rome.

The quarrel was arrested, but some time afterwards--not in the fight, as Gibbon says--the angry guards put an end to the reforms of Ulpian. The statesman fled before them into the palace, and sought the protection of the Emperor; but the insolent guards penetrated the sanctuary of the royal house with drawn swords, and murdered, in Alexander's presence, the most eminent and enlightened of his counsellors. The provincial troops were giving little less concern. We take our leave at this stage of the historian Dio. His work closes with a mournful lament of the condition of the army, and a just presentiment of impending calamity. He too had endeavoured to enforce discipline on the legions, and had found the authority of the Emperor insufficient to protect him from their murderous resentment.

As if this lamentable situation had been communicated to the countless peoples who pressed eagerly against the barriers of the Empire, we find a new boldness arising amongst them, and a serious beginning of those raids which will at last put the mighty power under the heel of the barbarian. The tragedy of the fall of Rome reaches a more certain stage. It is a singular and melancholy reflection that Rome suffered most under its most virtuous rulers.

During the reign of Marcus Aurelius the gods had seemed to make a war upon virtue. The new Stoic and his virtuous mother were destined to see the enemies gathering fiercely about their enfeebled frontiers, and to perish tragically in a futile effort to repel them.

The gravest trouble arose in the East. The ancient kingdom of Persia revived, and its vigorous rulers determined to regain the provinces which Greece and Rome had shorn from their once vast empire. Alexander, and probably Mamaea, went to the East. If we may believe the panegyrist of Alexander in the "Historia Augusta," he displayed an admirable firmness in enforcing discipline upon the troops when he arrived at Antioch. Gathering their sullen and spoiled officers from the haunts of Antioch and the licentious groves of the suburb of Daphne, he punished a number of them severely, boldly confronted the drawn swords of their demoralized followers, and set the legions in motion against the Persians. But the plan of the campaign was injudicious, and the execution weak. The Romans suffered a heavy reverse, and, before they could recover and check the advancing spirit of the Persians, Alexander was recalled to Europe with the news that the Germanic tribes were bursting through the northern frontier.

From the sunny lands of their native East the Emperor and his mother passed, in the year 234, to the banks of the Rhine. They had passed through Rome, where the citizens were easily persuaded to celebrate his triumph over the Persians. From the Capitol they had carried the young Emperor on their shoulders to his palace, his chariot with its four elephants walking behind them, and a great wave of enthusiasm went with him as he started for Gaul. He was now in his twenty-sixth year, and Mamaea must have felt that he was at the beginning of a glorious career.

They little suspected that they were going to meet their deaths at the hands of their own troops.

One of the commanders on the Rhine was a gigantic and powerful barbarian, half Goth and half Alan, of the name of Maximinus. More than eight feet in height, with a thumb so large that he wore his wife's bracelet on it as a ring, the giant had made his way in the army by sheer strength. A man who could eat forty pounds of meat in a day, drink a proportionate quantity of wine, and fell you with a finger, had the respect of the barbarian soldiers.

Elagabalus had repelled him, when he sought office, with salacious questions about his strength; Alexander had eagerly welcomed him, and put him in command of the younger troops. But Alexander had afterwards refused him an honour, which Mamaea desired to confer on him, and he probably heard this. He had given his son a good Roman education, and Mamaea thought that the young man was a suitable match for her daughter Theoclea.

Alexander protested that his sister would find the father-in-law too boorish, and the young Maximinus, now a tall, handsome, cultivated, and dissolute noble, married a granddaughter of Antoninus Pius, Junia Fadilla.

Whether this affront was remembered, or whether Maximinus acted from mere ambition, we cannot say. He began, in any case, to spread discontent in the army.

When Alexander practically bought peace from the barbarians, instead of conducting a vigorous campaign against them, the whispers were changed into open murmuring.

These effeminate Syrians, it was said, were unable to endure the sturdy North, and were eager to return to the East. The Emperor was a maudlin youth, who could not act without his mother's permission. He had abandoned the war against Persia in order to return to her side, and he was again sacrificing the honour of Rome out of regard for her comfort. Her palace at Rome was full of hoarded treasure, while the hard-worked soldiers were insufficiently paid. These complaints circulated freely in the camp during the long German winter. A lavish distribution of money might have defeated the plot of Maximinus, and a speedy retirement to Rome would certainly have saved the lives of the Emperor and Empress. But they remained in camp until the middle of March, 235, and then the end came.

They were at, or in the neighbourhood of, the small frontier town which is now known as Mainz. One morning, when Maximinus rode out to control the exercises, he was greeted with the name of Emperor. He feigned surprise and reluctance, but the soldiers--probably in pursuance of an arranged plan--drew their swords, and threatened to kill him if he did not take the power from the hands of the effeminate Syrians. He consented, promised a liberal donation in honour of his accession, and said that all punishments that had been inflicted on the soldiers would be remitted. He then led them toward the tent of Alexander.

The young Emperor came out to meet them, and

made an appeal that seems to have divided the followers of the usurper, as they went away to their tents. At night, however, the guards at the Imperial tent announced that the mutinous troops were gathering about it. Alexander rushed out, and called upon the loyal soldiers to defend him, making a tardy promise of money and concessions.

Many of them came to his side, but at last the massive figure of Maximinus was seen to approach at the head of a strong body of troops. For the last time the soldiers were urged to choose between the strong, generous man and the avaricious woman and her child. Alexander saw the faithful few pass sullenly to the side of Maximinus, and he returned to his tent. It is said that the last moments were spent in a violent quarrel between mother and son about the responsibility for the disaster. There was little time for it. The soldiers of Maximinus entered at once, and slew Mamaea, Alexander, and their few remaining friends.

A popular and spirited work of the fourth century described "the deaths of the persecutors," or the terrible fate which befell every Emperor who persecuted the Christians. No fate in the terrible series of Imperial calamities was so tragic as that of Alexander, though he had favoured the Christians, and had cherished a bust of Christ among those of the heroes and sages in his *lararium.*

No other Empress in the long line of murdered women so little deserved a violent death as Julia Mamaea. During the fourteen years of her son's reign she had solely studied the welfare of the Empire. The one charge that her murderers could bring against her was that she had hoarded money instead of spending it on, or giving it to, the troops. On public buildings, public works, and civic administration she had spent freely; she, or Alexander, had even expended large sums in providing surer sustenance and more effective transport for the troops themselves.

The charge is little, if at all, more than a cowardly subterfuge.

But it needed half-a-dozen strong and unselfish generals to restore the efficiency and docility of the legions, and they were not to be found. We pass into a period of anarchy, in which Emperors and Empresses rise and wither like mushrooms, and Rome stumbles blindly onward towards its doom. In that period of confusion, when every section of the army makes its Emperor, only two dominant personalities are found, and they are two Empresses of barbaric origin.

CHAPTER XV

ZENOBIA AND VICTORIA

THE Emperor Alexander Severus and his mother were murdered in the year 235. We may convey a just impression of the period that followed this odious crime by the brief observation that in forty years nearly forty Emperors appeared on the darkened stage of the Roman Empire, and that nearly every one of them perished at the hands of Roman soldiers. The anarchy was arrested for a time when, in the year 270, the energetic Aurelian came to the throne. People and Senate greeted the strong man with genuine enthusiasm, and among the cries of joy or hope with which the Senators hailed him we find this singular aspiration: "Thou wilt deliver us from Zenobia and Vitruvia." It is a piquant contrast with the disdain that their fathers had had for women--a confession that their vast Empire was now dominated by two women, without male consorts. But for the timely appearance of Aurelian there was a prospect that they would divide the rule of the world between them. One was a Syrian, the other a Gallic, queen; but each of them bore the title of Augusta, and they are the next commanding personalities to engage our interest.

Many years were to elapse between the death of Mamaea and the appearance of these two remarkable women, but we need do no more than glance at the many Empresses of an hour whose names are hardly discernible in that turbulent era. The huge barbarian who had purchased the throne by a brutal murder did not long enjoy it. The Empire heard with horror and disdain that this Thracian shepherd had seized the mantle of Antoninus and Marcus. The people of Rome, in particular, recollected with alarm the contempt they had shown him in his earlier years, and offered prayer in the temples that the gods might divert his steps from the south of Italy.

He met their disdain with vindictiveness, and ruthlessly executed those who remembered his humble origin, or whose wealth could add to his revenue. His Empress, Paulina, vainly endeavoured to restrain his bloody hand, and succeeded only in drawing it upon herself.[18] At length his exactions struck a spark of rebellion in Africa, and a new Emperor was appointed.

The African Proconsul, Gordianus, was an excellent Epicurean of the fine old Roman type. He had wealth, culture, character, and taste. After filling the highest offices at Rome with grace and applause, he was now quietly discharging the duties of Proconsul, and relieving the long hours of leisure with a tranquil enjoyment of letters, at the little town of Thysdrus, about a hundred and fifty miles to the south of Carthage. With him in Africa was his son Gordianus, an epicure rather than an Epicurean, who solaced his exile from Rome with the engaging company of twenty-two ladies. Their respective pleasures were violently interrupted in the beginning of the year 238. The father, a white-haired old man, with broad red face, was resting in his house after his judicial labours, when a band of men, with blood-smeared swords, burst into the luxurious villa, told him that they had rebelled against the tyrant, and peremptorily informed him that he was Emperor. His objections were unheeded, and he set out, with misgiving, for Carthage. But the pride of the Carthaginians was quickly chilled by the news that Maximinus's commander in Africa was advancing against their city. An armed force was hastily equipped, sent out under the lead of the younger Gordian, and cut to pieces. The younger Emperor had died on the field: the white-haired old man hanged himself.

Rome, meantime, had recognized the rule of the Gordians, and was now throbbing with a just apprehension of the vengeance of Maximinus. The certainty of punishment inspired it with a measure of courage, and two new Emperors were created--a vigorous son of the people, Pupienus Maximus, and a perfumed representative of the nobles, Balbinus. The choice did not please the people, who beset the Senate with sticks and stones, so a handsome boy, such as Rome loved, was associated with them.

He was a Gordianus, the fourteen-year-old son of the elder Gordian's daughter. The city rang with preparations for war, and in the early summer Maximus led out his weak and apprehensive force. The terrible Maximinus and his legions had crossed the Alps, and were descending on the plains of Italy. Luckily for Rome, they met a desperate resistance at Aquileia. Protected by strong and well-equipped fortifications, with ample provisions, the inhabitants repelled the fiercest attacks of Maximinus,

and jeered at him and his dissolute son from the walls.

When the thongs of their slinging-machines wore out, the women of Aquileia gave their long tresses to the soldiers to weave into cords. Maximinus vented his temper on his own troops, and one morning the besieged were delighted to see the soldiers advancing with the grisly heads of Maximinus and his son on the tips of their spears.

Maximus returned to gladden Rome with the news, but it was decreed that six Emperors were to die that year. The soldiers, who had had another fight with the Romans during the war, were sullen and treacherous.

Balbinus they hated for his effeminacy, Maximus for his rigour. The returning troops brought grievances of their own, and it was only the loyalty of the German soldiers that held the guards off the palace. Then there came a day when the delight of the games drew most of the soldiers away, and the guards marched upon the palace. Maximus hastily ordered the loyal troops to be summoned: Balbinus cancelled the order. Their relations had been strained for some time, and each looked upon this sudden onslaught as a device of the other. The German troops arrived at last, to find the palace empty, and learn that the three Emperors were in the hands of the guards.

They started at once for the camp, and found the bleeding remains of Maximus and Balbinus on the street. With them another ephemeral Empress passes dimly before us.

The coins seem to indicate that Maximus was the husband of Quintia Crispilla at the time of his death.

The youthful Gordian had been taken to the camp, and Rome was forced to acknowledge him as sole Emperor.

Intoxicated, as so many had been, by the sudden obtaining of so vast a power, he seemed at first inclined to the model of Caligula. His uncle's concubines and his mother's eunuchs were in a fair way to rule the ruler. But a wise tutor, Timesitheus, obtained a better influence over him, and he soberly chose his daughter, Furia Sabina Tranquillina, as his Empress. The whole prospect of the Empire changed with his marriage, in 241 or 242, but the evil genius of Rome intervened once more. The Persians had again crossed the eastern frontier, and the Emperor and his father-in-law went to Asia to take command. The war was proceeding with success, when Timesitheus contracted a mysterious illness and died. Gordian gave his command to a dashing cavalry leader named Philip--the man who, we have strong reason to think, had poisoned Timesitheus.

Philip was a handsome Arab, whose father had led a band of robbers in the desert. But the son was astute, and Gordian suspected nothing. Before many months the camps were simmering with discontent. Pay was reduced, and the troops were reluctantly informed by Philip that it was the command of the Emperor. Regiments found themselves quartered in districts where it was impossible to obtain sufficient food, and Philip begged them to regard the youth and military inexperience of Gordian. The plot culminated in the early spring of 244. Gordian was slain, and the son of the Arab pillager of caravans received the purple from the soldiers.

MARCIA OTACILIA SEVERA

The new Empress of Rome, Marcia Otacilia Severa, attracts our attention for a moment on account of the claim of the early Christian writers that she belonged to the new religion. The claim must have had some foundation, but the story on which it is generally based is regarded with reserve by historians. St. Chrysostom and others declare that, when Philip and Otacilia passed from the Euphrates, where Gordian had been murdered, to Antioch, they went to the Christian church for service on

Easter-eve; and that the bishop refused to admit them in any other character than that of penitents expiating a foul crime. Duruy ridicules the idea that a bishop would have dared so to address an Emperor in public before the middle of the third century, and it is certainly difficult to believe.

Indeed, historians generally suspect that, as the story itself implies, Otacilia supported her husband in his criminal ambition, and are reluctant to regard her as a Christian. Her nationality is unknown, and she hardly emerges from the obscurity in which the scanty chronicles have left the reign of her husband.

Let us hasten through the pages of ghastly adventure, and come to more interesting women. In the year 249 the troops in Moesia pressed the purple on one of the ablest Roman generals, Decius, and Philip was slain in the contest that followed. Otacilia fled with her son to the Praetorian camp, but the guards killed the boy in her arms, and sent her back sadly into the common ranks from which she had so unhappily risen. The wife of Decius, Herennia Etruscilla, who is known to us only from coins and an inscription, had little better fortune, since Decius perished in a war with the Goths two years later (251). His son and successor, Hostilianus, died in the following year, not without a suspicion of crime. The colleague of Decius and successor of his son, Gallus, was murdered in 253, together with his son Volusianus, with whom he had shared the Empire; and the rival and successor of Gallus was assassinated within four months. Then Valerianus, an aged and distinguished Senator, came to the throne, and we begin to have less fleeting glimpses of the ladies of the court, and to make acquaintance with the two remarkable women who will especially occupy us.

The elder Valerian does not long remain on the stage.

The weakness into which the Empire had fallen was soon observed by its enemies on every side, and the frontier provinces were being devastated. Investing his elder son, Gallienus, with the purple, Valerian went to the East to oppose the Persian monarch, Sapor, who threatened the whole of Roman Asia, and after a time fell, with his army, into the hands of the enemy. Whether or no it be true that the proud Persian used to step on the person of the aged Emperor to mount his horse, it is at least certain that Valerian died among the Persians after some years of ignominious captivity, and his skin, stuffed and padded to the proportions of a man, was long exhibited as the most glorious of Sapor's many trophies. There are later writers who assert that his second wife, the Empress Mariniana, was captured with him, and brutally treated until she died, but the authority is slender. Cohen, the great authority on Roman coins, warns us that, though there are coins of a certain Mariniana, who seems to have been a lady of Valerian's court, it is not certain that she was his wife.

So feeble did the Empire now become that its enemies made the most extensive and destructive inroads. The Persians advanced so far as to sack Antioch, the Franks overran Spain and reached Africa, the Alemanni spread terror in the north of Italy and even threatened Rome, and the Goths poured over Greece and Asia Minor. Gallienus received the news of each successive disaster with an insipid joke. Glittering with the jewels which encrusted his belt, his dress, and even his shoes, his hair powdered with gold dust, he dined from dishes of solid gold, in the company of his concubines, while his father suffered in captivity, and his subjects groaned under the hardship of invasion, famine, pestilence, and earthquake. His Empress, Cornelia Salonina, seems to have disdained his cowardly luxury, and she was replaced in his affection, though not in her position, by a charming barbarian. Attalus, King of the Marcomanni, had a beautiful daughter named Pipa or Pipara, whose attractiveness was brought to the notice of Gallienus. He frivolously submitted to the Senate that, since Rome had so many enemies, it were wise to disarm some of them; and he asked Attalus for the hand of his daughter. The shrewd barbarian stipulated for a large part of Pannonia, and in return for that valuable slice of the Empire permitted his pretty daughter to be the concubine of the Roman Emperor. She never appears on the coinage, while Salonina--whose grave, intellectual features suggest that she found solace in culture--remains Augusta to the end. Serviez finds an admirable trait of Salonina's character in the punishment of a man who had sold her some false jewels. He was sentenced to the lions; but when the terrible gates were opened, a harmless fowl flew out upon him, and he was discharged with the fright.

The Roman historian, however, ascribes the trick expressly to Gallienus.[19]

In the eight years of Gallienus's complete control of the Empire (260-268) it was distracted and worn with misery and anarchy. The "Historia Augusta" estimates that "thirty tyrants" arose in that short period to dispute the power of the corrupt Gallienus; Gibbon reduces the number to nineteen; Duruy counts twenty-eight claimants to the throne. There was, in any case, a period of profound demoralization, and as nearly all these generals met with a violent death, involved many others in their fall, and very frequently led their troops in civil warfare, the drain on the impoverished system was disastrous. It is amongst these "thirty tyrants" that we find Zenobia and Victoria.

Zenobia was the wife of Odenathus, the ruling man in the independent town of Palmyra. The town, which had become an important commercial centre, lay on the edge of the Syrian desert, and had long maintained a position of neutrality between the Romans on the west and the Parthians to the east. It had the title of a Roman colony, and Odenathus cannot have been more than its leading citizen and, perhaps, head of its Senate. To this little State came the news that the Roman Emperor was detained in ignominy by the King of Persia. Odenathus sent to Sapor a most polite suggestion that his conduct was improper, and gilded his remonstrance with a caravan of valuable presents. The presents were disdainfully thrown into the Euphrates, and the blustering Sapor threatened to punish his insolence. With great boldness the leading citizen of Palmyra formed an irregular army out of the neighbouring villages and the Arabs, with a few Roman troops, and inflicted a substantial reverse on the Persian troops. Gallienus gracefully acknowledged his service, and extended the Imperial title to him and his wife Zenobia, who became the representatives of Roman power in the East.

Zenobia was, says Trebellius Pollio in the "Historia Augusta," "one of the most noble of all the women of the East, and also one of the most beautiful." Her nobility rests upon her claim that she descended from Cleopatra, a point that we are unable to examine. The portrait-bust of her in the Vatican does not so much suggest exceptional beauty as exceptional power. It is a face of extraordinary strength and peculiar features. We can very well imagine her, as she is described for us, riding out on horseback before the assembled troops, her piercing black eyes aflame with spirit, a military helmet on her head, and a purple robe, embroidered with gems, so attached to her person as to leave naked the fine arm with which she emphasized her orders. She maintained a court of Persian magnificence, but was far removed from Persian insolence. She did not disdain to drink with her officers, and even to endeavour to surpass them in drinking. Yet it is uniformly stated that this remarkable independence of Syrian ideas as to a woman's position was united with a chastity of the most sensitive and peculiarly scrupulous character. When we add that she was a woman of exceptional culture, spoke Latin, Greek, and Egyptian, had so complete a command of the history of the East that she wrote a book on it, and enjoyed the daily companionship of the philosopher Longinus, who was tutor to her sons, we seem to have exhausted possible merit, and ventured into the province of legend. But we have still to say that her military and political ability was no less than her beauty, her culture, or her virtue. We shall see later that the finest Emperor of the age, Aurelian, spoke with extraordinary appreciation of her skill in warfare and in polity.

Even as the wife of Odenathus, Zenobia was not inactive.

She is said to have urged his bold attack on Persia, and she shared the longest marches of the soldiers when the campaign began. But she was soon the sole ruler of the East, in the interest, at first, of Rome. During the Persian war Odenathus quarrelled with a relative and officer, named Maeonius, and was only prevented by the intercession of his son, Herodes, from putting him to death. Herodes was the son of Odenathus by a former wife, and would be the natural heir to his dignity. The two sons whom Zenobia had borne him, Timolaus and Herennianus, were mere boys, but Zenobia had an older son, Vaballath, by a former husband. We can understand that there would be some jealousy in the family, now that the Roman purple and a practical sovereignty of the East were conferred on the "king of Palmyra." Zenobia could not but dislike and despise Herodes. He adopted the voluptuous ways of the East, and received from his father, as an immediate share of his heritage, the jewels, silks, and fair ladies which he had detached from the baggage of Sapor when that monarch retired before him.

Yet there is no ground for the assertion that Zenobia was privy to the conspiracy which removed Odenathus and Herodes. Maeonius was consulting his own ambition, as well as appeasing his hatred, in having them assassinated.

For a moment Zenobia was in a position of some anxiety, but she acted with vigour. She thrust her son Vaballath--the "Historia Augusta" at first says her two younger sons, but afterwards corrects this--before the Palmyreans as the most worthy heir of the power of Odenathus, and Maeonius passes into a significant obscurity. Vaballath was declared Augustus, and Zenobia became "Queen of the East," as she liked to call herself. The two younger boys were entitled Caesars. Within a short time it was felt at Rome that a new and rival power had arisen in the East.

The voluptuous Gallienus could at times start from his rose-strewn couches and the arms of his mistresses, and conduct an energetic raid upon the opponents of his Empire. The victories of Odenathus seem to have inspired one of these fits of vigour. The legions in Gaul had cast off their allegiance to their degraded ruler, put his son Saloninus to death, and chosen as Emperor their able and upright commander, Cassianus Postumus. Gallienus marched against him, pressed him hard for a time, and then returned to Rome to enjoy a magnificent triumph.

One hundred white oxen, with gilded horns, two hundred white lambs, several hundred lions, tigers, bears, and other animals, and twelve hundred gladiators, in superb costumes, preceded his car. The more serious Romans looked on in disdain. Some of the mimes, or comedians, dressed as Persians, and went about in the procession, staring in each other's faces, and saying that they were "looking for the Emperor's father." Gallienus had them burned alive.

But the chief interest of this dash into Gaul is that it first brings to our notice the famous Gallic princess Vitruvia or Victoria.[20] We find her supporting Postumus against Gallienus. When he is hard pressed, she persuades him to associate her son, Victorinus, with him in the Empire, and presently she herself becomes Augusta and "Mother of the Camp"--a proof that she accompanied the army. Victorinus is said by one of the contemporary writers to have been more manly than Trajan, more clement than Antonine, graver than Nerva, and a better financier than Vespasian; but this paragon of excellence had the one serious defect that he could not withhold his covetous eyes from the prettier wives of his officers. The responsibility of power sobered him for a time, but before long he led astray the wife of one of his officers, and was assassinated.

At his mother's suggestion he, with his dying voice, named his young son his successor, but the angry soldiers murdered the boy.

Victoria now put forward as candidate one of the soldiers themselves, a brawny officer named Marius, who had at one time been armourer or smith to the camp. He was accepted, but a slight that he was imprudent enough to put upon one of his old associates led to his receiving in his own breast one of the swords he had himself forged, after enjoying the delirious dignity of the purple for two days. The "thirty tyrants" were playing their parts with great rapidity. Tetricus, the commander of the troops and a Senator, was next put forward by Victoria, and he left her in control of the affairs of Gaul while he led the army into Spain. Victoria's power was not of long duration, and the references to her in the chronicles are too meagre to enable us to picture her remarkable personality. For many years her power in Gaul was so great that her fame ran through the Empire, and Zenobia, as she afterwards told Aurelian, had the design of communicating with her and proposing to divide the Roman world between them.

Her end is obscure. When Tetricus returned from Spain, he is said to have resented her domination and put her to death; though it is elsewhere said that her death was due to natural causes. She did not live to witness or share the humiliation of Tetricus a few years later.

We return to Zenobia, who had in the meantime become an independent sovereign. Gallienus had taken alarm at the growth of her power, and sent his general Heraclian with secret instructions to dislodge her. Zenobia divined the real intention of Heraclian and his troops, treated him as an invader, and destroyed his force. An invitation was then received, or obtained, from Egypt, and Zenobia sent 70,000 men to expel the troops of Gallienus from what she regarded as the kingdom of her fathers. Egypt was added to her dominions. Rome was now fully alarmed at the success of the two barbaric women, while every other province of the Empire was overrun by invaders or detached by locally-chosen Emperors. One of these rivals at length drew Gallienus from his palace once more, and gave an opportunity to remove his insolent weakness from the throne. The Emperor was besieging the pretender to the throne in Milan, when some of the leading officers conspired to assassinate him. He was drawn from his tent one night in March (268) by a false alarm that the besieged had made a sally, and, devoid alike of guards and armour, he was soon stricken with a mortal wound. Salonina is said by some to have perished with him, but of this there is no evidence.

His successor, Claudius, an experienced soldier of obscure descent but great personal merit, decided to leave Zenobia and Victoria in possession of their power until he had rid the Empire of the formidable Goths. They were said to have an army of 320,000 men, and the whole of Greece and the north of Asia Minor had been plundered by them. The instruments of Roman comfort or luxury that they took back into the bleak forests of the north seemed to be drawing an inexhaustible stream of marauders upon the debilitated south. Two years were occupied by Claudius in destroying their power, and he had just cleansed the Roman territory of their presence when he died of the pestilence, in the spring of 270. The obscure brother of so virtuous and valorous a ruler was deemed a worthy successor to the purple, but the army made choice of a strong and capable commander, Aurelian, and, after two or three weeks' timid enjoyment of his power, Quintilius opened his veins and gracefully yielded the throne.

The new Emperor was the bold and sturdy son of a provincial peasant, who had cut his way to the position of commander. Marriage with the daughter of a wealthy noble had further improved his position, and his temperance, zeal for discipline, skill, and bravery had made him a most effective leader. His first care was to complete the victory over the Goths, who were again advancing. After an exhausting struggle he entered into friendly alliance with them, drove back the other barbaric tribes who threatened or ignored the northern frontier of the Empire, and then turned his eyes toward the East. Gibbon makes him first apply himself to the restoration of Gaul, but the historians Vopiscus and Zosimus expressly say that he dealt first with the Queen of the East.

Zenobia had now, in 272, enjoyed her remarkable power for about four years, and seemed, owing to the preoccupation of Rome with the northern barbarians, to have established a solid and durable kingdom. Parthia and Persia respected her southern boundaries; Egypt peacefully acknowledged her rule; and even the cities of Asia Minor were beginning to bow to her title. But Palmyra was not a Rome, and provided too slender a base for so vast a dominion. As Aurelian and his formidable legions marched across Asia Minor, the cities returned at once to the Roman allegiance, and Zenobia prepared for a severe struggle. She led her army out in person from Antioch, and met the Romans near the river Orontes. Modern historians usually follow the account of the battle which describes Aurelian as stealing a victory by stratagem. He is said to have noticed the weight of Zenobia's heavily-armoured cavalry, drawn them into a wild gallop by a

feigned retreat, and then wheeled his troops, when they showed signs of fatigue, and scattered them. But the "Historia Augusta," the nearest authority, tells us that Aurelian's troops were really routed at first, and then recovered--owing to a miraculous apparition--and won.

Zenobia retired to Antioch. Her general, Zabda, deluded the inhabitants with a false report of victory, and trailed through the streets a captive whom he had dressed as Aurelian. But the Emperor was advancing, and they fled during the night to Emesa, where they were still able to put 70,000 men in the path of Aurelian. The second battle proved as disastrous to Zenobia as the first, and it was decided to retire at once on Palmyra. For a long time the city held Aurelian at bay, and he magnanimously allowed that its successful resistance was due to the sagacity of Zenobia. In the midst of the long siege he wrote to a friend at Rome:

"I hear that it is said that I do not the work of a man in triumphing over Zenobia. Those who blame me have no idea what kind of a woman she is--how prudent in counsel, how assiduous in arrangement, how severe with the troops, how liberal when it is expedient, how stern when there is need for sternness. I may venture to say that it was due to her that Odenathus put Sapor to flight, and advanced as far as Ctesiphon. I can assure you that she was held in such terror in the East and in Egypt that the Arabs, the Saracens, and the Armenians were afraid to move."

So difficult and protracted did the siege prove that Aurelian at length wrote to her, offering to spare her life if she would surrender. The answer seems to have been preserved in one of those libraries of valuable documents at Rome, from which the writers of the "Historia Augusta" obtained their material, as they tell us. It ran:

"Zenobia, Queen of the East, to Aurelius Augustus.

No one has ever yet made by letter such a request as you make. In matters of war you must obtain what you want by deeds. You ask me to surrender, as if you were unaware that Cleopatra preferred to die rather than lose her dignity. We are expecting auxiliaries from Persia, and the Saracens and Armenians are with us. The robbers of Syria beat your army, Aurelian. What will happen to you when our reinforcements come? You will assuredly have to lay aside the pride with which, as if you were a universal conqueror, you call on me to surrender."

The expectation of reinforcements was sincere, but was destined to be disappointed. Day after day Zenobia and her officers looked out over the desert from their invincible walls, and descried no sign of the deliverers. Persia was distracted by the death of Sapor; the Armenians and the Saracens had been seduced from her by Aurelian. Food began to fail, and the iron legions clung tenaciously to the little strip of country and intercepted whatever aid came to her. Zenobia resolved to go to Persia herself in quest of aid. Under cover of the night she stole out of the town, and fled toward Persia on a dromedary.

Within a few days the anxious Palmyreans again saw their Queen--a captive in the hands of the Roman soldiers.

It is probable that she had been betrayed. Aurelian, at all events, heard of her flight, and sent a company of horse in pursuit. They reached the banks of the Euphrates just as Zenobia and her attendants had entered a boat, and brought her back to the camp. She was one hour too late to save her liberty, or sacrifice her life. Palmyra sadly opened its gates, and Aurelian transferred its priceless treasures and rare curiosities to his wagons. Its chief officers and Zenobia he led away to Emesa, and put them on trial for rebellion.

The reader of Gibbon will expect that we have now reached a point where the virility of Zenobia faints and the eternal feminine reveals itself. Gibbon records, indeed, the bold answer which Zenobia made to Aurelian's complaint of her infidelity to Rome; but he goes on to say that, as the fierce demands of the soldiers for her death fell on her ears, she tremblingly pleaded for life, and, with a cowardice that her sex only could palliate, insisted that Longinus and the others had seduced her from her duty. Happily, we have a clear right to quarrel with the procedure of the great historian at this point. There are two versions of the behaviour of Zenobia: that of the Latin historians, Trebellius Pollio and Vopiscus in the "Historia Augusta," and that of the Greek historian Zosimus. The Latin writers, who lived at Rome in the generation after Zenobia, make her reply boldly to Aurelian, and do not say a word about her casting the blame on others. The Greek writer, a much later compiler, represents her as, in the words of Gibbon, "ignominiously purchasing life by the sacrifice of her fame and her friends." Gibbon affects to reconcile the two by making the woman's weakness follow upon the momentary show of courage.

To this method of reconciling contradictory and unequal authorities we may justly demur. The much later version of Zosimus is not only less entitled in itself to acceptance, but it is seriously enfeebled when he goes on to make the wildly erroneous statement that Zenobia died on the way to Rome, and her companions were sunk in the Bosphorus.

We have every right to follow the Latin historians.

Zenobia was brought before Aurelian, and the soldiers fiercely demanded that she should be put to death. Exasperated as the Emperor was, he refused to slay a woman, and asked her why she had dared to resist the majesty of Rome. "In you," she replied, "I recognize an Imperial majesty, because you have vanquished me, but I saw none in Gallienus." Her life was spared. What Roman general could have resisted the wish to grace his triumph at Rome with a greater than Cleopatra? The troops, with their vast treasures and their captives, moved slowly homeward, after executing Longinus and some others.

ZENOBIA

ENLARGED FROM THE COIN IN THE BERLIN MUSEUM

In the triumph which Aurelian had so splendidly earned, and no less splendidly celebrated, we catch our last certain glimpse of the Queen of the East, one of the most notable women of all time. Along the flower-strewn lane between the dense walls of citizens passes one of the longest and grandest processions that ever led a victor to the Capitol.

An immense number of tamed elephants, lions, tigers, leopards, bears, and other beasts move slowly and sullenly along, and eight hundred pairs of gladiators give promise of the impending spectacles. Then there are cars heavily laden with the gold, silver, and jewels of Palmyra, the rare presents of Persia, the purples of India, and the silks of China. Then there is the long and extraordinary train of captives, representing the nineteen nations which Aurelian has subdued, even women who have been taken, in male costume, in the sternest battles. At last the melancholy line is closed by the lithe bronzed figure, with brilliant black eyes and teeth like pearls, of the woman whose beauty, genius, and daring have been on the lips of Rome for several years. Clothed for the last time in the heavily-jewelled robes of a queen--she had complained that she was not strong enough to walk under the load of jewels--she drags along the golden chains which bind her hands and feet, and a slave sustains the weight of the gold band round her throat. Beside her, in scarlet cloak and Gallic trousers, is Tetricus, Victoria's last Emperor in Gaul. The whole Empire is again subject to Rome. And before the car of the conqueror three empty chariots are driven: one is the gold and silver car of Odenathus, one, of gold studded with gems, is a present from Persia, and the third is the car which Zenobia had made for her triumphant entry into Rome. Never had Emperor looked from his car on so superb a triumph. In less than a year Aurelian would be assassinated.

The last phase of Zenobia's life is not quite clear.

Zosimus is certainly wrong in his reproduction of a story that she died, or took her life, before she reached Rome. Still later and equally negligible writers ventured to say that she became a Christian, and even that Aurelian married one of her daughters. The "Historia Augusta,"

which we may follow, as it was written in Rome a generation later, tells us that Aurelian gave her a villa near Hadrian's palace at Tivoli, where she spent the rest of her life in the education of her children and the prosy duties of a Roman matron, and, we may conjecture, in looking back with sad but proud recollection on the stirring romance of her career. Bishop Eusebius observes briefly in his "Chronicle" that she lived to a great age, and was held in the greatest regard at Rome.

CHAPTER XVI

THE WIFE AND DAUGHTER OF DIOCLETIAN

ALTHOUGH we have already indicated the fate of Aurelian, we have not yet referred to the woman who shared his Imperial title and his great renown.

Her personality is, in fact, entirely unknown; even her name is preserved for us only on the coinage. We may fairly conjecture that she disliked the plebeian ways of her husband, and discharged the duties of a consort without enthusiasm. Daughter of a wealthy and prominent noble, Ulpius Crinitus, she had conferred a useful distinction on the ambitious peasant at a time when he was making his way in the Imperial service, and it is conjectured, on somewhat slender grounds, that she accompanied him on his campaigns. But his life at the palace was short and inglorious. He disliked its pomp and luxury, and found his chief delight in pitting his comedians against each other in eating-contests. He pampered the common citizens by increasing their free ration of bread, and adding pork to it. When he went on to meditate a free distribution of wine, one of his ministers sarcastically suggested that he might add geese and chickens. When the Empress, Ulpia Severina, thought it fitting that she should wear silk mantles, her husband forbade her to indulge in that rare and costly product of a precarious commerce with China.

Aurelian was, in fact, essentially a soldier. His manner, and even the reforms which he endeavoured to make, caused grave dissatisfaction at Rome, and a conspiracy against him was discovered within a few months of the magnificent triumph he had enjoyed. He crushed it with a fierceness that almost obliterated the memory of his great services, and then returned to Asia to meet the Persians. On his march he was assassinated, in the beginning of the year 275, and the great promise of his reign was unfulfilled. Ulpia Severina seems to have died before him, as the historian speaks only of a daughter who survived him.

Once more we pass swiftly over a number of turbulent years until we come to an Empress of whom we have a comparatively ample knowledge. It is generally admitted, though not entirely beyond doubt, that the throne remained vacant for the greater part of the year 275.

The "Historia Augusta," at least, which was written in the next generation, describes a situation in remarkable contrast to the earlier haste in appointing Emperors.

We are asked to believe that the Senate and the army spent many months in a most edifying encounter, each endeavouring to induce the other to choose a ruler. At length the Senators chose one of their number, the aged and upright Tacitus, who set out to take command of the troops in Asia. Within a few weeks, worn by the unwonted fatigue and pained by the unruly behaviour of the soldiers, he passed away. Some of the historians declare that he died of actual violence. There is no trace of an Empress. We read that Tacitus, like Aurelian, forbade his wife to wear sumptuous clothing, but this was probably in earlier days. The absence of coins leads us to think that she had died.

He was succeeded by a young and vigorous officer, of peasant extraction, named Probus, under whom the Empire recovered much of its strength. For six years he laboured successfully to restore the prestige of Rome, but his severity led at length to assassination. During a mutiny of the soldiers, in the year 282, "a thousand swords were plunged at once into the bosom of the unfortunate Probus," as Gibbon too floridly expresses it. From the absence of coins we may almost gather that his wife had died before his accession. Carus, who succeeded him, was an aged general of sixty years. He died after a year of strenuous warfare, and left the Empire to his sons Carinus and Numerianus. The younger Emperor was dispatched to the East, and Carinus virtually reigned alone.

Even the experience of our own time has so frequently taught us to expect a mediocre or effeminate issue from a distinguished and virile stock that we do not wonder at this happening constantly in the history of Rome. We need not refer it to the mystery of heredity. The vigorous sire had developed and enhanced his strength in the laborious climb to the heights of his chosen world. The son, finding the paths to the summit smoothed, and an engaging luxury at his command without exertion, allows it to degenerate. The finest steel and the purest gold yield and crumble in a corroding atmosphere. We cannot, therefore, affect astonishment at the almost invariable failure of the Roman practice of eagerly welcoming a son to the place of his gifted father.

The reign of Carinus affords one of the worst illustrations of the evil. Indolent, insolent, and luxurious, he saw in his Imperial power an opulent ministry to his depraved tastes. He did indeed provide Rome with the most splendid entertainments. The amphitheatre rang once more with the coarse applause of the ninety thousand spectators of its bloody contests; the Circus was transformed into a forest, in which the strange or beautiful beasts of remote lands lived under the eyes of three hundred thousand Romans. But this indulgence of the people's appetites was held to excuse an unbridled ministry to those of the prince. The whisper went once more through the fetid depths of Roman life that there were rich awards for the ingenious and industrious pandar to a sated voluptuary, and the palace exhibited again the loathsome spectacles that had long been expelled from it.

They have little interest for us, as although Carinus made and unmade nine Empresses in little over a year, they are lost in the riot of the time. One poor name, that of Magnia Urbica, has survived on a few coins. She is given by Serviez as the wife of Carus, because she is represented with two children on one of the coins. Cohen points out, however, that the group does not properly consist of a mother and two children, and he concludes that she was one of the nine wives of Carinus. In the number of his consorts Carinus surpassed the high record of Imperial license, and he was not less original in the grounds for his divorces. Sterility has often been pleaded by monarchs as a fit reason for repudiating their wives; it was reserved to Carinus to dismiss them the moment they gave proof of fertility. So the women of Rome succeeded each other rapidly in the dissolute palace, where the Emperor, surrounded by his courtesans, glittering down to his shoes with diamonds and emeralds, sat on rose-strewn couches to his costly banquets.

The new pestilence was blown out of the Imperial city by a storm from the East. The younger Emperor, Numerianus, was a gentle, cultured, and delicate youth.

As he led the troops home from the East, he sheltered his eyes from the burning sun by keeping to his tent or his closed litter. At length his complete seclusion gave rise to suspicion, and the soldiers broke into his tent, only to find a mouldering body. The ambition of Aper, his father-in-law, who commanded the guards, fastened the guilt upon him, and a general assembly of the soldiers appointed one of their abler officers, Diocletian, to judge him. Diocletian, possibly with reason, preferred to execute rather than to try Aper, and he was at once saluted as Emperor by the troops. The son of two slaves, he had educated himself and pushed his way to the highest offices and commands; and he now composedly donned the purple mantle which the soldiers offered him, and led the legions toward Rome. Carinus marched out against him, but was assassinated by an officer whose wife he had appropriated, and a new chapter opened in the annals of Rome. A strong man and judicious statesman had come to the throne, and he would occupy it for twenty years.

From our point of view it is disappointing that the wife of Diocletian does not come to our notice until his reign is nearly over. Her very name was disputed for ages; even now her personality is only faintly illumined by the adventures of her later years. Her daughter is a more commanding figure, and other Imperial ladies stand out in the chronicle of the times. Some of these, such as the mother and wife of Constantine, we reserve for the next chapter; and we may compress into a few lines the story of the twenty years' reign of Diocletian.

A year after his accession, which took place in the year 285, Diocletian chose a colleague to share the control of the vast Empire. This friend and partner, Maximian, was the son of peasants, rough, ignorant, and unscrupulous, but an effective commander. He was entrusted with the care of the West, Diocletian passed to the East, and several years were profitably spent in restoring the crumbling frontiers. The task proved so formidable that, in 292, they chose two officers for the inferior dignity of "Caesars"--a title which implied that they would probably one day be Augusti, and should meantime wear the purple, but have no power to make laws or control finance. Of the two, Galerius again was a child of the soil, while Constantius was the son of a provincial noble; and they were compelled to dismiss their humbler wives, and wed the daughters of the Emperors. Four courts were thus set up within the Empire, while Rome found itself coldly neglected, its palace deserted, and its Senate impotent.

To the court of Galerius we shall return presently, while we leave the affairs of Constantius and his wife to the next chapter. The court and the Empress of Maximian need not detain us. He chose Milan as his seat, and began to adorn the northern town with the marble edifices that befitted its new dignity. His wife was a very attractive Syrian woman, Galeria Valeria Eutropia. Her name has led some to conjecture that she was related to the father of Constantius, Eutropius, one of the chief nobles of Dardania, though the connexion is feeble. She seems, in any case, to have regarded her uncultivated husband with disdain, and sought more genial company. Her son Maxentius is said by some to have been the issue of a liaison with a compatriot, while others declare that he was a boy substituted for the daughter she bore, because Maximian desired a son. We may leave these disputable scandals and come to the court of Diocletian.

The son of a Roman slave had created a glittering court at Nicomedia. His palace, round which the city quickly grew in size and magnificence, was adorned and served with an Oriental pomp. The successive approaches to the chamber of the Emperor were guarded by splendid officials, and when the suppliant or ambassador penetrated at length to the inner apartment, he found the stately Diocletian in purple and gold robes, his brow encircled by a glistening diadem, and was compelled to prostrate himself before the divine majesty. It was not, however, the vanity or folly of a Caligula, but a calculated policy, that had prompted Diocletian to clothe himself with this Olympic dignity. Earlier Emperors, of the same mean extraction, had refused to put a barrier of royal ceremony between themselves and their subjects or soldiers, and had invariably fallen by the hand of the assassin. Diocletian was too shrewd, too much attached to life, and too sensible of his beneficent use of power, to incur the risk. He had restored Egypt to obedience, humiliated the Persians, and devoted an even greater ability to the reform of the administration. Co-operating with his vigorous colleague in the West, he had brought peace and prosperity back to the Empire.

In the settled years of his reign we begin again to recognize the various personalities of the court. The Empress herself is more or less involved in a piquant obscurity. Until the end of the seventeenth century her name was unknown, and a great deal of romantic legend was reproduced in regard to her. Cardinal Baronius found in "Acts of St. Susanna" that her name was St. Serena, a martyr for the Christian faith. Other "Acts" of the martyrs furnished a St. Eleuthera and a St. Alexandra as consorts of Diocletian. He seemed to have been an Imperial Bluebeard.

But in 1679 the manuscript was found of an early Christian work, "On the Deaths of the Persecutors," and the earlier writings were proved, in the words of the learned Franciscan, Father Pagi, to be fictitious and full of untruths. The many saintly martyrs gave way to an Empress Prisca, who broke down lamentably at the first test of her faith. It is very curious that we have no coins whatever of Prisca, though she must have lived through the whole reign of Diocletian. This, and the fact that she left him many years before his death, suggest either that she was not married to him at all or that he had little regard for her. She was, in any case, a woman of weak and retiring character, and is mentioned only in association with her daughter.

Valeria was a beautiful, attractive, and spirited young woman, with a good deal of the strength, and not a little of the ambition, of her father. She was married to Galerius, the Caesar whom Diocletian had chosen, and remained with him by the side of the Emperor. Galerius was, as I said, of peasant origin, and never laid aside the uncultivated roughness of his class. Diocletian had, by diligent education, erased the traces of his own lowly origin, but his peasant colleagues had gone straight from the soil to the camp, and the work of a soldier had not given them the least inclination to seek culture. The character of Galerius has been painted in the most lurid colours on account of his persecution of the Christians, but it is significant that both Valeria and Prisca clung to his court when Diocletian retired. His mother, Romula, and other rustic relatives were attracted to his court. There was, it is clear, a most incongruous group of personalities about the court of Diocletian, and in the nineteenth year of his reign they were shaken by a severe storm. The great and final struggle began between the old faith and the new, and Prisca and Valeria favoured the latter.

Christianity had not been persecuted for half a century, and had made great progress. The cult of the old gods was palpably insincere, and half-a-dozen Asiatic creeds were steadily supplanting it. On the streets of Nicomedia, as on the streets of Rome or any other large city, one might meet any day the white-robed shaven priests of Isis, the painted and effeminate ministers of Cybele, the Persian representatives of the popular cult of Mithra, and--until they were expelled by Diocletian--the black-garbed clergy of the Manichaeans and the Christians. The Christians were now advancing. There had been some slight and irregular repression of them from time to time since the days of Nero, but more than forty years of toleration, and the knowledge that their adherents were now occupying high places in the camp and the court, and that even the wives of the Emperor and the Caesar favoured them, gave them strong confidence. One of their churches occupied a central and commanding position in Nicomedia. Four influential officers of the court attended it, and it seems that Valeria and Prisca were, if not Christians, openly disposed to the new religion. All we know in that regard is that they were "compelled" to sacrifice when the persecution began.

Persecution on account of religion, as such, was not natural to the cosmopolitan builders of the Pantheon, and Diocletian was a broad-minded statesman, so that the origin of the persecution is not so clear as it was once held to be. The literary remains which we have to use have to be handled with caution. The "Historia Augusta"

has ended with Carinus, and we shall greatly miss its minute and gossipy descriptions. Zosimus, a pagan writing in a Christian age, has an appearance of sullen reticence at times and a perceptible bias. Aurelius Victor and Eutropius are scanty, and the immediate Christian writers are used very cautiously by modern historians. Bishop Eusebius says frankly, in his "Life of Constantine," that he will write only what tends to edify, and the little work "On the Deaths of the Persecutors" is obviously imaginative in many pages and inaccurate in others. Experts still differ as to whether it comes from the pen of the brilliant Christian rhetorician Lactantius, but all warn us to take account of its strong feeling. Our authorities, in a word, now belong to two antagonistic and bitterly hostile creeds, and, as all subsequent historians favour one side or the other, we have to proceed with caution. I have endeavoured, in the remaining chapters, to make my way between them with more than ordinary care and independence.

A few incautious hints given in Lactantius throw a faint light on the origin of the great persecution. The writer of the treatise has himself a very positive theory.

The root of the evil was, he says, Romula, the peasant-mother of the Caesar. Fanatically attached to the gods of her native mountains, she inspired her son with a hatred of Christianity, and Galerius bullied the older Emperor into issuing the Edict of Persecution. We feel that the policy of Diocletian would hardly yield to the prejudice of a superstitious woman. There is more enlightenment in the incidental statements that Romula was stung by the disdain of Christian officers in the palace, and that Diocletian was greatly annoyed at seeing Christian soldiers disturb the harmony, if not the efficacy, of his sacrificial ceremonies by making the sign of the cross. Galerius may have been moved by the growing reluctance of Christians to bear arms, and the very pronounced rejection by some of the arms they bore. There is no need to trust the imaginary conversation which Lactantius puts in the mouths of Diocletian and Galerius. They agreed that the zeal of the Christians was impertinent or dangerous, and, in the month of February (303), a troop of soldiers was sent to raze to the ground their large and commanding church. On the following day Diocletian published an

Edict forbidding the cult under grave penalties. When the Imperial decree was torn down by a zealous Christian, and this act of treason was openly applauded by his fellows, Diocletian was embittered, and blood began to flow. During the next fortnight the Emperor's quarters in the palace were twice found to be in flames. Diocletian was convinced that the fire was kindled by Christian officers, and gave a full sanction to the work of repressing them.

Prisca and Valeria were not among the heroines of the persecution. Lactantius destroys all the myths of martyred Empresses by telling us that they consented to burn a few grains of incense in honour of Jupiter, and impotently witnessed the dark roll of the wave of persecution through the provinces. He does not even say that they joined, or rejoined, the Church when the persecution was over, and we lose sight of them for a few years. Probably they went with Diocletian to Rome for his triumph in November, and returned with him to Nicomedia in the summer of 304.

He was confined to the palace by a serious illness during the following winter, and as soon as he recovered he abdicated the throne. It is untrue that the threats of Galerius forced him to do this. He had expressed the intention years before.

On a wide plain near Nicomedia the army assembled on May 1st, 305, for the unexampled ceremony of the abdication of an Emperor. A little hill in the centre was surmounted by a lofty throne and a statue of Jupiter, and the ageing Emperor--he was in his fifty-ninth year--surrendered the power he had wielded so well for more than twenty years. By a previous arrangement, Maximian was abdicating on the same day at Milan. The two Caesars became Augusti, and two new Caesars were appointed. In their selection we recognize the partial and unskilful hand of Galerius. He handed his own Caesarean dignity to a rustic nephew, Daza--"who had just left his herds in the forest," Lactantius scornfully says--and sent a loyal and undistinguished friend to receive that of Maximian in Italy.

From that selfish act would develop one of the greatest civil wars since the founding of the Empire. In the ranks of the officers by the platform was the tall, handsome, gifted, and disappointed young man who would one day be known as Constantine the Great.

Diocletian retired to Salona, in his native province of Dalmatia, and built, close to the town, what was for the age a magnificent palace. Valeria remained in the palace of Galerius, and it seems that Prisca stayed with her, as we shall presently find her sharing the hard lot of her daughter.

Why the mother, at least, chose to remain in Nicomedia is left to our imaginations. The religion they had favoured was cruelly suppressed, and, if we are to believe Lactantius, their virtue must have been outraged by the unbridled license of the new Emperor. He is described as an ogre, dragging the noblest women of Nicomedia from their husbands, feeding his bears on innocent citizens, and "never taking a meal without a taste of human blood."

Yet Valeria clung to her husband even through the painful and repulsive illness which ended his life; and her name was given by him to a part of his Empire. The picture is evidently overdrawn, yet life in the palace, with Galerius and his boorish relatives, cannot have been very congenial, and the temper of Galerius would be soured by the events that followed.

The first mishap was the flight of Constantine. He had been living for some years at the court of Diocletian, and was deeply disappointed and rightly indignant at the choice of the new Caesars. By birth and ability he had the clearest title to the purple. He was now a tall and manly young officer, handsome, popular, and successful, and anxious to join his father Constantius in Gaul. There is little doubt that he fled during the night, though the romantic story told by Lactantius is now generally regarded as a clumsy piece of fiction. It describes Galerius as failing to take the youth's life by engaging him in dangerous contests, and at length devising an ingenious scheme. He one night gives Constantine permission to depart after he has seen him in the morning, and warns him that he will be put to death if he is still in Nicomedia at noon. Then the ogre gives orders that he is not to be awakened before noon on the morrow; but the young hero steals all the horses in the stables--there were probably hundreds--cripples all other horses along his route, and flies to his father. The only authentic point is that Constantine fled. He would wade back through a sea of blood. Within a few months his father was dead, Constantine was chosen by the army to succeed him, and Galerius was forced to recognize him as Caesar.

Galerius gave the title of Augustus, which Constantius had left vacant at his death, to his loyal Severus, but he was soon informed that the troops, the people, and the Senate had chosen another Emperor at Rome. A brief outline of the stirring events that followed will suffice here.

The new Emperor was Maxentius, son of the retired Maximian. The father issued from his retreat to join in the fray, and Galerius was bound to support Severus.

Diocletian looked on quietly from his gardens at Salona.

When Maximian urged him to return to power, he said that if Maximian could see the vegetables he was growing he would not make such a request. Briefly, Severus was treacherously taken by Maximian, and induced to ease the complication by taking his life. Maximian, Galerius, and Diocletian met at Carnuntum, on the Danube, and it was settled that Galerius and Licinius (one of his officers) should be recognized as Emperors, and Constantine and Maximin (Daza) as Caesars. Maxentius was disregarded, and Maximian was persuaded to retire once more. How the restless and ambitious old man then clung to Constantine, and attempted to murder and displace him, we shall see later.

The expedition of Galerius into Italy proved disastrous, as he returned in bad health and temper to his dominions.

He died in 311, of an unpleasant disease, of which the morbid reader may find a luxurious description in Lactantius.

Valeria remained with him to the end, and then a new and more romantic chapter opened for her and her mother. The two Emperors of the East made rival offers of their hospitality; for Maximin had exacted an equal dignity with Licinius. Valeria was at that time in her early thirties, and her mourning garments did not detract from her ripe beauty of face and figure. She is represented as weighing the respective immoralities of the two Eastern Emperors, and considering to which of the two it would be the less dangerous to entrust her virtue. Lactantius does not tell us why she was forced to choose at all; why she and her mother did not retire to the luxurious and unsullied palace of Diocletian. The end of his life was approaching, it is true, but the palace would still shelter them. On the other hand, Maximin and Licinius are both very thickly tarred with the brush of Lactantius. We shall see something of the conduct of Licinius later. As to Maximin, if one half of what Lactantius and Eusebius say is true, he must have been known over the whole Empire as an erotic maniac.

He may not have been this romantic combination of Nero, Elagabalus, and Carinus, but we know from other writers that he was much more vicious than Licinius. When, therefore, we find Valeria choosing to live in his palace, we cannot repress a suspicion that the beautiful widow was not quite so unworldly as she is represented to have been.

She had not been long in her new home when certain officers came to tell her that Maximin loved her, and was prepared to divorce his wife and wed her. When she refused, the baffled passion turned to rage, and mother and daughter were expelled from the palace. When we learn, from a later passage, that Valeria refused to yield her right to the property of Galerius, the episode seems more human.

A story of adultery was invented, a Jew--the villain of early Christian literature--was suborned to give false evidence, and several of Valeria's friends were implicated.

A number of ladies of high rank were publicly executed, and the Empresses, spoiled of their goods, were driven from province to province, until they found themselves lodged in a mean village on the edge of the Syrian desert.

Valeria contrived to acquaint her father with their situation, but the rough Maximin rejected his feeble entreaties. They seem to have spent the winter (312-13) in this miserable exile. The only comfort was that they had with them Candidian, a natural son of Galerius, whom Valeria had adopted, and Severian, the son of Severus.

SALONINA

VALERIA

ENLARGED FROM COINS IN THE BRITISH MUSEUM

In the early spring the little group were inspirited by the news that the tyrant had fallen in a struggle with Licinius, who was now sole Emperor in the East. What follows, in the narrative of Lactantius, is even more obscure, and suggests still more strongly that much is concealed from us. Candidian went openly to the court of Licinius, and was cordially received and promoted. The other young man followed. Licinius was naturally hostile to all who had taken the side of Maximin, but he could hardly be angry with these poor victims of Maximin's rage.

Valeria, however, went in disguise to Nicaea, where the court was, to follow the fortunes of her adopted son.

Suddenly something happened which brought upon them all the sword of the executioner. What it was we can only conjecture. A writer like Lactantius is so accustomed to regard a savage outbreak on the part of one of the last pagan Emperors as a natural event that he disdains to enlighten us. A part of the story has been concealed, and it would not be fantastic to suppose that the spirited, young, and ambitious Valeria meditated an intrigue for the advancement of Candidian to the throne.

It is plain that Licinius suspected this. The royal birth and manly bearing of the youth might suffice to draw such a suspicion on him, but do not plausibly explain the treatment of the Empresses. Nor is there any apparent reason for her disguise. She was willing, Lactantius says, to cede her rights to Licinius, and the sentence unjustly passed on her by Maximin would have no weight with him.

Whatever the cause of the trouble was, Valeria learned one day that Candidian and Severian were arrested, and they were presently executed. She fled to the remote Syrian village, but she was so plainly implicated, in some way, that she dare not remain there. Dressing in the rough robes of the common people, the aged mother and her brilliant daughter set out on a painful and aimless journey. Either a sentence of death had been passed on them, or they had ground to apprehend one; for their flight would certainly elicit it. Lactantius says that they wandered in this disguise for fifteen months, but it is difficult to believe that they could so long evade the Imperial troops who hunted them.[21] At length they were recognized and arrested in Thessalonica, and the tragedy of their unfortunate and, so far as we know, innocent lives was brought to a close. Under the eyes of the assembled citizens the wife and daughter of the great Emperor were beheaded, and their remains were contemptuously flung into the sea.

CHAPTER XVII

THE FIRST CHRISTIAN EMPRESSES

THE fourfold power which Diocletian had prudently set up ensured for the Empire twenty years of uneventful prosperity. The two Emperors and their Caesars guarded and repaired the frontiers, at which the strong young nations of the hills and the forests were now gathering in ominous numbers, while the body of the Empire tranquilly pursued its sluggish and debilitated life.

But no sooner had the balanced mind and the firm hand of Diocletian relinquished their control than the system revealed its weakness. The multiplication of dignities led to a multiplication of aspirants; the distribution of power inflamed the ambition of the stronger and less scrupulous.

In one year eight generals claimed and bore the title of Augustus, and our stage is crowded with Empresses.

Most of them, however, are so poorly outlined in the records of the time that we may neglect these faint conjugal shadows of inconspicuous rulers, and select for consideration the three or four more prominent consorts of the Emperors.

Possibly the most widely known of all the Roman Empresses, more familiar even than the very different figure of Messalina, is Helena, the mother of Constantine.

The first Christian Empress, the generous supporter of the early Church, the first royal woman to find a place in the list of the canonized, we turn to her with eagerness to discover the contrast with her pagan predecessors. She does not bear the Imperial title, and does not properly fall within our range, until she is advanced in years, but we cannot understand her character unless we glance first at her earlier years.

In one of his more important sermons ("De Obitu Theodosii," SS 42) St. Ambrose observes that she "is said to have been a maid at an inn," and he so clearly accepts the statement that historians, sacred and profane, have not hesitated to follow him. The claim of another Roman writer, that Constantine had illumined Britain "by originating there," gave rise at one time to a theory that she was British, and our learned commentators furnished so august a lady with a royal pedigree. The phrase is, however, generally understood to refer to the beginning of Constantine's Imperial career, and the native town of Helena is sought either in Dacia or in Nicomedia. Since Constantine gave her name to Drepanum, in Nicomedia, we may presume that her first humble home was in that town, and that she moved from there to Naissos, in Dacia, where the birth of Constantine is usually placed.

A *stabulum* was, in the language of the time, one of the meaner inns in the towns through which the Roman roads ran. A *stabularia*--the epithet used by St. Ambrose--was a woman or girl connected with the inn; and those temporary resting-places for soldiers or merchants on their journeys were so easy in their ways that the word was sometimes used in an unpleasant sense. We may follow the early tradition that Helena was the daughter of a man who kept one of these inns, possibly a quite respectable establishment, at Drepanum, on the way to the city of Nicomedia, which Diocletian had made his capital. Here, in or about the year 273, the young Roman officer Constantius--later, for some obscure reason, called Constantius the Pale (Chlorus)--saw and fell in love with Helena. The road that ran through Drepanum was much used by the troops, and the encounter is placed at the time when Aurelian was conducting his campaign against Zenobia.

Constantius, an excellent officer and the son of a provincial noble of some distinction, would then (273) be in his twenty-third year. Helena, who was over eighty at her death in 328, must have been two or three years older.

Historians have left us a lengthy and learned debate on the question whether she was the wife or the concubine of Constantius, and the grouping of the combatants is singular.

In the Migne edition of the works of the Fathers we find a note appended to the passage of St. Ambrose, which I have quoted, in which the Benedictine commentators observe that "all the writers on Roman affairs declare that Helena was the concubine, not the wife, of Constantius," and they adopt that view. Yet the critical Gibbon defends "the legality of her marriage" with a rare and edifying chivalry, and Mr.

Firth, in his recent biography of Constantine, asserts that it is "beyond question." With such weighty encouragement ecclesiastical writers have confidently deserted the Benedictines and followed Gibbon. Let us first hear the authorities, and we may not find the problem insoluble.

Bishop Eusebius, the chaplain of the Imperial family, as one may term him, would not mention such a circumstance in his "Life of Constantine," even if he knew it to be true; but it is not quite accurate to say peremptorily that the bishop *never* mentions it. In the second book of his "Chronicle" (*ad annum* 310) we read that Constantine was "the son of Constantius by his concubine Helena." We have no means of determining if these words were written by Eusebius or added by St. Jerome.[22] Even in the latter case it is a weighty testimony.

Another Christian historian of Jerome's time, Orosius--who does not follow Zosimus, as Gibbon says, but precedes him--makes the same statement (c. xxv), and it is later repeated in the "Chronicle" of Cassiodorus. A writer of the generation after Constantine, commonly known as "Anonymus Valesii," says (c. ii) that Constantine was "born of Helena, a very common [*vilissima*] woman, in the town of Naissus." Zosimus, a century later, and a pagan critic of Constantine, says (ii. 8) that he was "born of a woman who was not respectable semne and not legally married to Constantius," and he later observes that Maxentius resented the raising to the throne of a man whose mother was "not a matron." Finally, the early mediaeval monk, Zonaras, says ("Annals," xiii. i): "Some say that she was lawfully married to Constantius and divorced ... others that she was not a legitimate wife but a paramour." The grave and weighty Eutropius, writing in the generation after Constantine, says that he was born of "a somewhat ambiguous [*obscuriori*] marriage."

The Benedictines had an ample authority, both Christian and pagan, for their view, and only one argument is advanced in disproof of it by modern writers. Several of the historians tell us that, when Constantius was made Caesar, he was compelled by the Emperor to "divorce" Helena, and, it is said, divorce implies marriage. The argument is hardly conclusive. When Eusebius (or Jerome) tells us that the Caesars were compelled to dismiss their "wives," he adds, on the same page, that Helena was not a wife, but a concubine. He means merely that Constantius was forced to dismiss Helena and wed the daughter of Maximian, and does not imply that any legal form of divorce was employed. It is quite open to us to interpret the other authority, Aurelius

Victor, in the same way; and Zonaras, the only other writer who could be quoted, expressly leaves it open whether Helena was married or not. In any case, the single authority of Aurelius Victor cannot outweigh the others, and even his words do not necessarily imply a legal divorce on the part of both Caesars.

But there is another aspect of the question, which is usually overlooked. Could there be a valid marriage between Helena and Constantius in Roman law? When we regard the subject from this point of view, we see that Constantius could not possibly have married Helena before the birth of Constantine, and, unless her legal condition was subsequently altered by a special enactment, their union could never become a valid marriage. As I have earlier observed, the strict and ancient forms of Roman marriage had fallen very generally out of use under the Emperors. They had had the effect of putting the wife under the despotic power of the husband, and Roman feeling in regard to the position of woman had entirely changed. Looser forms of marriage, which evaded the older tyranny of the husband, were generally employed and legally recognized. If a man and woman lived together uninterruptedly for twelve months--without three nights' interruption--their union might become a valid marriage.

Below this was the legally recognized concubine. The ease with which Christian writers admitted that Helena was a concubine is due to the fact that the Church, as well as the law, permitted a concubine, if a man had no wife. As late as the year 400, the important provincial Council of Toledo decided that such a man and his concubine were to be admitted to communion. St. Augustine, we shall see, went even further. Below these, again, were the ordinary paramours, the mistresses of a month or the playthings of an hour, which Stoic and Christian equally condemned.

The real question we have to decide is, therefore, whether the long association of Constantius and Helena could ever be recognized as a valid marriage in Roman law. That they went through any form of marriage in 273 could only occur to a writer who knows nothing of Roman law or practice. A young officer, taking a girl from a tavern in a small provincial town on his route, would not dream of any such ceremony; and no ceremony would have been valid in Roman law. Whatever the legal condition of Constantius was, Helena was, to Roman law, a barbarian, or *peregrina*, and could not contract a valid marriage.[23] We need little acquaintance with Roman life to imagine what happened. Constantius felt for the young woman he found at the country inn a more tender sentiment than that usually entertained by the young centurion or tribune on travel, and he took her to live with him. I do not see how this relation ever could become a valid marriage, nor is there any clear proof that they were ever *legally* divorced. At the most, it remains "a questionable marriage," as Eutropius calls it, and it began as a free union.

From Nicomedia Constantius's troop seems to have passed, possibly after sharing Aurelian's triumph at Rome, to Thrace, where Constantine is said to have been born in the year 274. Helena narrowly missed the dignity of Empress a few years later, as Carus had some disposition to leave the purple to Constantius. The mother of Constantius had been a niece of the Emperor Claudius, and his father was one of the chief nobles of Dardania. But the accession of Carinus dispelled this hope, and Helena followed her husband from province to province, and grade to grade, until, in 292, he was selected for the lofty position of Caesar of the West. But with the purple came a command that he must dismiss his concubine, and marry the stepdaughter of Maximian, Flavia Maximiana Theodora.

From that date until the year of her son's brilliant triumph Helena passes into complete obscurity.

Meantime other Empresses occupy the pages of the historian. Theodora, of whom we have just spoken, is one of those Empresses whose propriety of conduct and mediocrity of person have not attracted the lamp of the historian. She was the daughter of Eutropia, the Syrian wife of Maximian, by a former husband. Three boys and three girls came of her union with Constantius, and she seems to have been a worthy consort of that judicious and happy ruler. The full Imperial title passed to them when Maximian abdicated in 305, and the handsome and spirited Constantine joined them at Gessoriacum (Boulogne), after his romantic flight from Nicomedia, in that or the following year. They crossed to Britain, and suppressed a rebellion that was in progress. But Constantius died at Eboracum (York) in the summer of 306, and the unambitious Theodora passes from our sight.

Constantius had, with a last display of prudence, preferred his eldest son to the legitimate children of his wife, and probably little money needed to be distributed among the legions to ensure that they should recognize his superiority. Constantine was then in his early manhood, a commanding and graceful figure, in the finest phase of his character, and the troops followed him with alacrity from the cold mists of north Britain to more genial and more cultivated Gaul. From Gaul the young Caesar watched with close interest the quarrels in which his colleagues prepared to devour each other. In February of 307 he heard that Severus had opened his veins, and left the purple in the hands of the crafty Maximian and his son Maxentius. Within a few weeks Maximian was in Gaul, seeking an alliance with Constantine. He brought with him his pretty and charming daughter, Fausta, and presently she was married at Arles, with great pomp, to Constantine, the stepson of her half-sister. The old man returned to his intrigues in Italy, from which he was shortly ejected by his son: Galerius expelled him from Illyricum, where he had taken shelter; and he returned to the court of his son-in-law in Gaul.

The portrait-bust of Maximian might be confused with that of a modern pugilist, but he had, in addition to strength and ambition, a restless disposition to intrigue.

To rust in a court full of women--for we may confidently place in the court of Constantine his wife, mother, stepmother, mother-in-law, and three young half-sisters, if not also his concubine--was to him an intolerable experience, and he took the first opportunity of enlivening his surroundings. An inroad of the barbarians in the north drew away the young Emperor with much of his army, and Maximian rebelled. He gave out a report that Constantine was dead, emptied the treasury into the hands of the soldiers, and assumed the purple mantle once more. But Constantine returned with the stride of a giant, and Maximian shut himself in Marseilles, which was presently surrendered. The aged intriguer returned to the palace, tried to corrupt the loyalty of his daughter, and brought upon himself the punishment of his crimes.

It is a peculiarity of the time that, the more remote an historian is from an event, the more he knows about it.

Eutropius and Zosimus merely know that Fausta revealed her father's plots to her husband; Zonaras, of the twelfth century, is able to tell us the whole story. Maximian, he says, persuaded his daughter to have the guards removed from the Imperial chamber at night. Then, telling the night-attendants that he wished to relate to Constantine a remarkable dream he had had, he entered the chamber and plunged his dagger into the sleeping figure on the bed. Rushing out to announce the fall of the tyrant, however, he found himself in face of Constantine, Fausta, and the guards. Fausta had been true to her husband, and it was "a vile eunuch" that Maximian had slain in the Emperor's bed. Whatever truth there may be in this romance, we may accept the statement that Fausta betrayed his plots, and Maximian came to the end of his career. Zosimus sends him into exile, and makes him die a natural death at Tarsus. Lactantius, with a stronger sense of propriety, tells us that he strangled himself, and it is the general belief that Constantine did not permit him to leave Gaul alive.

Galerius died in the following year (311), leaving the Eastern Empire to Licinius and Maximin, while Maxentius ruled in Italy and Africa. Four Empresses now lived in the court of Constantine, but before we seek to penetrate the mystery of their relations to each other, we must briefly accompany Constantine in his rise to the position of supreme monarch. Maxentius, who had expelled his father from Italy, now affected a filial anger against his destroyer, and, after some exasperated correspondence, sent toward Gaul an army of nearly 200,000 men. Constantine boldly led 40,000 of his soldiers across the Alps, wore down the strength of his opponent in successive encounters, and, within a few months, exhibited the grisly head of Maxentius to the astonished and delighted Romans.

He was now master of the Western Empire. Devoting two months to the settlement of Roman affairs, he returned to Milan to meet his Eastern colleague Licinius. His half-sister Constantia was married there to Licinius, who returned to Asia with his bride, to crush Maximin, and to perpetrate the melancholy tragedies over which we shuddered in the last chapter. Anastasia, the second daughter of Constantius, was married to the Senator Bassianus.

Constantine made him Caesar, but put no troops at his command--he had just suppressed the Praetorian Guards at Rome--and refused to grant him the authority that had hitherto been associated with the title of Caesar. Bassianus corresponded angrily with Licinius, and before the end of 315 the Emperors of the East and West were in arms against each other.

It would be interesting to know what share the daughters of Constantius had in promoting these disorders.

The correspondence of Bassianus and Licinius suggests a correspondence of their wives, and, when Bassianus was deposed and disgraced, we may assume that Constantia was not insensible of the misfortune of her younger sister.

The superior age and ability of Constantine would hardly reconcile the legitimate children of Constantius to their position of dependence. Constantia is sometimes represented as a pious peacemaker, but we do not find her in that character until her husband's power is irremediably broken, after the second war with Constantine. She fled in great haste with her husband after the first defeat, and returned with him to Nicomedia, to rule his reduced dominions.

The court-life of the West flowed with uneventful smoothness in the eight years between the first and second war with Licinius. The only break in the monotony is the birth of three sons and three daughters in quick succession.

Zosimus emphatically asserts that these were not the children of Fausta, but of a concubine, whom Constantine put to death on a charge of adultery. We are naturally disposed to regard this as a piece of reprehensible malice on the part of the pagan writer, but even the most cautious judgment will find ground for reflection in the circumstance that Fausta had borne no children whatever for the first nine years of her marriage, and then children begin to appear with astonishing rapidity. We know that Constantine had had a concubine, named Minervina, before he married Fausta. Her son Crispus lived at the court.

It would not be entirely surprising if Minervina had returned to the court, to rear the Imperial dynasty which Fausta failed to provide, and was eventually destroyed in one of Constantine's bursts of temper.[24]

In the Eastern court the young Empress had, if we trust the authorities, a more adventurous career. Constantia cannot have been more than seventeen or eighteen at the time of her marriage, but she was a woman of spirit and ability, as well as virtue and beauty. It is said that she, with the whole court, became a Christian after Constantine's victory over Maxentius, but the story of the miraculous sign in the heavens--a story that is not found in any form until thirty years afterwards--is now rejected, and the conversion of Constantine is spread over many years. At Nicomedia, however, where Constantia occupied the magnificent palace built by Diocletian, she met the accomplished and courtly Eusebius, and induced Licinius to allow him the position of Bishop of Nicomedia. Two things, it is said, then transpired in the character of Licinius to excite her disgust. He not only persecuted the Christians, but made equal war upon virtue. In brief, he, like all the other persecutors, is depicted by the flowing pen of Lactantius as an erotic ogre. His eye falls on a Christian maiden, of dazzling beauty and virtue, in the suite of Constantia, and he sends an officer to corrupt her. She tells Constantia, who dresses her as a young military officer, and sends her, with a splendid equipage, to take an imaginary Imperial commission to a remote region. In the distant city of Amasia she is embarrassed by her masculine hosts, and confides in the bishop.

Finally, a letter of hers to Constantia is intercepted, and she escapes by a very timely death from the embraces or the tortures of Licinius.

Of these wicked ways, and of her husband's hostility to the Christians, Constantia is said to have kept her brother well informed, and, when Licinius committed the greater enormity of refusing to surrender fugitive offenders to the vengeance of Constantine, the legions were once more led toward the Bosphorus. Several disastrous battles crippled the power of Licinius, and he retired sullenly to Nicomedia. Whether at his request or no, Constantia interceded for him, and Constantine swore to respect his life. In assigning the blame for the war we may, perhaps, hesitate between the contradictory charges of the opposing schools of historians, though modern writers usually follow the neutral and sober Eutropius, and ascribe it to the ambition of Constantine. But there is a sharper indictment of Constantine's conduct after the war. Licinius, in surrendering, had relied on the oath of the conqueror.

He had been stripped of the purple, and exiled to Thessalonica, but he was put to death there shortly afterwards.

Zosimus and Eutropius say that this was done "in spite of the oath," and the statement of Constantine's more resolute admirers, that Licinius was discovered in treasonable intrigue, has not carried much conviction with later historians.

Constantia passed, with her daughter Helena and her boy Licinius, to the court of her brother, who was now (324) master of the whole Empire. The remark of Zosimus, that Constantine degenerated into the most wilful license after his attainment of supreme power--a remark feebly supported by the assurance of the cautious Eutropius that "prosperity somewhat altered his character"--contrasts quaintly with the circumstance that he now became the Imperial patron of the Christian religion. Here, again, we hesitate between conflicting accounts, or rival romances.

According to the mediaeval Christian writer Zonaras, who supplies a remarkable amount of detail that was unknown to contemporary historians, the conversion of Constantine had a picturesque origin. On his return to Rome, after crushing Licinius, he was afflicted with a painful eruption, and his pagan physicians prescribed a bath in the warm blood of children. "At once," says the lively writer, "children were collected from the whole Empire," and dispatched to the palace. The lamentations of the mothers fell on the ear of Constantine, touched his heart, and he left paganism in disgust for Christianity.

The pagan Greek, Zosimus, who at least faithfully reproduces the pagan gossip of his time--as, on this point, we know from Sozomen--gives us the legend of *his* school.

After committing certain murders, which will occupy us presently, Constantine applied to the priests of the temple of Jupiter for purification. The priests sternly replied that their lustral water had no power to obliterate the trace of such a crime, and Constantine turned in despair to an Egyptian who was known to "the women-folk" of the palace. The Christian priest, as he seems to have been, declared that his religion contained the desired remedy, and Constantine embraced it.

It will be seen that we now pursue our biographic way amid a forest of legends. Happily, we may reject both these stories as, at least, anachronisms. Constantine was already a Christian in 324. He had abolished the decrees of persecution in the year 313, and had taken a keen interest in Church matters for some years. The whole court gradually accepted the new faith. Helena, Eusebius tells us, and Fausta for some time opposed the change of religion, but Helena at least was converted. Eutropia appears in the East a few years later as a zealous opponent of paganism. From their several and ample purses the money poured into the lean coffers of the Church, and the conversion of the Empire proceeded rapidly. Villages that embraced Christianity were raised to the dignity of cities; nobles and officers were encouraged by promotion; and ordinary citizens were rewarded with a baptismal robe and a piece of gold.

It is not for us to inquire into the obscure question of Constantine's real attitude. Professor Bury and other eminent authorities believe that his creed was a liberal, or vague, one until his death. Years afterwards we find him building pagan temples at Constantinople, and he did not disdain the Imperial title of Sovereign Pontiff of the old religion. On the other hand, the details collected by Mr. Firth show a very real interest in the Church. He opened the great Council of Nicaea in the year 325, and reverently kissed the wounds of those who had suffered in the persecution. Yet even amid this evidence of orthodoxy the hesitating student will find trace of his liberality.

In the letter which he sent to the Catholic bishops he complained that the subject of their vehement quarrel with the Arians was "quite insignificant, and entirely disproportionate to such a quarrel." The question at issue was the divinity of Christ. His experience at the Council would give him a larger sense of its importance.

From the benedictions of the prelates and the embraces of the martyrs Constantine returned to Europe, and, within a year, apparently, his court was rent by a tragedy that has left an irremovable cloud on his memory. He had gone to Rome, with the court, to celebrate the twentieth anniversary of his accession. The city exulted in the rare indulgence of his presence, and the games and festivities warmed it with its old enthusiasm. The Empire was united and at peace, and the growing brood of children gave promise of an unending dynasty. Crispus, Constantine's eldest son, was now a popular and promising

commander, clothed in the mantle of a Caesar. Two of the sons of Fausta, or her substitute, were Caesars. Then there was the twelve-year-old son of Constantia. Over these watched the aged Helena and Eutropia, and the mothers and aunts of the younger children.

In the middle of the festivity Rome was startled to hear that Crispus had been arrested, by his father's command, and exiled to Pola, in Istria. From that remote and solitary region the report at length came that he had been put to death. Every eye was turned on the palace, and before long--most of the historians say--the gay figure of the beautiful young Empress disappeared, and the report spread that she had been brutally suffocated in the steam of a dense vapour-bath. The horror was increased, and the prospect of a humane interpretation lessened, when it was learned that the innocent child of Constantia also had been put to death. Such is the grave and mysterious tragedy of Constantine's mature years. As Fausta has been heavily indicted by those who have sought to defend her husband, and Helena impeached by his accusers, we may glance at the evidence on which one's verdict must be based.

There are partisan historians who would cast doubt on the whole story; there are more serious historians, such as Gibbon (who again gallantly opposes the critics), who say that Fausta, at least, was not slain; and the rest are divided in opinion as to whether it was a just execution or a ghastly crime. The first two opinions are now untenable. There is no serious dispute that Crispus and Licinius were put to death. That Fausta was killed is now equally established. Gibbon relied upon a certain anonymous writer to show that Fausta was living long afterwards, but it has been shown that the writer is not speaking of Fausta and Constantine. Moreover, Dr. Seeck, in a special study of the evidence ("Die Verwandtenmorde Constantins des Grossen," *Zeitschrift fur Wiss. Theol.*, Bd. 33), has shown that the coins of Fausta and Crispus, unlike those of the other members of the Imperial family, end before the year

330. Dr. Gorres, who held Gibbon's view, consents that this proof is decisive. The only serious question is that of motive or justification.

Let us glance at the authorities, in the order of their nearness to the event. Bishop Eusebius is naturally silent; he professes to give only the things that edify in the life of Constantine, and is writing almost in his son's court. Eutropius, the soundest and most impartial writer of the next generation, says (x. 6) that the character of Constantine "was somewhat changed with prosperity,"

and that "following the exigencies of the situation [*necessitudines rerum*], he put to death, first his excellent son and the son of his sister, a boy of promising character, then his wife and a number of friends." St. Jerome, in his Latin version of the "Chronicle" of Eusebius, writes, at the year 329, that "Crispus, the son of Constantine, and Licinius the younger, the son of Constantia, are most cruelly put to death in the ninth year of his reign," and three years later we read: "Constantine put to death his wife Fausta."[25] Dr. Seeck believes that we have here only an echo of Eutropius, but Jerome would hardly add "most cruelly" on so cautious a narrative. Aurelius Victor, a contemporary of Eutropius, says that Crispus "was put to death by his father for some unknown reason,"

and Orosius, the Christian historian, merely observes that Constantine put Crispus and Licinius to death.

From these earlier writers we learn only that the deaths were cruel, and the motive unknown, but later writers have successively built up a story that has provoked endless discussion. Sidonius Apollinaris, the most cultivated and liberal Christian writer of the fifth century, says, with the confidence of a parenthesis (Ep. v), that Crispus was poisoned, and Fausta killed in a vapour-bath; and that a couplet was fixed on the palace-gate recalling the crimes of Nero. The epitomist of Aurelius Victor declares that Crispus was put to death at the instigation of Fausta, and Fausta was "thereupon" killed in a vapour-bath, as Helena bitterly reproached Constantine for the death of Crispus. Zosimus (ii. 29) says: "With no regard for the law of nature he put to death his son Crispus, on the ground that he was suspected of intimacy with Fausta,"

and, when Helena heavily reproached him, he, "as if to console her," suffocated Fausta in an overheated bath.

Philostorgius, a Christian writer of the same (fifth) century, declares that Fausta was put to death because she was caught in adultery with a groom. The story culminates in the twelfth-century annalist Zonaras. After telling his incredible legend about Constantine and the babies, he represents Fausta in the character of Potiphar's wife. She conceived a passion for the handsome Caesar, was repelled by him, and then denounced him to Constantine as having offered violence to her. Crispus was put to death. Then Constantine learned in some way--Helena is left to the imagination--that he had been deceived, and he angrily killed Fausta in a vapour-bath.

It is remarkable how many grave writers have favoured this legend of the mediaeval writer,[26] yet, besides its obvious growth through the centuries, it has the fatal weakness of throwing no light whatever on the murder of Licinius, the son of Constantine's most cherished sister. We are reduced to conjecture in face of this mysterious and terrible tragedy. That the youths met with some violent death at the hands of the Emperor, that Helena bitterly remonstrated with him, and that the savage suffocation of Fausta followed this remonstrance, seems to be clear.

We may further conclude with some confidence, from the persistent rumour of amorous relations, that this charge was allowed to reach the outside world in extenuation of the murders. But it is suspected by many historians, and seems to be suggested by the obscure language of Eutropius, that the real motive was political.

FAUSTA

FLAVIA HELENA

ENLARGED FROM COINS IN THE BRITISH MUSEUM

Crispus was in great favour with both the people and the troops, and had distinguished himself in the war with Licinius. If anything happened to Constantine, who was in his fifty-second year, Crispus had a clear prospect of the throne. It would not be unnatural for Fausta to resent this, and one is tempted to see, either an effect of her importunity or a proof of Constantine's jealousy of his son, in the fact that Constantine took away the province of Gaul from Crispus, without compensation, in 323, and gave it to the eldest of his legitimate sons.

From that time Crispus was retained in idleness, and probably discontent, under the eye of his father. He would be a natural focus for all the dissatisfaction in the Empire, and the Romans, and pagans generally, regarded Constantine and his family with anger and disdain on account of their abandonment of the old religion. By the year 326 Constantine was in a state of extraordinary nervousness and suspicion. Before going to Rome he issued an edict in which he revealed his frame of mind to the whole Empire. At Rome he flouted the most cherished customs of the city, and may well have incurred fresh murmurs. Something occurred that brought his suspicion of Crispus--who may not have become a Christian--to an acute stage, and he condemned him to exile and death. This theory is also the only one to explain, with any plausibility, the execution of young Licinius.

He was the only other rival of Constantine's legitimate sons. It is impossible for us to say whether Crispus had incurred any guilt or no, but the silence of the earlier writers and panegyrists is a grave circumstance. If there had been plausible evidence of conspiracy they would not have remained silent. In any case, the sentence on Crispus was harsh and unjustifiable, and the execution of a twelve-year-old boy was a piece of brutality that only the worse Emperors would have perpetrated.

The murder of Fausta is even more perplexing. Even if the late and negligible stories of Philostorgius and Zonaras were true, she was not executed, but brutally murdered. The only firm point in the conflicting evidence is the persistent association of her death with the anger of Helena. We have no evidence of any value in regard to her relation to Crispus; but the words of Zosimus, which are not inconsistent with the earlier writers, enable us to extend the above theory to her. Constantine, on this view, put Crispus and Licinius to death because they were possible nuclei of the conspiracy which he believed to pervade the Empire. Adopting a familiar device, however, he concealed his motive under a charge of amorous irregularity, or too great a familiarity with the Empress. Helena, who was greatly attached to Crispus, seems to have insisted that, if there was any guilt, both were guilty, and Constantine savagely completed his work by murdering his wife. The Christian historians describe Fausta as opposing Constantine's progress in his new faith, and, as we have no evidence that Crispus had embraced it, one may not implausibly wonder whether the two did not attract the favour of the pagan Romans, to the extreme anger of the Emperor. No charge against Fausta was made public. During the lifetime of Constantine's eldest son, Julian described her, in one of his orations, as not only one of the most beautiful, but one of the most virtuous and noble ladies of her time. Even if we make allowance for the licensed flattery of a panegyrist, the description would be too glaringly inconsistent with any Imperial theory of her infidelity. She was probably in her thirty-fourth or thirty-fifth year at the time when she met her appalling death.

Constantine hastened to remove the gloomy, stricken court from the disdainful eyes of Rome. The pagans pointed with fierce scorn to these fruits of the new religion, as they expressed it. One day it was found that some one had fastened a Latin couplet--written, the pagans of a later day boasted, by the hand of the Emperor's chief counsellor, Ablabius--on the gate of the palace:

Say ye the Golden Age of Saturn breaks again?
Of Nero's bloody hue these jewels are.

Either at once, or in the course of the next year, the court broke up. Constantine went to direct the building of the new capital of the West, which was to bear his name. Later pagans said that he fled from the theatre of his crimes and the scorn of Rome, but the ample lines of Constantinople had been traced long before, and the site had been chosen for its strategical importance. Helena sought the land in which Christ had lived and died, and her pious munificence won for her the halo of sanctity. The legend of her finding the cross does not appear until seventy years afterwards, and Eusebius tells us that it was Constantine, not she, who found the sepulchre and built a church over it. But Helena, who had now great wealth, covered the land with churches, and returned with a great repute for piety. She died soon after her return--in 328, Tillemont thinks--having passed her eightieth year.

Europia also went on a pilgrimage to Palestine, and seems to have settled in the East. We find her a few years later urging Constantine to scatter the pagans who are defiling some sacred spot with their impure ceremonies.

Theodora seems to have died, at some unknown

date, before the year of the murders. Constantia died in, or about, the year 329. Her Arian friend Eusebius had been banished, at the triumph of the Athanasians, but she obtained his recall, and adhered to his Unitarian creed. In her last hours she succeeded in recommending an Arian priest to Constantine, and prolonged the religious struggle. We pass to a new generation of Empresses, and may dismiss briefly the ten years which remain of Constantine's rule and introduce us to the events of the next chapter.

In the month of May of the year 330, the new city of Constantinople was solemnly dedicated. The curious reader will find in Gibbon a splendid restoration of its princely proportions, its stores of art gathered from all parts of the Empire, its superb palace, its great hippodrome, its churches and temples, its spacious fora, and its lofty column of porphyry, surmounted by a gigantic statue, in which the head of Constantine replaced that of Apollo, and the various attributes of the god he still admired were hesitatingly redeemed by emblems of the jealous God of his new faith. The enormous sums absorbed in the building of the new city were regarded by the pagans as one of the causes of the decay of the Empire, and the bitter strife of Arians and Athanasians, which distracted it, irritated their resentment. But their day was closing. The arguments with which they clung to a Jupiter and a Venus in whom they no longer believed were hollow; the rewards of conversion were

great. The grey gods saw their crowds of worshippers becoming thinner and less joyous. The Empire lifted the humble cross into the sunlight from Persia to Britain.

The last decade of Constantine's life was inglorious.

We might distrust the partial and severe accusations of Zosimus, but the substance of his charge is found in the other authorities. His vast and hurried enterprise in building forced him to lay heavy burdens on his enfeebled Empire, and we have the authority of Ammianus Marcellinus that he "encouraged those about him to open

devouring jaws" in a lamentable degree. Conversion was the first right to favour and wealth. The later Emperor Julian, we are not surprised to find, pours acrid satire on him. In the treatise ("Caesares") in which he introduces the Emperors of Rome to the Olympic court, he makes Constantine turn to the goddess Luxury, as the one congenial deity, and she introduces him only to her sister Prodigality. He ridicules Constantine's womanly finery in dress and jewels, his elaborate crown of false hair, his complete lapse into effeminate ways.

Aurelius Victor gives us the proverbial judgment of the next generation on Constantine: in his first decade he was admirable, in his second decade thievish, in his third decade a squanderer. He made the final blunder of--without naming a successor--dividing the Empire among his sons and nephews, of gravely unequal character, and died in 337, leaving them and their supporters to engage in a murderous struggle for supremacy.

CHAPTER XVIII

THE WIVES OF CONSTANTIUS AND JULIAN

WHEN the announcement of Constantine's death had been borne by swift couriers to the distant provinces, and the body, in its golden coffin, had been transferred to Constantinople, there was a nervous rush of aspiring Emperors and Empresses to the capital.

The unification of the Empire under Constantine had cost the State some hundred and fifty thousand of its finest soldiers, who perished in civil warfare while powerful nations pressed against its yielding frontiers. In his later years he had so distributed these provinces, whose unity had been so dearly purchased, among his sons and nephews, worthy and unworthy, that dismemberment was certain to follow his death. His eldest son, Constantine, now in his twenty-first year, ruled Gaul and Britain; Constantius, the second son, a youth of twenty, was the Caesar of the East; the third son, Constans, aged seventeen, held sway over Italy and Africa. His nephew Delmatius, also entitled Caesar, controlled Thrace, Macedonia, and Greece, and the younger nephew Hannibalian bore the ornate title of King of Kings in Pontus and Cappadocia. The two brothers of Constantine, and the husbands of his two sisters, were not left without a share of the Imperial provision.

The race to Constantinople after the death of the Emperor may be imagined, but the suddenness and horror of the consequent tragedy must have sobered even the most frivolous. Constantius, the second son, was the first to arrive, and to him the conduct of the impressive funeral was entrusted. The members of the family gathered round the marble palace from all quarters of the Empire, and the shade of Constantine continued for some months to rule the State, until their conflicting claims should be adjusted.

Julius Constantius and Delmatius, the legitimate heirs of Constantius Chlorus, who had been thrust aside thirty years before by the vigorous son of Minervina, were now men in the prime of life. The younger son of the latter, Hannibalian, the "King of Kings," strutted in a scarlet and gold mantle, and had married the fiery and ambitious young daughter of the late Emperor, Constantina. Anastasia, Constantine's sister, brought her husband, the "Patrician"

Optatus. The partition of power seemed a formidable task. But in the weeks that succeeded Constantine's death a new and sinister power arose, and its secret designs prepared a ghastly simplification of the problem.

Constantius became insensibly the central figure of the drama. A callous youth, with little strength of character, he was selected by the eunuchs and corrupt officers of Constantine's court as a likely instrument of their plans.

It was agreed that the interests of these officers and of the sons of Constantine would be best served by a removal of all the other competitors, and a diabolical plot was devised.

The details are given at length only by the Christian historian Philostorgius, of the next century, and are regarded with reserve; but an Arian writer would hardly inculpate an Arian bishop and an Arian monarch without some just ground. His story is that Constantine left a will in which he declared that he had been poisoned by his two half-brothers. The will was given to Bishop Eusebius.

When the brothers were eager to see the will of Constantine, Eusebius is said to have discovered a fine piece of casuistry.

He put the will in the hands of the dead Emperor, and covered it with his robes, so that he might, without injury to his delicate conscience, assure the brothers that Constantine had indeed shown him a will, but he had returned it into his hands. The will--or a will--was now produced, and the people and army were assured by their dead ruler that he had been poisoned by his family.

The story is regarded with suspicion by most historians.

For the reason I have given, and because it is the only plausible explanation of what followed, it seems probable that such a will was produced and published by Constantius.

It was probably forged by the palace officials. Whether they and the sons of Constantine used this device or no, they somehow directed the tempestuous anger of the troops upon the older princes and their families, and extinguished their claims in a brutal massacre. Julian casts the blame on Constantius, admitting that he acted under compulsion, and the other fourth-century writers do not differ. Constantius "permitted," rather than "commanded." The corrupt power behind the throne directed the murders, and the sons of Constantine purchased a larger dominion by the blood of their uncles and cousins. The two uncles, seven cousins, and other distinguished men, were included in the bloody list. Then the three Imperial youths divided the Empire between them, and departed to their provinces.

The wives of the eldest and the youngest of the brothers are unknown to us, and the first wife of Constantius is so little known that we may pass rapidly over a number of years. The Imperial sisters of Constantine--except Constantia, whom we have considered --enter little in the history of the time. Anastasia disappears after the murder of her husband. Eutropia will presently mingle her blood with that of her insurgent son on the soil of Italy. Constantina, the daughter of Constantine who had married

Hannibalian, and who already bore the title of Augusta, retired into a long widowhood, from which we shall find her emerging later in a monstrous character.

Constantius had been married to his cousin Galla in 336. She seems to have been the daughter of Julius Constantius, since Julian says that her father and brother were included in the massacre. Her personality is never outlined for us in the historical writings of the time, and we are left to imagine her shuddering or languishing in the arms that were stained with the blood of her family.

She died some time before 350, as Magnentius offered his daughter to Constantius in that year. We have, therefore, no Empress who can engage our attention until 353, and may be content with a slight summary of the events which lead on to the appearance of Eusebia and the reappearance of the repulsive Constantina.

Three years after the partition of the Empire Constantine and Constans quarrelled about their territory.

The elder brother led his troops into the dominion of Constans, and was slain; and his provinces were added to those of Constans. The character of the youngest son of Constantine was gross and intolerable. He revived the lowest vice of his pagan predecessors, and his open parade of the handsome barbarian youths whom he bought, or attracted to his frivolous court, disgusted his officers.

In the beginning of the year 350 they rebelled against him. A banquet was given at Augustodunum (Autun) to the notables of the town and the officers of the camp, and at a late hour, when the abundant wine had warmed the hearts and obscured the judgment of the diners, the commander of two of the chief legions, Magnentius, was brought before them in a purple robe. Constans awoke from his vices to find that he had lost the throne and the army, and fled toward Spain. He was overtaken and slain. Some blood-curse seemed to hang over the house of Constantine. Constantius, who had been long occupied in resisting the Persians, now wheeled round his troops, and faced the usurper.

In the long struggle that followed there were two incidents of interest for us. Constantina, the Imperial widow, was living in restless impotence at the time.

Between the rebellious provinces of the West and the loyal provinces of the East was the intermediate district between the Danube and the Greek sea. Constantina, it is said, instigated the commander of the troops in these regions, Vetranio, to assume the purple. What we shall see of her character presently will dispose us to believe that she meditated a return to power through Vetranio, but Constantius astutely disarmed and exiled him, and accepted her explanation that she had acted with the pure aim of resisting the advance of the Western usurper. Constantine's sister Eutropia also appears in the struggle. Her son Nepotian assumed the purple at Rome, and led out a motley army to attack Magnentius. They were quickly annihilated, and mother and son--two of the few remaining members of Constantine's family--were slain.

The interest of the student of the time is divided between the clash of armies and the not wholly bloodless conflicts of theologies. We are concerned with neither, and need only observe that Constantius defeated Magnentius, after a long and costly struggle--in one battle 54,000 Roman soldiers perished in civil warfare--and reunited the Empire under his sole dominion. The young Empress of the defeated Magnentius retired into widowhood, and will be restored to us in the next chapter. In the meantime Constantina has returned to the field, and her Imperial adventures call for our notice.

Two children, the sons of Julius Constantius, had survived the massacre at Constantinople. Gallus was in his twelfth year, Julian in his sixth. They were hidden until the fury of the soldiers had abated, and then their tender age induced the murderers to overlook them. The jealous eye of Constantius fell on them when they approached manhood, and they were confined in a fortress, or ancient palace, in Cappadocia. In the solitude of Macellum no company was offered them but that of slaves and soldiers.

Julian, in whose mind the seeds of an elevated philosophy had taken root, resisted the pressing temptations, and devoted the long days to culture; but Gallus, a sensual and ill-balanced youth, adopted the coarse distractions of his spacious jail. After six years (in 351) they were not only set at liberty, but Gallus was amazed to find himself clothed with the dignity of Caesar and married to the Emperor's sister Constantina. Constantius was compelled to leave the East in order to face Magnentius, and he needed a Caesar to rule in his name.

The three years' rule of Gallus and Constantina was an Imperial scandal. Unscrupulous and unbridled, the daughter of Constantine lives in the literature of the time as a monstrous perversion of womanhood. With her begins the historical work (as we have it) of Ammianus Marcellinus, a retired general, one of the most scrupulous and ample chroniclers of his time. He bursts at once into a vivid denunciation of her vices. She was "a mortal Megaera," an ogre, swollen with pride and thirsting for human blood. It is unfortunate that Ammianus gives us no personal description of the women of his time. His work contains charming vignettes of the Emperors and princes, but he seems never to have looked on the face or figure of their wives. Gallus, he tells us, was a superb youth in figure and stature, his handsome features crowned with soft golden hair, and bearing a look of dignity and authority, in spite of his vices. The strain of cruelty and coarseness in him was provoked to excesses by his wife.

When his savage conduct had exasperated his subjects he used to send his spies, in the disguise of beggars, to gather the secret whispers of discontent; and he even stooped to the practice of wandering himself, in disguise, from tavern to tavern on the well-lit streets of Antioch to discover his critics. Antioch had been noted for centuries for its freedom of speech, and the prisons and torture-chambers of Gallus were busy.

Constantina not only encouraged this criminal conduct, but enlarged on it. A woman of vicious character came one day to disclose some plot, or pretended plot, to her.

She rewarded her heavily, and sent the harlot out into the city in the royal chariot, to encourage others. An Alexandrian noble distinguished himself by resisting the guilty passion of his mother-in-law. The woman presented Constantina with a pearl necklace, and the noble was put to death. We need not prolong the disgusting narrative.

Flavia Julia Constantina, a beautiful and able woman, who can scarcely have passed her thirtieth year, was one of the worst Empresses in the Imperial gallery. One can but suggest, in some attenuation of her guilt, that the murder of her husband by her brother when she was a young girl in her early teens, and the fourteen years of young widowhood that followed, had provoked the worst elements of her nature.

As long as Constantius was occupied with the struggle against Magnentius, he overlooked the excesses of his Caesar and his sister in the East. His opponent, Magnentius, was not so compliant, though he wasted no legions in an effort to dethrone him. He sent a soldier to assassinate Gallus and seduce the troops. As the man resided, however, in a tavern near Antioch, he became less cautious over his cups, and boasted to his associates of his mission. The old woman who kept the tavern seemed too far removed from politics to be taken into account, but she promptly denounced her guest at the palace, and he was put to death.

Then Magnentius fell, and committed suicide, and Constantius turned to consider the scandalous conduct of his viceroy and his sister.

Constantius proceeded, as he usually did whenever it was possible, by craft instead of force. The Prefect of the East had been slain by the people of Antioch, with the guilty connivance of Gallus, and a new Prefect, named Domitian, was sent to Antioch, together with the Prefect of the Palace, Montius. Domitian had orders to secure, by the most tactful and seductive means, that Gallus should visit Italy, and walk into the pit dug for him. He was, however, a sturdy officer, more sensible of the just substance than the form of his instructions. Gallus and Constantina were at once insulted because, on the day of his arrival, he drove insolently past the gate of the palace, and went straight to his villa. They then condescended to invite him to the palace. In the presence of the hated rulers he laid aside all pretence of diplomacy, and roughly ordered the Caesar to proceed at once to Italy, or incur the just resentment of the Emperor. Gallus, stung by his insolence, at once gave the Prefect into the custody of the soldiers. Montius, who was present, and who also had lost all feeling for diplomacy in the passionate encounter, remonstrated with Gallus, adding the taunt that a man who had no power to dismiss one of his magistrates had no right to imprison a Prefect of the East. We are assured by Philostorgius that Constantina flew at the official, dragged him from the tribunal, and pushed him into the hands of the guard. We may prefer the more sober version of Ammianus. Gallus impetuously called upon the troops and the people of Antioch to defend their ruler, and they responded with surprising alacrity. The distinguished officers of Constantius were bound hand and foot, dragged through the streets until the last spark of life was extinct, and then flung into the river.

Still Constantius hesitated to enter upon a civil war with the East, and the unscrupulous cunning which dictated his policy discovered an alternative procedure. First, the commander of the cavalry in the East was summoned to Milan, that the danger of a rising might be lessened.

Then, a series of letters, couched in the most friendly and mendacious terms, were sent to the Caesar. Constantius was eager to see his beloved sister once more, and to confer with his Caesar. For some time they resisted the invitation, but at length Constantina, less apprehensive of personal injury, set out for Italy. She died on the journey, at Coenum in Bithynia, of fever, and her remains were buried at Rome. She was still in her early thirties at the time of her death. The single deed that is recorded in praise of her is that she and Gallus planted a Christian church in the dissolute grove of Daphne, and drew the austerity of the new faith upon that region of sensuous superstition and sensual license. Her share in that act of piety may be put in the scale against her avarice, cruelty, selfishness, and unbridled temper.

The fate of her husband may be briefly recorded. Lured at length by the deceitful professions of Constantius, he set out for Milan with his princely retinue. As soon as he reached Europe, the retinue was brushed aside, and he discovered himself a captive. When the little party arrived in Pannonia, he was stripped of the purple, and conducted to the remote prison at Pola, where Crispus had been executed. There he was "tried" by a eunuch of Constantius's court, and within a few days a breathless courtier--he had ridden several horses to death--rushed into the presence of Constantius with the shoes of the slain Caesar.

The Empire was reunited under Constantius, at a cost of the deaths of twenty princes and princesses of his house and their dependents, and fifty thousand soldiers; and the eunuchs and courtiers filled the palace at Milan with the incense they offered to the young conqueror.

Constantius had, meantime, married again, and a more worthy and commanding Empress engages our attention.

Toward the close of his struggle with Magnentius, in the year 352 or the beginning of 353, the Emperor married a Macedonian lady, Aurelia Eusebia, of remarkable beauty, no little ability, and dignified personality. Her father and brothers had had consular rank in their province; her mother had been distinguished for the propriety of her conduct and the careful rearing of her children after the death of her husband. The language in which the Emperor Julian describes her is enhanced by gratitude, and enjoys the license of a panegyric; some would say that it is warmed by a more tender sentiment. But Ammianus, who also knew her, pronounces that the beauty of her character was not less splendid than that of her form, and, beyond a peevish complaint of a later writer that she did not confine herself to the proper and restricted sphere of a woman, she maintains her high repute among the conflicting writers of the time. The one grave imputation, which Ammianus seems to find quite consistent with his superlative praise of her, we will consider later.

We find Eusebia established in the court at Milan at the time when the heads of the last of Constantius's rivals are falling. When Gallus has disappeared, he proudly takes the title of "Lord of the World," and endeavours to live up to it, amid his company of eunuchs and fawning attendants. In the hands of those astute and concordant schemers the weak and vain monarch was easily persuaded to arrive at decisions which he attributed to his own judgment, and it is, perhaps, the most indulgent plea that we can make for him that he was governed by a power so subtle and insinuating that he never perceived it. The high merit of a scrupulous chastity is claimed for him; but the monastic writer Zonaras somewhat detracts from this by affirming that his coldness deprived him of a dynasty and forced his beautiful and accomplished wife into a fatal decline. His piety, at least, might be praised; but it rested on a basis of Arian creed and is exposed to the scorn of the orthodox, who called him Antichrist.

We may concur in the strictures of Zonaras so far as to admit that Eusebia cannot have been happy in his court. The eunuch Eusebius, who had tried and executed Gallus, was the most powerful man in the Empire.

Ammianus observes, with heavy irony, that Constantius was believed to be not without influence with his emasculated chamberlain. A hierarchy of lesser, but hardly less corrupt, officials led up to this favoured minister, and Ammianus, from personal acquaintance with the court, assures us that their rapacity and unscrupulousness grew with the power of Constantius. A Persian officer, Mercurius, had the nickname of "The Count of Dreams," from the skill with which he could make the most innocent fancies of the night bear a treasonable complexion, and bring destruction and spoliation on the dreamer. Paulus, who had risen from the lowly position of table-steward, was called "The Chain," because of the art with which he could involve a man in a charge of plotting. Torture and confiscation became common experiences once more, and men began to shrink from even the most innocent conversation.

This unpleasant tenor of the Imperial life at Milan was relieved by the great controversy of the Arians and Athanasians, which was brought to Italy for decision.

How Constantius and his officers induced the Latin bishops to condemn Athanasius, in 355, by "stroking their bellies instead of laying the rod on their backs," to use the vigorous phrase of St. Hilary, does not concern us, but it is interesting to see how Eusebia came in contact with the prelates. When the Roman bishop, Liberius, bravely--for a time--incurred exile rather than condemn Athanasius, Eusebia sent him a sum of money. He returned it with the suggestion that her husband might find it useful for his troops or his Arian bishops. A new power, besides that of eunuchs, was rising. Suidas preserves a story that may be given here, though it may or may not refer to this Council. As the bishops, he says, came to the town where the court was, for the purpose of holding a Council, they called to salute the Empress.

Leontius, Bishop of Tripoli, refused to visit her, and she sent word that, if he would call, she would give him the funds to build a large church. The saintly prelate replied that he would condescend to visit her if he were assured that she would receive him with fitting respect--if, he explained, she would rise from her throne at his entrance, bend for his benediction, and remain standing, while he sat, until he permitted her to resume her seat.

In the same year (355), however, a more pleasant diversion alleviated the weariness of Eusebia, and another Empress is introduced to our notice. We have already said that the unhappy Gallus had for companion in his Cappadocian jail a young half-brother of the name of Julian. Imbibing his early culture at the alternate hands of Bishop Eusebius and the philosophical eunuch Mardonius, Julian had come to prefer the Greek culture of the latter to the theological lore of the prelate. He had come out untainted from the lonely fortress at Macellum, and had passed to Constantinople and then to Nicomedia.

There the distinguished pagan Libanius attracted his allegiance, and from the three years in which he studied at Nicomedia his mind was wholly given to the older culture, however much he might be compelled to dissemble his aversion for the new religion. After the execution of Gallus he was brought to Milan. With growing apprehension he awaited the decision of "the eunuch, chamberlain, and cook" who, he says, directed the bloody counsels of Constantius. But he found an unexpected and powerful friend in the Empress.

It seems clear that Eusebia first espoused his cause in a pure feeling of humanity. The officials had impeached the innocent youth of twenty-three or twenty-four, chiefly on the ground of having visited Gallus, and his life was gravely threatened. Eusebia threw all her influence in the scale against the malignant officials, and, though they prevented Constantius from hearing him, she saved his life. He was housed in the suburbs of Milan, and was taken one day to see Eusebia. "I seemed to see, as in a temple, the image of the goddess of wisdom," he afterwards wrote in his "Letter to the Athenians." The splendid figure of the beautiful Empress can easily be imagined to have made a remarkable impression on the bookish youth. Eusebia was differently, but favourably, impressed.

Julian was a well-made youth, of moderate stature and broad shoulders. He had the soft curly hair of his brother, a straight nose, large mouth, and brilliant eyes. The humane feeling of the Empress assumed a more tender and personal complexion, and she set to work to make Julian's fortune.

He was sent for a time to Como, and, as her influence prevailed, recalled to Milan, and permitted to reply to his accusers before the Emperor. He was then permitted to retire to his mother's small estate in Bithynia, but Eusebia induced Constantius to impose on him the pleasant sentence of an exile to Athens. From the beloved schools of Athens he was, after a few months, recalled to Milan, to hear the astounding news that he was to receive the purple robe of Caesar and the hand of the Emperor's sister Helena.

He shrank in tears from the political world that opened to him, but Eusebia tactfully overcame his opposition and guided his conduct. Her eunuchs ran continually between the palace and his lodging. The beard and cloak of the philosopher were laid aside, and Julian blushed to find himself accoutred in the splendid trappings of a commander. The jeers and intrigues of the court were at length silenced, and, on November 6th, 355, he stood on a lofty platform before the troops while Constantius invested him with the purple and exhorted him to sustain the honour of Rome. The marriage with Helena followed, and in December Julian and his bride, with a valuable collection of books as the gift of Eusebia, set out for Gaul.

Julian never saw Eusebia again, and cannot have had the least correspondence with her. Even in Milan he had, on reflection, torn up a letter in which he modestly wished his patroness the reward of a succession of children.

On his side there was nothing but a pure feeling of gratitude and reverence. She was, says Zosimus, "a woman of erudition and prudence above her sex"; a shining example of spiritual and bodily beauty, according to Ammianus. She had most probably saved his life, and most certainly made his fortune. But it is believed by many writers that Eusebia's feeling for Julian was of a less ethereal nature. Gaetano Negri, whose life of Julian is one of the most distinguished biographies of a Roman Emperor, justly repudiates the suggestion of improper feeling on her part, and it is a superfluous inference. But one may, without casting the least reflection on her virtue, hesitate to think that the only link between them was a sympathy of culture. Such sympathy we may well assume between a cultivated Greek lady and an ardent Hellenist, but so cold and spiritual a relation may very naturally and pardonably have been strengthened by a warmer feeling. Julian had no sensuous attractiveness for a beautiful woman. But his manly person and character, his vast superiority to the crowd of ignoble parasites she daily encountered, and to her weak and mediocre husband, must have excited an admiration less purely intellectual than an appreciation of his learning.

The person of Flavia Julia Helena remains faint and elusive in the ample chronicle of the time. She was much older than Julian, who was in his twenty-fifth year, while Helena cannot have been less than thirty.[27] She had not been previously married, Ammianus says, and the long maidenhood would not tend to make her attractive. The marriage was arranged by Eusebia in the political interest of Julian, and it probably retained the chill that a *mariage de convenance*, with such disparity of age, would naturally bear. In Julian's abundant, and largely autobiographical, writings she is barely mentioned. It was the marriage of an old maid--for the Roman world--with an austere, if conscientious, philosopher. The gradual discovery of Julian's secret loyalty to the old gods would not make their relations more cordial.

We may, therefore, regret that the single line of inquiry which we pursue will compel us to leave almost unnoticed the brilliant episode of the reign of Julian. The more liberal taste of our time has removed the violent and conflicting colours which the partisan writers of the fourth century laid upon the portrait of Julian. To Gregory of Nazianzum he was a faint impersonation of Antichrist; to the pagan writers a modest incorporation of Apollo.

In modern history he is a most conscientious thinker, a humane and unselfish ruler, a very capable commander, a conceited and unattractive personality. His character, in spite of the shade that clings to it as a trace of the enforced dissimulation of his early years, is great: his ability and achievements are just entitled to be called brilliant.

Helena and Eusebia appear little in the years that follow, and we must narrate the necessary events very briefly. The frame of mind in which Constantius sent Julian to Gaul as Caesar is not at all clear. The frontier was obliterated; the barbarians overrunning the country in formidable strength; the military force inadequate, except with fine control. Some writers are disposed to think that Constantius was sending his cousin to death.

At all events, the faith of Eusebia, that her young and shrinking scholar would surmount these difficulties, was great; and it was rewarded. Julian at once discovered a bravery that none had suspected. He cut his way through a region occupied by the barbarians, surveyed the devastated frontier, and passed the first year of his inexperience with only one small disaster. The difficulty of his task seemed greater when, in the winter, he was besieged in Sens, and the commander of the troops in the neighbourhood refused to go to his relief. In the trouble that followed Eusebia obtained for him the full command of the troops, which had been withheld from him, and from that moment he entered on a career of victory.

It is probable that Helena did not share his peril in this winter (356-7). We find her at Rome in April, with Eusebia and Constantius, and a curious story of their relations is put before us. Constantius in that month bestowed his first and only visit upon the ancient capital of the Empire. Sitting in a chariot that glittered with gold and gems, preceded by officers whose spears bore silken dragons, so fashioned as to hiss in the breeze, on their golden and bejewelled tips, followed by his legions in battle-array, their breastplates and shields gleaming in the sun, the Emperor passed with affected indifference between the dense lines of spectators and the great monuments of Rome; though both the vast crowds and the ancient structures, shining with a beauty that his decaying Empire could no longer produce, wrung from him in private an expression of astonishment. Eusebia had invited Helena to join them in this visit to Rome.

At a later point in his narrative Ammianus makes a reference to this visit that has perplexed every thoughtful reader. When he comes to record the death of Helena, he says that it was due to a poisonous drug administered to her by Eusebia, during the visit to Rome, to prevent her from having children, and that in the previous year, when she was pregnant, Eusebia sent a midwife to destroy the child under pretence of attending her. It does not seem to occur to Gibbon and other historians, who adopt this story, that it suggests in Eusebia a character in complete contradiction to that ascribed to her by Ammianus himself and every other Roman writer. A jealousy of Helena, whether on account of her own childlessness or on account of Julian, that could force her to such a malignant course, is utterly inconsistent with the description we have quoted of her. The story is peremptorily rejected by Miss Gardner and Signor Negri, and its discord with all that we know of Eusebia is noticed by most writers.

One is tempted to inquire if it may not be an interpolation, but the text of Ammianus lends no support whatever to the idea. We can only suppose that Ammianus incorporated a piece of idle gossip, and was inattentive to its inconsistency with his high moral praise of Eusebia. Many legends, we shall see, sprang up after the death of Helena.

Some of them assail Julian, and are easily traced to their source. It is possible that the courtiers who opposed Eusebia, and doubtless misrepresented her zeal for Julian, started the rumour, and Ammianus heard it in Italy years afterwards. It is a mere feather in the scale against the authorities for the high character of the Empress.

From Rome Constantius was summoned to repel fresh invasions in the East, and Helena returned to Gaul. She remains unnoticed until the spring of the year 360, and we will not follow Julian through the brilliant campaigns in which he reduced the most powerful tribes of the barbarians, and restored peace and prosperity to his stricken province. But while Julian succeeded in the West, the campaign of the troops of Constantius in the East won for the Emperor few laurels, and entailed grave disasters.

The intriguers now doubled their charges against Julian, and plausibly suggested that he would be prompted to claim a higher title than that of Caesar. It was decided to reduce his power by removing a number of his finest legions to the East.

Julian was in winter quarters at Paris--as Lutetia was beginning to be called--when the grave summons reached him. The island on the Seine, which now bears the Cathedral, had from early times offered a secure settlement, and, as the province became more settled, the adjoining slope, where the Latin Quarter of a later age began, was occupied with a palace, an amphitheatre, and a few of the customary institutions of a Roman town. Julian loved the little settlement on the broad silvery river, surrounded by dense forests, and he was spending the winter there, attending with equal judgment and humanity to the civil welfare of his province, when the officers of Constantius arrived.

He has described at length the painful perplexity into which he was thrown. Not only would the sacrifice of four of his best legions seriously impair his strength, but they were local troops and had enlisted only for local service. He decided to obey, and ordered the troops to prepare for departure. An angry murmur arose from the camps, as the men reflected on the fate that might befall their families in the ill-protected country. Julian provided that their wives and children should accompany them, and they gathered at Paris for the dismissal. In affecting language the Caesar conveyed to them his thanks and his admonitions, entertained their officers at a banquet, and retired to his palace.

The sincerity of Julian has been made the theme of an acrid discussion between his violent critics and his resolute admirers. But we may, without serious reflection on his character, doubt whether he entirely wished the troops to go. Such an order, from such a source, would plausibly relieve a Caesar from obedience. Only excessive virtue or uncertain prospect of the issue would counsel a man to obey it. Both feelings were at work in Julian's mind, and there is not ground to accuse his later account of hypocrisy. But we may surmise that, at the time, his decision was accompanied by unsanctioned hopes and dreams of a more satisfactory issue. In those days of anxious deliberation his imagination, however he might curb it, must have depicted for him the revival of culture, the arrest of superstition, the purification of the court and Empire, that would follow his elevation to the throne.

He retired to his palace, where, as he incidentally observes somewhere, Helena lived with him. But shortly after midnight a great tumult arose from the direction of the camp, and from the windows one could see the troops, the light of their torches gleaming on their drawn swords, coming toward the palace. The doors were at once closed, and Julian refused to show himself, but the cry of "Imperator" easily penetrated to his ears. On the following morning they broke into the palace, and forcibly conducted Julian to the camp. He resisted, threatened, and supplicated, but the troops were consulting their own interest, now gravely threatened by their revolt, and there was no other course possible but to consent. He was raised up on a shield, and the legions broke into a frenzy of delight at their escape from exile.

A diadem only was needed to complete his new dignity, and Helena, who was present, seems to have offered a pearl necklace of hers. Julian refused to wear the feminine adornment, and an officer provided a rich golden collar, studded with gems, for the coronation.

With the struggle that followed, and the dramatic chapter that opened in the annals of Rome, we have no concern. Both our Empresses die before a decisive stage is reached. The date of the death of Eusebia is not known. It was some time between the beginning of 359

and the middle of 360, as Constantius married again toward the end of 360. She is said to have died of an inflammation of the womb, brought on by taking drugs for procuring fertility. That such drugs were familiar at the time, and that the Empress would naturally try their effect, we readily admit, but we need not entirely overlook the statement of Zonaras that the conduct of her husband and the unhappiness of her circumstances brought the beautiful Greek into a decline. Had she shared the throne with Julian, and adopted his views, the story of Europe might have run differently.[28]

That Helena was won to the views of Julian is improbable. She would, no doubt, discover soon after her marriage that he secretly cherished the cult of the old gods. From his first month in Gaul he had, with one assistant, set up a private shrine to them. There are coins that bear the names of Julian and Helena and the figures of Isis and Serapis, but they yield no inference.

Nor can we learn the attitude of Helena in the struggle between her husband and her brother. The complete silence of Julian suggests that she remained moodily silent or hostile. Several months were spent in negotiation with Constantius. In December Julian celebrated, at Vienne, the fifth anniversary of his promotion, and wore the splendid diadem of an Emperor as he presided at the games and exercises. In the midst of the festivities Helena died. Zonaras, who also gives a ridiculous rumour that she had been divorced by Julian, says that she died in childbirth. We are tempted to think that the painful development of her unprosperous marriage weighed heavily on her, and her pregnancy had a premature and fatal delivery. Her remains were conveyed to Rome, and laid by those of her sister Constantina. We need not notice the charge of one of Constantius's officers that Julian had poisoned her, and paid the guilty physician with his mother's jewels. Julian, honestly, professes no grief at her death, and he never married again.

A third Empress makes a brief appearance at the time when Helena passes away. Passing from his long campaign on the Danube to the stricken regions of the East, Constantius had, toward the close of 360, married for the third time, at Antioch. Maxima Faustina, his third Empress, had little time to make an impression on history, if she were capable of it. As Constantius at length set out from Antioch, in the autumn of 361, to crush the mutiny in the West, as he affected to regard it, he contracted a fever, and died before he reached the European frontier. Faustina was left with the unborn wife of the future Emperor Gratian, and will come to our notice again. The Roman Empire was once more united under a strong, upright, and accomplished ruler. But Julian was now wedded to his ideals, and, as no woman shared his ascetic life and arduous labours, we must pass over the reforms, the campaigns, and the religious struggles of the next two years.

CHAPTER XIX

JUSTINA

THE splendour of Julian's reign was soon overcast.

In the summer of 363, as he was skilfully extricating his troops from a dangerous position in Persia, he was pierced with a javelin, and he expired, with dignity and serenity, amongst his saddened supporters. Amid the noisy intrigue for the succession that followed, the name of Jovian, a popular and handsome officer of no distinction, obtained the loudest support, and the mantle of the brilliant young Emperor was conferred on him.

How he secured the retreat of his troops by humiliating concessions to the Persians, and the Roman soldiers and Roman settlers sadly evacuated the provinces on which the blood of their fathers had been freely spent, and the emblem of the cross was borne again at the head of the legions, need not be told here. Not only is the wife of Jovian, Charito, no more than a name to us, but Jovian himself died before he reached the luxury of the capital.

His brief enjoyment of power had been adorned by neither courage nor temperance. Charito sank back into obscurity, with her infant son, and was years afterwards laid by the side of her husband in the Church of the Apostles at Byzantium.

The next reign will introduce us to the stronger and more prominent personality of the Empress Justina and other Empresses of some interest. The hum of intrigue had arisen again in the camp, and the struggle of Christian and pagan was resumed. The choice of the army at length fell once more on an officer whose chief distinction was that he had a large and handsome person, and had had an energetic father. Valentinian had been an officer in Julian's guards, and had one day, as he attended the Emperor at sacrifice, cuffed the priest for dropping some of the lustral water on his coat. Julian banished him for this violent desecration of his cult, but, though the more lively writers of the time promptly dispatch him to remote and contradictory regions, even Tillemont doubts if the sentence was carried out. It is probable that Julian had merely dismissed him from the body-guard, as we find him in the army at the time of Julian's death. With two other officers he was sent by Jovian to secure the allegiance of the troops in the West. One legion, devoted to the memory of Julian, rebelled, and Valentinian had to fly for his life. He returned to the East, and resumed his post in the army, as it trailed some miles in the rear of the retreating Emperor. And in the middle of February (364) he was amazed to learn that Jovian had died, after a too liberal supper, and he himself was called to the throne. He was compelled by the troops to share the power with his brother Valens, and, leaving the shorn Eastern provinces under the care of Valens, he went on to Milan to take possession of the Western throne.

Valeria Severa,[29] the first wife of Valentinian, is one of those shadowy Empresses whose form can hardly be discerned in the records of the time. She had borne him a son, the future Emperor Gratian, five years before, but she does not seem to have secured his affection, and we shall find her retiring in disgrace as soon as the beautiful Justina appears at court. Albia Dominica, the wife of Valens, is not more interesting, but an Empress whom we have dismissed in a former chapter at once reappears at Constantinople in opposition to her.

Before they separated Valens and Valentinian had fallen ill together, and, under the pretence that Julian's friends had attempted to poison them, they turned with some vindictiveness upon the pagan officials. The aged and respected Sallust firmly controlled the inquiry, and no blood was shed; but large numbers of Julian's officials were displaced--in many cases quite rightly, as Julian's zeal for paganism had had the same evil effect in encouraging hypocrisy as the zeal of other Emperors for

Christianity--and driven into sullen discontent. Further, Dominica's father, Petronius, a deformed and repulsive person, had risen to power with his daughter, and was grinding the faces of the citizens of the East with the most extortionate demands. A spark soon fell on this inflammable world. Procopius, a relative of Julian's, had published a very hazy claim to the Empire after Julian's death. He had hastily withdrawn and disowned it, but Valens sent men to apprehend him. Ingeniously escaping the soldiers, he fled to Constantinople, and seems there to have fallen into the hands of abler intriguers. Two legions were bought for him, and they made him Emperor. There was no purple mantle to be obtained, so they clothed him in a stagy tunic bespangled with gold, put purple shoes on his feet and a piece of purple cloth in his hand, and conducted him, amid the amazed and derisive spectators, to the Senate and the Palace.

His force grew so quickly that the weak and nervous Emperor of the East was disposed to yield him the throne, but his older officers urged him to resist. In the short struggle that followed we meet again the third wife, and widow, of Constantius. Faustina had been *enceinte* at the death of her husband, and she was living at Constantinople, with her four-year-old daughter, when Procopius made his romantic attempt on the throne. With some shrewdness he withdrew her from her retirement, and associated her with him in his claim. The legitimate dynasty seemed to be wresting the throne from usurpers when the widow and daughter of the son of Constantine appeared at the head of the troops. Even when they marched out to meet the forces of Valens, Faustina, in a litter, accompanied them. But the new hope of Faustina died away as quickly as it had been born. The soldiers were persuaded to return to their allegiance, and the power of Procopius swiftly melted away. Faustina sank again into obscurity, and the adventurous career of Constantia was postponed for some years.

Dominica returned to her position in the enervated and luxurious court, and the rest of her life offers little interest. The ecclesiastical historians describe her as egging her husband to persecute the Trinitarians, but we must read the charge with discretion. There is little positive trace of persecution. One day eighty Trinitarian priests came to plead their cause at the court, and Valens is said to have ordered them back to their ship. At some distance from port the vessel was found to be aflame, and the priests were burnt to death. The orthodox writers declare that the vessel was purposely fired, at the command of Valens, but it is impossible to adjust the conflicting statements of the rival schools of theology. Valens was an ardent Arian, but he upheld the principle of religious toleration, and confined theologians to the use of theological weapons. The only occasion on which he is known to have ordered or countenanced violent persecution was in the suppression of magic. In some obscure chamber of the capital a group of men resorted to this dark means of discovering who would be the successor of Valens.

Some say that a ring dangling from a mystic tripod spelt out the name on painted letters; some that grains of corn were placed on letters of the alphabet, and, when a cock was admitted to peck them, the order of the letters which it first attacked was noticed. In either case, the result was to give the letters Th E O D. It would be a remarkable forecast, if the story did not belong to a generation after the accession of Theodosius. However, the attempt became known, and a searching inquiry and savage persecution followed. The despicable trade of the informer was encouraged, whole libraries of valuable books were destroyed, and numbers of innocent philosophers and matrons were included in the bloody lists of the condemned.

The name of Dominica occurs only in one authentic connexion during the reign of Valens. The Emperor passed the winter of 372-3 at Caesarea in Cappadocia, where he encountered the stern and uncompromising champion of orthodoxy, St. Basil. Strong no less in his personal haughtiness--St. Jerome calls it pride--than in his glowing zeal for his Church, Basil emphatically refused to obey him, and was threatened with banishment. At once Dominica and her boy fell ill. Besides two daughters, she had had a son in 366, and this boy fell into a dangerous illness. It is said that Dominica learned in a dream that the illness was a divine punishment, but it is not impossible that her waking intelligence could arrive at that conclusion.

Basil was summoned to the palace once more.

Theodoret would have it that the bishop courteously breathed on the boy, and declared that he would recover if he received Trinitarian baptism. The earlier ecclesiastical writers, however, ascribe to him a firmer attitude. He asked Valens if the boy would receive orthodox baptism, and was told that he would not. "Let him meet whatever fate God wills then," said the bishop, quitting the palace. The boy was baptized by the Arians, and died during the following night. A power even greater than that of eunuchs, and more imperious than that of Emperors, was rapidly growing. When, some days later, one of the favourites of Valens, who had risen from the kitchen, attempted to intervene in a discussion between the bishop and the Emperor, Basil curtly told him to confine himself to sauces and not interfere in Church matters.

Five or six years later Valens perished in the war with the Goths, and Dominica passed to the fitting obscurity of private life. The one indication of spirit that is recorded of her is that, when the victorious Goths pressed on to Constantinople and invested it, she paid the citizens out of the public treasury to arm themselves against the barbarians. We turn from her vague and retiring personality to the more interesting figure of Justina, who had some years before begun to share the throne of Valentinian.

Valentinian was as fierce and choleric as his brother was timid. A tall and powerful man, with stern blue eyes, a brilliant complexion, and light hair, he enlisted and encouraged his native cruelty in the service of what he regarded as the interest of the State. The pagans he refused to persecute, and he did much to promote the higher culture of Rome, which was so closely connected with the pagan beliefs. But, like his brother, he fell with truculence upon all who could be brought under a comprehensive charge of magic and divination, and the blood of Italy flowed very freely. His hard, covetous, and brutal officers enriched themselves in the work of torture, spoliation, and execution, and--though the statement recalls rather the savagery of Nero or Domitian--we are assured by the contemporary Ammianus that he kept two monstrous bears in cages near his chamber, and fed them on human victims. The slightest offence might incur sentence of death. "You had better change his head,"

he is said to have ordered, in brutal playfulness, when some official desired to change to another province.

It is, perhaps, a circumstance of credit to Severa that she failed to retain the affection of Valentinian, though a less flattering reason is assigned by some of the authorities.

The truth is that, since Valentinian is described as most chaste and most Christian, the accession of Justina to his palace has caused the ecclesiastical historians no little perplexity. The Church was peremptorily opposed to divorce, and regarded as adultery a second marriage contracted while the first wife lived. Baronius conveniently removes Severa by death, but Ammianus

informs us that Severa was living long afterwards at the court of her son,[30] and the Alexandrian Chronicle expressly says that Gratian recalled his mother to court. Tillemont acknowledges this, and can only blush for the guilty connivance of the clergy of the period.

If we could believe the ecclesiastical historian Socrates, Valentinian avoided the sin of divorce and adultery by promulgating a decree to the effect that it was lawful to have two wives, and promptly marrying Justina in addition to Severa. Of such a law, however, we have no trace, and most writers follow the alternative theory of the authorities.

Aviana Justina was the widow of the usurper Magnentius, who had so dramatically stolen the throne of the worthless Constans, and had been crushed by Constantius in the year 353. She was a woman of great beauty, the daughter of a high provincial official, a spirited and ambitious young woman. She would be in her later twenties, at least, in 368, when she entered the suite of Severa in some capacity. She was soon associated so intimately with the Empress that they bathed together, and Severa made the fatal mistake of describing what Socrates curiously calls her "virginal beauty" to the sensual Valentinian. Before long it was announced that Severa was divorced, and Justina occupied her bed. A late authority throws a thin mantle over the action of Valentinian. Severa, he says, used her Imperial position to compel a lady of Milan to sell her an estate at a most inadequate price, and Valentinian was unable to endure her avarice. The vague description we have of Justina's dazzling beauty will, perhaps, suffice.

This remarkable conduct on the part of Valentinian and Justina is put in the year 368.[31] The succeeding years of war and religious controversy throw no light on the character of Justina, and we need not describe them. Valentinian died in 375. Some delegates of the barbarians had come, with deep humility, to implore his clemency for their invasion of his dominions, and Valentinian burst into one of his appalling storms of rage. So violent was his fury in addressing them that he burst a blood-vessel, and left the Western Empire to his son Gratian. Gratian had married in the previous year. His Empress was the daughter of Faustina, who had been borne in her mother's arms at the head of the troops of Procopius. In crossing the provinces to meet Gratian, Constantia had had a singular adventure. While she was dining at an inn, some twenty-six miles from Sirmium, the tribes broke across the Danube and occupied the village. There was just time for the Governor of Illyrium to snatch up the thirteen-year-old princess and make a dash for Sirmium. She married Gratian in 374, and became Empress of the West in the following year. But Flavia Maxima Constantia has left only the faint impress of her early adventures on the chronicles of the time, and the few years of her Imperial life have no interest for us. The next mention of her is that she died some time before her husband, who was assassinated in 383. He had married again, but his widow, Laeta, is a mere name in history. Theodosius gave a comfortable income to Laeta and her mother Pissamena, and they were distinguished for their charity in the later misfortunes of Rome.

When Valentinian had died in a fit of rage at Bregetio, Justina and her four-year-old boy, Valentinian the younger, were in the town of Murocincta, a hundred miles away.

Justina hastened to the camp, and it was presently announced that the army had decided to associate the boy with Gratian in the rule of the West. Gratian, the most temperate and promising of the Emperors of the period, published his consent. A refusal to acknowledge the boy, and an attempt to punish the intrigue by which Justina retained her power, would have involved a civil war, and the whole of his forces were now needed to stem the flood of barbarism that surged against the northern frontier of the Empire. The last days of Rome were fast approaching.

From the remote deserts of Asia a fierce and numerous people, the Huns, had entered Europe, and were sweeping the Goths and other Teutonic tribes southward.

Gratian appointed an Emperor of the East, whom we shall meet presently, in the place of Valens, and spent his strength in heroic efforts to defend the threatened frontier.

Justina returned with the boy-Emperor to Milan. As long as Gratian lived, Justina was restricted to the life of the palace, but in 383 the throne was usurped by Maximus, and Gratian was murdered by one of his emissaries. Gibbon generously traces the general dissatisfaction out of which this revolt emerged to a deterioration of the character of Gratian. This deterioration cannot be questioned, but one particular outcome of it, the active persecution of the pagans, was probably his most fatal error. Milan was now dominated by the imperious and zealous St. Ambrose, and the two young Emperors were expressly under his control. At the suggestion of Ambrose, Gratian abandoned Valentinian's policy of toleration. He rejected the title of Pontifex Maximus, ordered the removal of the statue of Victory from the Roman Senate, and confiscated the estates of the temples. He even admitted the abusive epithet "pagans" (or "villagers"), which the more forward Christians were beginning to use, in his official decrees.[32] This must have inflamed the general discontent, and the army of Maximus marched peacefully over Gaul, and occupied the Empire as far as the Alps. The Emperor of the East, Theodosius, consented that Britain, Gaul, and Spain should remain under the rule of Maximus, and Justina continued to rule the curtailed dominions of her son.

It was now discovered that Justina was an Arian. Whether she had concealed her beliefs during the life of Valentinian, or had been recently won to the sect, it is impossible to say; but Ambrose now found that he had a stubborn opponent of his religious ambition. The trouble culminated in 385, when scenes were witnessed that effectively impress on us the change that had come over the Roman Empire. Justina ordered that one of the Christian churches of the city should be put at the disposal of the Arian clergy. Ambrose sternly refused, and, when he was summoned to the palace, and a sentence of banishment was apprehended, the people flocked to the palace and intimidated the Empress and her counsellors.

A little later, the Gothic (Arian) soldiers were sent to occupy the church, and orders were given that it should be prepared for the Empress's devotions. A renewal of the riot, and the showering of the vilest epithets upon the person of the Empress, forced her to retire once more.

In the following year, 386, she passed sentence of exile on the bishop, and her spirit was expended in a final struggle. For the first time in the history of Rome--a true index of its profound demoralization--the troops were prevented by the people from carrying out an Imperial decree. Ambrose was guarded day and night by thousands of his followers. The chief church and the episcopal house were fortified as if for a siege, and the troops of "Jezebel"

had to stand inactive before a mob of citizens. On the advice of Theodosius, Justina refrained from any further attempt. Indeed, her attention was soon violently withdrawn to a very different danger.

The ambition of Maximus had once more outrun its bounds, and he coveted the remaining provinces of Valentinian.

Justina's conduct betrays that her ability was inferior to her spirit. Duped by the treacherous diplomacy of Maximus, she was suddenly informed that the hostile forces of Maximus were close to Milan, and she fled hastily to the coast. At Aquileia she and her son took ship for the East. The soldiers of Maximus followed them on swift galleys, but they rounded the south of Greece in safety, and landed at Thessalonica. Her task now was to induce Theodosius to espouse their cause, and it proved to be one of nearer proportion to her talent.

Her pressing appeals to Theodosius for aid were parried or unheeded for some time. If we may believe Theodoret, the only reply which she received was a painful assurance that the heresy she entertained, and in which she was educating her son, was a sufficient cause of all the evils that had come upon them. She was directed to await a visit from Theodosius at Thessalonica, and the visit was much delayed. Historians usually depict the Emperor as held in suspense by a painful dilemma. Not only would it be a serious thing for the Empire, surrounded as it was with peril, to engage the forces of the East and the West in an exhausting civil war, but Theodosius would, in such a war, be attacking an orthodox Catholic in the interest of a fanatical Arian and enemy of the Church; and Theodosius was a most zealous Trinitarian. The difficulty must have occurred to him, and it would not be fantastical to assume that there had been some correspondence between the prelates of the East and the prelates of the West, to ensure that the point did not escape him.

The pagan Zosimus has a different theory of the delay of Theodosius. The character of that Emperor was, he says, a singular union of contradictions. He could blaze with the fury of a Valentinian, or bend his head meekly for the blessing of a bishop; he could lead the troops through a campaign with the most signal dexterity, energy, and success, and then relax into the most ignoble indolence; he could embrace the rigour of a soldier's life without the least effort to soften it, and then resign himself to the most voluptuous day-dreams in his Imperial palace. Justina, Zosimus says, was so unfortunate as to need his aid during one of his periods of luxury and "insane pursuit of pleasure." He resented the effort to awaken him from it.

His deep indebtedness to Gratian, however, who had conferred the Empire on him, at length forced him to cross the Greek sea, and visit Justina at Thessalonica. From the time of that visit his pulse was quickened, and he began a vigorous preparation for war with Maximus. Justina had with her at Thessalonica, not only the insipid boy Valentinian, but a pretty young daughter, Galla, and Theodosius had fallen in love with her. Justina promptly perceived, and artfully used, her opportunity, and it was arranged that the pretty princess should be his reward for restoring the Western Empire to Valentinian and his mother.

AELIA FLACCILLA

HONORIA

ENLARGED FROM COINS IN THE BRITISH MUSEUM

Theodosius, who is incomparably the leading ruler of the fourth century, had come from the same part of Spain as Trajan, to whom some of the writers of the time compare him--with no little flattery. His father, Count Theodosius, had been an able commander and a just administrator, but had been unjustly disgraced and executed owing to some obscure jealousy. Later writers, thinking of the magical Th E O D of Antioch, believed that his name led to his undoing. The younger Theodosius, a cultivated and skilful officer, retired to his estates in Spain, from which he was drawn by Gratian, and presently clothed with the purple. He had, in 376 or 377, married a Spanish lady, AElia Flaccilla, who is believed, on slender grounds, to have been the daughter of the consul Antonius.

Their son Arcadius, the future Emperor, was born during the retirement in Spain. A daughter, Pulcheria, was born in Spain, while Theodosius was on campaign. Then Flaccilla found herself transferred from the quiet Spanish estate to the pomp of Constantinople, and the second son, Honorius, was born in the purple.

Although Flaccilla is canonized in the Greek Church, it does not appear that she had a marked individuality.

She is one of the crowd of fourth-century Empresses who live in the chronicles only as generous benefactors of the Church. Theodosius was the first Emperor to persecute his pagan subjects on the ground of religion, and his successive decrees quickly changed the religious aspect of the East. His modern biographers, Ifland and Guldenpenning ("Der Kaiser Theodosius"), lay much of the blame for these violent measures on Flaccilla, but they point out that the coercive legislation begins just after Theodosius came under the influence of Bishop Acholius during a severe illness, and that his efforts to crush paganism by violence relaxed with his advance in age and experience.

All that we learn of Flaccilla is that she was generous to the Church and the poor, and that she occasionally curbed the fiery and vindictive temper of Theodosius. She seems to have died in the year 385, and the Greek ritual celebrates her memory on September 14th.

Theodosius was, therefore, a middle-aged widower--his biographers put his birth in 346--when, in the autumn of 387, Justina presented her daughter Galla to him. Dr.

Ifland admits that the young girl probably turned the hesitating scale of his judgment. He returned to Constantinople, and made energetic preparations for war. A

two months' campaign in the following summer (388) completely destroyed the forces of Maximus, and the full Empire of the West was restored to Valentinian. But Justina had little personal profit by the victory. Zosimus tells us that she "supplied the deficiencies of her son as well as a woman can" after the return to Milan, while Sozomen declared that she died before the return. The point is obscure, but the evidence suggests, on the whole, that she returned to Milan. It was, however, to a different Milan from that she had quitted. Theodosius accompanied them, and the strong, earnest character of Ambrose made a deep impression on him. Valentinian was "converted" to the true creed, and the policy of persecution was introduced into the Western world. Justina must have remained a powerless and embittered spectator of the ascendancy of Ambrose. So great did it become that the coldest decisions of the Emperor were reversed by him, and his transgressions were ignominiously punished. The news came

to Milan that the monks and populace of a small town in Persia had burned the synagogue of the Jews, and that the prefect had ordered them to rebuild the synagogue and restore its property. Theodosius confirmed the just sentence, but Ambrose assailed him so strongly, in letter and sermon, that he was obliged to give complete immunity to the offenders; and the wave of violence--the burning of temples and synagogues, and the despoiling and slaying of unbelievers and heretics of all shades--continued to roll destructively over the East. The more impressive incident of Theodosius, the greatest ruler of his time, standing in the humble attitude of a penitent in the church at Milan is well known. The people of Thessalonica, stung by the heavy taxation which the extravagant rule of Theodosius imposed on the East, and the quartering of barbaric troops on them, took some occasion to riot, and slew the representatives of the Emperor. In a fit of passion Theodosius turned his troops upon the defenceless people, whom he had treacherously invited to the Circus, and a horrible and unexampled massacre was perpetrated. Ambrose nobly insisted that the Emperor must expiate his crime like the humblest member of his flock. The world was entering upon a new era.

How much of these proceedings Justina lived to see it is impossible to determine. She died some time between 388 and 391; the obscurity of her death is a sufficient proof of her powerlessness in her last years. Valentinian, whose weakness was hardly compensated by the propriety of his conduct and his docility to St. Ambrose, was instructed in the elements of government by the older Emperor, who remained three years in Italy, to the lasting grief of its pagan citizens. He visited Rome, where the majority of the leading citizens still clung to an idealized version of the old cult, and appealed to the Senate to abandon the dying gods. No answer was made to his appeal, and he resorted to the growing practice of coercive legislation. In 391 he returned to Constantinople.

Galla had married Theodosius soon after the destruction of Maximus. The Chronicle of Marcellinus puts the marriage in 386; Zosimus, more plausibly, implies that it took place in 387 or 388. From a curious statement in the Chronicle of Marcellinus it seems that she was sent to live in the palace at Constantinople while Theodosius remained in Italy. The statement is that the elder son of the Emperor, Arcadius, a boy of thirteen years, drove her out of the palace. Commentators are loath to believe that so young a prince could do this, but it is not in the least impossible, and the authority is respectable. We shall see that Arcadius was a peevish and worthless prince, indolently guided by eunuchs and servants, and capable of very cruel decisions. Theodosius had departed from the finer Imperial tradition of appointing a grave and distinguished scholar as the tutor of his sons, and had committed them to the care of a Roman deacon, Arsenius, who had a repute for piety. We can hardly regard the authority of a late Greek writer (Metaphrastes) as weighty enough to commend the statement that Arcadius set his servants to take the life of Arsenius for whipping him, but the unhappy events of the next chapter will show that the only result of this kind of education was to leave the character unformed, and throw the stress on external observances.

In 391 Theodosius returned to Constantinople, and Galla entered upon her brief Imperial career. Whether or no we accept the biased picture which Zosimus offers us of the Eastern court, it is clear that it sustained a soft and excessive luxury at the cost of the enfeebled Empire.

Large numbers of eunuchs found employment, and, with the genius of their class, intrigued for favour in the sleeping quarters, and in the service of the Empress and the Imperial children. The kitchen employed a regiment of ministers to the heavy and voluptuous table; the circus and theatre supported vast numbers of mimes, dancers, and charioteers.

Besides this large army of ministers to the Imperial pleasure, a second army of idle and avaricious place-seekers beset the palace, and extorted a generous revenue from the offices which were created for them in the army and the administration. It is even said that such offices were openly sold in the public places and in the palace of Constantinople. Strenuous as Theodosius was in the field, he was not strong enough to sustain the burden of peace, and he unconsciously prepared the Empire for the avalanche that was soon to be cast upon it.

But the drowsy indulgence of Theodosius was soon startled once more by a call to arms from the West. In the spring of 392 Valentinian was slain, or in despair slew himself, and a Frankish commander had put his purple robe upon the shoulders of a Roman rhetorician. The young Emperor had been so overshadowed by the power of his general that he had attempted to dismiss him, and had then been found dead with a cord round his neck.

Theodosius again hesitated to exchange the softness of his palace for the rigours of a campaign. Galla "filled the palace with her lamentations," but Theodosius sent away the ambassadors of the usurper with pleasant words and presents, and continued for nearly two years to resist the appeals of his young Empress. It was not until the summer of 394 that he led out his legions for the punishment of the murderer, as Argobastes was believed to be.

Galla did not live to see her brother avenged. She died in childbirth just as the army was about to start, and Theodosius is said to have mourned for her one day and then started for Italy.

The issue does not now concern us. We pass on to a fresh generation, a new and more interesting group of Empresses and princesses. Suffice it to say that, partly by valour, partly by accident and treachery, the forces of Argobastes were destroyed, and the empurpled rhetorician was slain. The younger son of the Emperor, Honorius, was summoned from the East, and placed upon the throne of the West. Arcadius remained in feeble charge of the throne of Constantinople. And within a few months the powerful Emperor sank into the grave, and the Empire entered upon the unhappy reigns of Arcadius and Honorius.

CHAPTER XX

THE ROMANCE OF EUDOXIA AND EUDOCIA

WITH the Imperial ladies of the courts of Arcadius and Honorius we enter upon the final act in the tragedy of the fall of Rome. The sun is sinking rapidly to the Western horizon; the long shadows trail across the record of events; the chill of evening contracts the life of the historic Empire. The only aspect of that tragedy that concerns us is a consideration of the part that women played in the gradual enfeeblement of the Roman Empire. While taking full account of the various causes assigned by historians, it may be said that the fall of Rome was due to a coincidence. The invasion of Europe by the fierce Huns had pressed the Germanic tribes against the Roman frontier just at the time when the Empire was particularly feeble. That it was inwardly outworn and doomed--that the organization of a State has an appointed term of decay, like the frame of an individual--may be confidently challenged. Egypt maintained its vigour for close on 8,000 years; Babylon for nearly 6,000.

The only question we may touch here is whether the personality of the later Empresses counted for anything, either for good or evil, in this enfeeblement of the Empire; and the answer is clear that, with one or two exceptions, they counted for neither. They had no deep or large influence on the life of the Empire, even through their husbands. The Roman ideal of womanhood was changing once more. As in the early days, they were diverted from interest in public affairs, except in so far as the cause of the Church called for their interference. We must not conceive them as powerless witnesses of the gradual dissolution of the Empire. No one, man or woman, saw that the Empire was dissolving, or dreamed of its fall, until it lay in ruins under the feet of the northern tribes.

None reflected that, since Constantine had assumed the purple, thirteen Emperors out of twenty had been either executed or murdered; that the blood of able officers or servants had generally been mingled with that of the fallen ruler; and that hundreds of thousands of soldiers had been wasted in civil war. None reflected that, while they were distracted with religious quarrels, a formidable avalanche was gathering on the hills; or that, while the courts absorbed enormous sums in Oriental display, the fiscal machinery of the State was running down. In any case, it was no longer the place of women to notice these things. Their duties were to rear the Imperial family, wear pretty robes of cloth of gold, and build churches. The age of Livia, Agrippina, or Plotina, was over.

These reflections will be enforced by the lives of the interesting Empresses whom we have next to consider.

The new Emperors were unmarried youths at the time when their father died. Arcadius, a little, dark, unpleasant-looking youth, whose laziness appeared in his dull, lustre-less eyes, was in his eighteenth year. Honorius was a boy of eleven, and as, during a reign of twenty-eight years, he never rose above the character or intelligence of a boy, and his two Empresses were timid young girls, we must dismiss them in a page; though that page must contain an event that sent a thrill of excitement through civilization--the fall of the city of Rome. So little had our Imperial characters to do with it that a later age amused itself by saying that, when Honorius was told that "Rome was taken," he wept for the supposed loss of his favourite fowl, which bore that name.

The real master of the Western world, over which young Honorius had nominal sway, was a powerful and gifted commander, Stilicho, of Vandal extraction. He had married Serena, the beautiful niece of Theodosius, and he led the armies and governed the Western Empire until his death. In 398, in his thirteenth year, Honorius was directed to wed Maria, the elder daughter of Stilicho. It was said that Theodosius had desired the union. Serena, at all events, desired it, and, although her daughter was yet immature, the wedding took place at Milan in 398. All that we have to say of her is that she died some time within the next ten years--probably, as Tillemont calculates, in the year 404. Her body was embalmed and buried in a Christian church at Rome, where the poor crumbling frame, laden with gold, was discovered in 1544.

In the year 408 Honorius married his deceased wife's sister, Thermantia. Tillemont very properly laments that he finds no record of any protest on the part of the Bishop of Rome--who probably celebrated it--against this irregular marriage, but the modern reader will be more seriously concerned to hear the argument with which Serena urged it upon her reluctant husband. Maria, she said, had died a virgin. Before entrusting her immature child to the bed of Honorius, she had had some obscure operation performed on her, which would guard her virginity. Certainly, Maria had had no children. Thermantia was equally unprepared for marriage, Zosimus says, and the operation was repeated. It was a superfluous sacrifice to the ambition of Serena, because Stilicho fell, in a palace intrigue, a few months later, and the little maid was restored to her mother.

Such was the short and melancholy story of the Empresses Maria and AEmilia Materna Thermantia, as an inscription calls the younger. Their monument was terrible. Within a few months the avalanche of the Gothic army descended from the Alps and devastated Italy; and Serena was, with the consent of her cousin Placidia, the Emperor's sister, strangled by the Senate on the light, and probably false, charge of communicating with the enemy.

Zosimus, at least, says that she was innocent; but he is not surprised at her fate, as she had one day appropriated a jewelled ornament from the statue of one of his goddesses.

Within two years Rome was sacked by the Goths, and Placidia was carried off by them.

We turn to the East, to follow the less tragic, but hardly less interesting, fortunes of Eudoxia and Eudocia. In the East, as in the West, Theodosius had left a powerful minister to guide the hands of his young and unpromising son. But the eastern minister, Rufinus, had not the manly qualities of Stilicho. He had entered the palace by craft, not by military exploits, and had easily dissembled his vices from the too indulgent eye of Theodosius. When that Emperor died, he cast aside the cloak, and pursued his native avarice, and exercised his cruelty, without restraint. By fines, taxes, despoilments, and the unscrupulous ruin of his opponents, the hated Gaul amassed wealth and power, and ruled like an autocrat. He had a daughter of marriageable age, and Arcadius seemed to listen in compliant mood when he proposed that she should become his Empress. The task of destroying an opponent took him for a time to Antioch, and he returned to hear that the Emperor was preparing for marriage. He awaited the appointed day with eagerness. At length the hymeneal procession set out from the palace, and the people gathered to witness its passage to the house of Rufinus, a superb villa in one of the suburbs. To the intense surprise of all, it stopped at a house in the city, and the blushing and beautiful daughter of a Frankish chief was announced to be the choice of the Emperor.

While Rufinus was pursuing his vengeance at Antioch, the eunuchs of the palace had conspired to defeat his plan and undermine his power. The chief of them was Eutropius, a slave by birth, castrated immediately after birth that he might bring a bigger price, and rising in time from the occupation of hair-dresser to the daughter of General Arintheus to the position of high chamberlain at the palace. Such were the rulers of Emperors in the fourth century. Eutropius knew that Arcadius had no attraction to the daughter of Rufinus, and chafed under the authority of her burly father. He cast about for a prettier companion, and soon had the affection of Arcadius safely engaged. The temporary absence of Rufinus gave them an opportunity, and Constantinople was enlivened by the rare spectacle of an Imperial marriage, and the still rarer spectacle of the defeat of Rufinus.

Eudoxia--such is the Greek name under which the new Empress is presented to us--was the beautiful daughter of Bauto, chief of the Franks. Historians, politely accepting the assurance of some of the writers of the time, say that she was being "educated" at Constantinople, her father having died in the service of the Eastern army. It is, perhaps, a pity to disturb the plausible phrase, but the duty of a biographer is stern. The house in the city from which she was taken to wed the Emperor was occupied by two young men of wealth. They were the sons of the commander Promotus, who had been one of the first victims of Rufinus. One of these young men, Zosimus says, "had a beautiful maid" in the house. We will not inquire too closely. The stern ideals of the Germanic tribes had relaxed as they came into closer contact with civilization, and it became common for them to lend or sell their daughters to the Romans. We remember the adventure of Pipera a century before. Eutropius submitted an adequate picture of the girl to Arcadius, whose pulse was quickened, and the son of Promotus easily parted with his tender pupil when he learned that it was for the purpose of discomfiting the destroyer of his father.

Eudoxia had no less spirit than beauty of person, and she would watch with interest the duel between the wily eunuch and the powerful Gaul. Arcadius, "whose feeble and stupid goodness," says Tillemont candidly, "brought frightful evils on Church and State," was a pawn in the game. But the big, wealthy, powerful Gaul now found a sterner opponent in Stilicho, of the Western Empire, and within a year his head was separated from his body, and his wife and daughter were permitted to remain alive at Jerusalem. Eutropius and Eudoxia now "led Arcadius like a dumb beast," in the words of Zosimus, and sucked the resources of the Empire. The people of Constantinople gained nothing by the revolution. They had carried in triumph the grisly, extortionate hand of Rufinus through the streets of the city, but the supple hand of the eunuch proved as formidable. He surrounded himself with spies and informers, filled the prisons with men whose property he desired for himself or his friends, scattered statues of himself through the city, and assumed every title of honour short of that of Augustus. He would press his deformed person and painted face into the armour of a man, to review the troops, and would harangue the Senate with a feeble imitation of the authority of a statesman. While his exactions and the luxury of the court enfeebled the Empire of the East, he alienated the power of the West, and had Stilicho branded as a public enemy. And the Goths and Huns crept nearer.

Arcadius, lazily riding in his gold-plated chariot, studded with large gems, in robes of silk embroidered with golden dragons, or playing the monarch on a throne of solid gold, with a crowd of adoring eunuchs before him, had no more appreciation than a peasant of a Cappadocian village of the true situation of the Empire. Eudoxia, beautiful, haughty, spoiled, revelling in the luxury of the palace, generous to the Church and the poor, floated soothingly with the stream. She lived the languid life of an Oriental princess, within the confines of the palace, and was rarely seen even by the greater part of the palace servants. The only occasion when the populace saw her quit the marble city, which the palace of Constantine had become, was when, in 398, she walked humbly, with downcast eyes, but clothed in purple silk, with a glittering diadem on her head, by the side of St. Chrysostom, as he transferred certain relics of the saints. Chrysostom would find her in a different temper in a few years.

The arrogance of Eutropius at last passed all bounds, and he ventured in the year 400 to threaten to expel Eudoxia from the palace. Whether she knew it or no, the time was ripe for the destruction of the repulsive minister. The people groaned under his terrible exactions, his infamous legislation, and his bloody tyranny; the leaders of the troops were prepared to sacrifice him.

Eudoxia took her baby girls, Pulcheria and Arcadia, in her arms, and fled in tears to the Emperor. Arcadius, "becoming an Emperor for a moment," says Philostorgius, signed the sentence of his favourite, and the eunuch soon found people and soldiers pressing, like wolves, for his destruction. He took refuge in a church, where Chrysostom protected him from the fiery crowd, but quitted it after a time, apparently on the oath of either Eudoxia or Arcadius that his life would be spared. He was exiled, recalled, tried, and--oath or no oath--put to death by the public executioner.

Eudoxia's title of *nobilissima* ("most noble") had been elevated to that of *Augusta* at the beginning of the year 400, and her second daughter was born in April of the same year.[33] She was now complete mistress of Arcadius and the Empire, and she published her dignity with such extravagance that the Western court sent an angry protest

that, in causing her statues to be borne through the provinces, she had exceeded the privileges of her sex. In the following year she completed her ascendancy by giving birth to a boy, Theodosius II, and seemed to have a prospect of a long and luxurious, if useless, reign. But she had meantime quarrelled with Chrysostom, and she was to pass through a period of humiliation to a premature grave.

In 398 Eutropius had transferred the austere and eloquent Chrysostom from his presbytery in Antioch to the archiepiscopal palace at Constantinople. The stern monk--as

John of the Golden Mouth always remained at heart--was horrified from the first at the vice and luxury of the Christians of the Imperial city, and even of their clergy, but he allowed two years to elapse before he began his fiery campaign against the sins of the laity.[34] He applied himself first to the reform of the priests and the control of the monks. With that we have no concern.[35] It is enough to say that the clergy bitterly resented his reforms, and were ready to co-operate with Eudoxia in an effort to get rid of him. In 400 he began to attack the easy ways of the laity more sternly, and it is probable that some feeling was created between him and the Empress over the massacre of the Gothic Arian soldiers, which took place in that year.

Their commander Gainas had rebelled, and Arcadius had virtually surrendered to him. He marched his troops to the city, obtained the use of a church for them, and allowed them to roam about, to the irritation of the people; until at last the people rose and slew seven thousand of the heretics.

It seems that Eudoxia was alienated from Chrysostom, who had resented the grant of a church, from that time.

When, in the following year, St. Porphyry of Gaza came to the capital to obtain an Imperial order to destroy the pagan temples of his town,

Chrysostom declined to introduce him at court, and referred him to the eunuch Amantius. The sequel is not without interest in a study of the Empress.

The holy man was presented to Eudoxia, and promised that she should bear a boy if she would secure the destruction of paganism in Gaza. She promised to do so, but Arcadius, who seems to have resented religious wrangles, refused to grant permission. Then the boy was born, and Eudoxia felt an obligation to secure Porphyry's request.

She instructed him to draw up a formal petition, and present it to the baby-Caesar as he was carried from the baptismal font. The noble who carried the baby was then instructed how he was to behave, and a little comedy was arranged.

Porphyry presented his paper to the infant Caesar. The noble read a little of it to the baby in a low voice, so that Arcadius should not hear, and then bobbed the child's head as a sign of assent. Arcadius wearily overlooked the trick, eight beautiful temples were burned at Gaza, and Eudoxia supplied the funds for building a large church on their ruins. Tillemont, whose admiring course through the fourth century is much tempered by groans, complains that "this kind of piety favours only the demons."

Chrysostom then went on to denounce, in unmeasured language, the vicious and luxurious ways of the wealthy women, especially widows, of his church. He had diverted the coins of the laity from the army of monks, deprived the clergy of their mistresses, and declared that the great majority of the bishops of his province were hopelessly corrupt. With the aid of his rival, the Bishop of Alexandria, they conspired against him, and they reached the ear of the Empress through the courtly and comfortable bishop, Severian. The other ear of the Empress was now assailed by the wealthy widows who smarted under the preacher's fierce lash. Such fine ladies as Marsa and Castricia would not be likely to sit under the Socialistic oratory of the archbishop, but shorthand (*notatio*) was as commonly used in those days as in our own, and he could thus irritate the eye of the rich as well as gladden the ear of the poor.

They brooded darkly over his impersonal strictures, and no doubt detected occasional references to the luxurious Empress in them. In fine, Archbishop Theophilus was summoned from Alexandria; the bishops of the province eagerly drew up and passed a lengthy indictment of their superior; and, before the orthodox population could gather what was happening, their orator was on the way to exile.

EUDOXIA

PULCHERIA

ENLARGED FROM COINS IN THE BRITISH MUSEUM

But the triumph of Eudoxia was as brief as that of Justina. The people rose in fury, and, after the slaughter of seven thousand trained soldiers, made a light matter of the monks and sailors of Theophilus. When, in addition, an earthquake shook the province, Eudoxia prudently yielded to the human pressure, under the decent pretext of obeying the divine will. Chrysostom returned to his church, and the sight of the gay fleet that set out to meet him, the flaring illumination of the shores, the frenzied rejoicing of the returning procession, must have filled the palace on the heights with bitterness. Such a truce could be observed with cold discretion by neither party, and it was not long before the struggle was renewed.

In honour of the birth of the third daughter of the Empress, Marina, a silver statue of her was erected, on a column of porphyry, at the door of the Senate. The Prefect of the city commemorated the event with games or other rejoicings in the square before the statue, and they were naturally accompanied by profane, if not licentious, gaiety. Straight opposite, across the square, was the door of Chrysostom's church, and the devout regarded this demonstration as an outrage on religion. Chrysostom's sermons become more explicit. In a later age a sermon was published under his name, in which the people--or the readers--were reminded of the infamous Herodias clamouring for the head of John. The sermon is generally regarded as spurious, but we have the weighty authority of Socrates for the fact that the extempore preacher did utter the fatal name of Herodias. The conflict ended with the exile of the archbishop (June 404), but on the following night his church was found to be in flames, and the fire spread to, and almost destroyed, the Senate-house, a building adorned with the most exquisite marbles and works of art.

The condition of Constantinople, the anxiety of Eudoxia, during the following months, may be imagined. It is enough to know that Eudoxia met a painful death, through miscarriage, in the month of September of the same year (404). I will not reproduce the horrible details that a more orthodox age discovered in connexion with her death.[36] If Chrysostom spoke from "a bitter disillusion," as Dr. Puech holds, Eudoxia had not less cause to be embittered. Even her religious zeal had led her into the most painful experiences. For the State, in which she had high power, she did nothing. The vultures gathered on the hills, while the court absorbed its little soul in voluptuous pomp, and the people fought each other over creeds. We may dissent from the hard verdict of Gibbon, that Eudoxia indulged her passions while the Empire decayed, and we must regard as too frivolous for consideration the suspicion of unchastity which he reproduces; but we must grant that, where Eudoxia's action was not selfish, it was generally useless, and frequently mischievous.

We have carried the slender story of the Empresses in the West as far as the year 410, and we shall find no other Empress there until 421. We may, therefore, continue the record of the East, and consider the romantic story of Eudocia, before we proceed to the last scene in the Empire of the West.

After an ignoble reign of thirteen years the elder son of Theodosius died in his bed in the year 408. His only son, Theodosius II, was clothed with the purple, in his sixth year, and a prudent and experienced minister controlled the State for the next seven years. In 415 Pulcheria, the elder sister of Theodosius, was named Augusta, and gradually assumed the guardianship of her brother and the control of the State. She was as yet only in her sixteenth year, and Theodosius was only two years younger, but her cold, decisive temper compensated in some measure for the strength which Theodosius wholly lacked, and she held the reins of the Empire. Deeply religious, she took herself, and induced her younger sisters to take, a vow of chastity, which was written in gold and diamonds on the wall of the public church. The palace offered the singular spectacle of a nunnery within a luxurious court. Only pious eunuchs and women were allowed to approach the Imperial virgins, in whose sober apartments no music was ever heard save that of the psalm and sacred song; while the weakly youth was educated in the pomp that befits a king, as well as the propriety that adorns a Christian. He learned both lessons with success; but we cannot avoid a suspicion that less earnest and assiduous efforts were made to fit him for the task of taking in his own hands the levers of the heavy machinery of the State. It is proper to add, however, that, partly from circumstances, partly from the prudence and care of Pulcheria, that machinery ran with unaccustomed ease, and the Empire enjoyed a span of peace and prosperity.

At length the anxious question of the Imperial marriage arose, and the virginal Pulcheria confronted it with her usual coolness and decision. The task was simplified, in a sense, by Theodosius. He declared that he would marry only a young lady of exceptional bodily charm, and would pay no attention to wealth or dignity. It may have occurred to Pulcheria that an Empress thus elevated would be less likely to dispute her power than some woman who had been born into the world of large action. She began her search, with the aid of Paulinus, a youth who had been educated with Theodosius and was his intimate friend.

One day, at this period, a young Athenian girl was brought into her presence with a petition. She was of the fairest Athenian type; a supple and graceful young woman, with skin of a snowy complexion, large intelligent eyes, and a beautiful head of golden hair. Further, she pleaded her cause, in perfect Greek, with a surprising restraint, eloquence, and art. She was Athenais, the daughter of an Athenian teacher. He had cultivated her mind and her beauty with all the resources of his art, and had, at his death, left her only a hundred pieces of gold, on the pretext that she was wealthy enough in her advantages. She begged her brothers to share the inheritance more justly, but they refused. She had therefore come with a relative to the house of an aunt at Constantinople, and asked for a just distribution of her father's money. Pulcheria's interest was, not in the case, but in the girl. She took the aunt aside, and prudently inquired if the girl was a maid and a Christian. Athenais was declared to be a virgin, though a pagan; but the defect was one that could easily be removed.

Pulcheria joyfully told her brother that she had found the beauty he desired, and described her. They arranged a second visit, during which Theodosius and Paulinus should inspect the maiden from behind a curtain. In a short time Athenais had changed her name into AElia Eudocia, changed her religion into that of Christ, and changed her condition into that of wife of the Emperor.

She was married on June 7th, 421, in, it is believed, the twentieth year of her age. There was consternation in the home she had quitted at Athens, and her brothers hid themselves in the provinces. Eudocia had them sought and conducted to Constantinople. There they learned to their surprise that she thought herself indebted to their conduct for her fortune, and they were richly rewarded.

From these pleasant girlish traits we pass to the inevitable struggle with Pulcheria. Theodosius remained

an Imperial nonentity. He could hunt, paint, and carve, but public business so bored him that he signed documents without reading them. One day Pulcheria put a parchment before him, and he, as usual, blindly appended his name. Shortly afterwards he summoned Eudocia, and was told that she was now the slave of Pulcheria, and awaited *her* orders. The document he had signed was a deed of sale of his wife, but it does not appear that the little stratagem made much impression on him.

Pulcheria still held the reins. Eudocia had her first child at the end of 422, and was, in the following January, entitled Augusta. The court had a visit, too, from the Empress of the West, Galla Placidia, and her daughter, and large matters were discussed. In 433 we may, perhaps, trace some influence of Eudocia on legislation. An edict imposing the death-sentence on the remaining pagans may be confidently ascribed to Pulcheria; but an edict reforming and enlarging the higher schools of Constantinople seems rather to remind us of the Athenian scholar's daughter. She occupied much of her leisure in writing historical and religious poetry, and the little that survives of it has been recently edited by Ludwich.

It is correct in form and devoid of inspiration.

The years passed tranquilly until 437, when we begin to suspect that there is friction with Pulcheria. Few things had happened, beyond the echo of the stormy movements of the West, and the disquieting advance of the Huns, to disturb the life of the court. One year (434) had, indeed, brought a strange thrill into the Imperial nunnery. A princess of the Western Empire, Honoria, came to Constantinople, *enceinte* by her own steward.

But the hard lot of Honoria, and the romantic devices by which she sought to enliven it, will occupy us later.

Pulcheria promptly enclosed the fiery young princess in a convent, and the scandal would be mentioned only in whispers. Three years later (437) the Western Emperor, Valentinian III, came to Constantinople, and led away Eudocia's beautiful daughter, Licinia Eudoxia, to share his trembling throne. The next detail is that, in 439, Eudocia made a lengthy pilgrimage to Palestine, and there can be little doubt that her absence from the palace for a year--which is unconvincingly connected by Gibbon with the marriage of her daughter, two years before--was due, in part or entirely, to some quarrel with either Theodosius or Pulcheria, most probably the latter.

At Antioch, on the journey, Eudocia enjoyed the prestige of her solitary and independent dignity. From a golden throne she delivered a studied oration to the Senate, and the tumultuous applause and voting of statues to her must have greatly increased her self-consciousness.

The shower of gold she rained upon the churches and monasteries of Palestine, and indeed all along her route, elicited a no less stimulating demonstration. She returned to Constantinople, apparently about the end of 439, with a larger sense of her importance, and with such priceless relics as the arm of St. Stephen and the authentic picture of Mary which Luke the Physician had painted. It is only at a much later date that Greek writers add to her luggage a phial of the Virgin's milk, some underclothing of the infant Christ, and similar treasures.

The pilgrimage was the turning-point in the career of Eudocia. So far her life had been one of splendid and powerless prestige; it now rapidly darkens with intrigue, is overshadowed by tragedy and suspicion, and soon ends in a virtual exile. We are sufficiently acquainted with the writers of the time to expect that they will throw very little light on this fresh Imperial tragedy, but, using the later and less weighty Greek writers with discretion, we may obtain a fairly confident idea of its main features.

Two facts are related by writers of the time, and are beyond question. In the year following Eudocia's return, her friend, and the intimate friend of the Emperor, the charming and accomplished Paulinus, was exiled and put to death without public trial. The second fact is that, a few years later, Eudocia left the palace for ever, to spend the remainder of her life at Jerusalem.

The later Byzantine writers give a rounded story of these events, and, on the whole, one is disposed to think that in this case they are revealing the suppressed truth.

Theophanes (in his "Chronographia") says that a eunuch named Chrysaphius rose into favour, and urged Eudocia to secure the dismissal of Pulcheria. They persuade Theodosius that, since Pulcheria has taken a vow of virginity, her proper place is among the deaconesses of the Church, and Archbishop Flavian is instructed to take her away. Flavian, however, prefers to have her in the palace, and he directs her simply to live apart for a time and wait. Then, in 440, occurs the execution--one may almost say murder--of Paulinus. These later Greek writers all give a romantic story in connexion with it. As Theodosius and Eudocia go to church on Epiphany morning, a peasant presents the Emperor with a remarkably large apple. He gives it to Eudocia, who privately sends it to Paulinus. Unluckily, Paulinus in turn presents it to the Emperor, who sternly asks Eudocia what she has done with it. She declares, and repeats with a most solemn oath, that she has eaten it. Paulinus is at once sent away, and decapitated. A much nearer and more weighty authority, John Malala, confirms, in substance, this story of the apple, and says that Paulinus was suspected of intimacy with the Empress. There is no serious reason to doubt it, nor is any other reason suggested for the murder of Paulinus; but whether Eudocia was guilty, or the suspicion was inspired by the servants of Pulcheria, we are unable to determine.

The eunuch then, says Theophanes, presses Eudocia to attack Flavian and Pulcheria. He reminds her of "all the bitter things she had endured from Pulcheria," and covers the human motive with a pretence of religious zeal. We know, at least, that Eudocia embraced the Eutychian heresy, which Chrysaphius had adopted, and that a Church-council was summoned in 441 that put an end to Flavian.

The intrigue, however, runs on in obscurity until Eudocia suddenly asks permission to retire to Jerusalem. Theodosius could not divorce her, but we can easily believe that, as these writers say, he treated her with such severity, repeatedly reminding her of Paulinus, that she was driven into exile. Pulcheria returned to the palace, and resumed her control of the Emperor and the Empire.

Gibbon scouts these "Greek fictions," but, not only has he not taken sufficient account of John Malala, whose authority he recognizes, but a detail he adds from the still more authoritative Chronicle of Marcellinus (which is almost contemporary) gives a very serious confirmation.

In the suite of Eudocia, when she set out for Palestine, were a priest named Severus and a deacon named John, favourites of hers. They had not long left Constantinople when an officer named Saturninus, of the faction opposed to Eudocia, came upon them with an order to put Severus and John to death. It appears that they too were executed for supposed intimacy with the Empress. Eudocia lost her self-control at this brutal outrage, and bade her servants make an end of Saturninus. When Theodosius heard, he stripped Eudocia of her Imperial prerogatives, and left her in the position of an ordinary citizen. These authentic statements of Marcellinus strongly confirm the story, and it is clear that the Byzantine court was stained by a sordid quarrel and several brutal murders.

The romance of Eudocia's career was not yet over.

Marcellinus sends her to Jerusalem in 444: the later writers in 442. However that may be, in the year 445

we find her again embarking on an unhappy adventure.

The monks of Palestine were infected with the Eutychian heresy, and they welcomed so powerful a patroness.

With the aid of her servants they ousted the orthodox bishop of Jerusalem, and a vigorous monk was put in his place. The monk-bishop, with his militant army of ten thousand monkish followers, held Jerusalem for twenty months, in spite of the Imperial troops, drove all the orthodox bishops out of Palestine, and slew and cast to the dogs a number of their followers. In this quaint company the delicate Greek Empress continued to build churches and monasteries for three years, but when she hears at length of the misfortunes of her daughter, which the Bishop of Rome, as well as the courts of Ravenna and Constantinople, ascribe to her heresy, she sends to consult the famous hermit of the pillar, Simeon Stylites.

Simeon recommends her to confer with a certain saintly monk of the desert. The monk will neither leave his desert for her, nor permit a woman to enter it. She therefore builds a tower on the hill some miles away, and in that safe and public elevation the monk enlightens her out of her heresy.

Eudocia brought her adventurous career to a close in 460, protesting with her last breath that she was innocent of the charge of unchastity. Pulcheria continued to rule the Eastern Empire in the name of Theodosius until he died, in the year 450, inglorious and unhonoured. It was now seen that the prosperity of the Empire in her earlier years was a hollow truce of circumstances. When the fierce and rapacious Huns approached it, in 446 and 447, the Eastern Empire tremblingly purchased peace by the most ignominious concessions. When Theodosius died, she assumed sole control of the Empire, and the head of the eunuch Chrysaphius was at once removed from his shoulders. But the pressure of her people forced her to marry, and an aged Senator, Marcian, engaged to share her throne without sharing her virginal bed.

To his more vigorous hands the affairs of State now passed, and Pulcheria maintained her virtue and piety to the end. But we must now leave the Oriental pomp, the emasculated frame, and the splendid piety of the Byzantine court, to conclude our story in the West.

CHAPTER XXI

THE LAST EMPRESSES OF THE WEST

THE course of our inquiry has led us through five centuries of change. We have passed from the sober and virile integrity of the first Imperial pair, the golden age of Roman life and letters, to the successive depths of the Caesars. We have then seen the decrepit and corrupt city refreshed with an inflow of sound provincial blood, the enervated patrician families replaced on the throne by vigorous soldiers, and a new period of sobriety and prosperity open under the Stoics, to sink again under the burden of vice and luxury. Diocletian restores its strength, and then a singular and momentous change comes over the face of the Empire. The white homes of the gods perish or decay, the gay processions no longer enliven the streets, the cross of Christ heads the legions and towers austerely above the public buildings and monuments. The ante-chambers of the Emperors are filled with Christian bishops, and the rulers of the world bend meekly before the ragged figures of monks and tremble at the threats of lowly priests.

We return to the Western world to find another and a greater change. Rome has fallen, the frontiers are obliterated, the provinces, even to Africa, are cowering under the armies of the barbarians. Poverty, misery, and violence are scattered over the Empire, as if the departing gods had sown its fields with salt or with dragons' teeth as they retired to Olympus. Civilization, law, culture, art, seem to be doomed, and the end of the world is confidently expected. But amid the crumbling frame of the vast Empire a few shades of Emperors and Empresses linger for a generation, and we may glance briefly at their sobered features and adventurous experiences.

The chief figure of interest is AElia Galla Placidia, the sister of Honorius, whom we found visiting Constantinople in 423. Her adventures began when the Goths invested Rome in 408. She is then mentioned as concurring with the Senate in the pitiful execution of her cousin, the widow of Stilicho. Placidia was then in her eighteenth year. Bearing a heavy ransom, the Gothic army went away to harass her useless and trembling brother at Ravenna, and Placidia thought fit to remain at Rome.

It still contained wealth enough to capitulate to barbarians on fair terms. But the Goths returned in 410. Rome was awakened in the dead of night by the blare of their trumpets, and looked out to find palaces in flames, the streets filled with the terrible Goths, and the work of looting already begun. After six days of pillage they retreated northward, taking Placidia with them. We cannot follow her closely in that extraordinary march.

She was treated as a princess, however, and two years later was sought in marriage by the new king of the Goths, Ataulph. Ataulph was a barbarian only in name; a large, handsome man, princely, intelligent, and amiable.

He aspired to be a Roman Emperor. Honorius weakly resented the proposal, and demanded that he should prove the friendship he offered to Rome by returning Placidia. For two years she had wandered over Italy in the Gothic army.

It appears that Placidia was attracted to the graceful and courtly Goth, and they were married at Narbonne--the Goths having now returned to Gaul--in 414. When she reflected on the splendour of the wedding gifts, she may have thought that even an alliance with a Roman prince could not be more magnificent. Fifty beautiful youths, clothed in silk, brought to her one hundred dishes laden with the gold and jewels which the Goths had brought from Rome. But Ataulph was assassinated in the following year, and Placidia sank again to the position of captive. She had to walk twelve miles on foot, amid a crowd of captives, before the victorious barbarian who had slain her husband. Within another year her persecutor was slain, and his more humane successor restored her--or sold her--to the court at Ravenna.

The Roman commander Constantius, into whose hands she was committed, at once claimed her in marriage.

Honorius had promised that he should marry her if, by whatever means, he recovered her from the Goths. Placidia shrank resentfully from his embraces, and found his coarse, large, surly person a poor exchange for her handsome Gothic husband. The wedding took place, however, in 417, and Placidia settled down to the prosy duties of a matron, giving birth, in succession, to the princess Honoria and the future Emperor Valentinian III. In 421 her husband compelled the weak-minded Honorius to clothe him with the purple. Placidia received the title of Augusta, and a better prospect seemed to open before her. But Constantius died within a few months, and it was not long before she fell into a violent quarrel with Honorius.

The cause of the quarrel is, as usual, obscure. Some of the later writers suggest that Honorius became enamoured of his sister in her young widowhood. We know only that the palace at Ravenna was filled with bitter recriminations, its courts were stained with the blood of their followers, and Placidia fled to Constantinople with her children.

PLACIDIA

ENPHEMIA

ENLARGED FROM COINS IN THE BRITISH MUSEUM

Honorius died a few months later (August 423), and Placidia, confirmed in her title of Augusta by Theodosius, was sent in the following year to claim the throne for Theodosius, at the head of a considerable force. A secretary had usurped the vacant throne during her absence. It was the spring of 425 before they set out from Thessalonica for Italy; Placidia was with the cavalry, which reached and took Aquileia with great speed. There, after a short time, she received the captive usurper. His hand was cut off in the public Circus, he was placed on an ass and conducted round the town, amid the jeers of the crowd and the actors of the Circus, and was finally beheaded.

They then proceeded to Ravenna. Valentinian, a boy of six years, was created Emperor of the West, and Placidia settled down to a long period of government in his name.

As the legislation which followed, bearing the name of Valentinian but breathing the spirit of Placidia, was mainly of an ecclesiastical character, we will not linger over it. She fell ruthlessly upon Pagans, Jews, Pelagians, Manichaeans, and every other class who were obnoxious to her clergy. As in the case of most of the later Empresses, her piety so impressed the writers of the time that her personality is almost entirely hidden from us.

Apart from her decrees of religious coercion, we know her only as experiencing, not doing, things. Procopius, not a biased historian, severely complains that she reared her son in a luxurious softness that led inevitably to his later vices and his violent death; and it is frequently suspected that she had no eagerness to see him fitly educated in the duties of a prince. Cassiodorus pronounces that she conducted the affairs of the State with wavering and incompetent counsel, just at the time when Rome most urgently needed a firm and enlightened ruler.

Tillemont, after praising her piety, admits sadly that she brought great evils upon her afflicted Empire.

Though Rome had been looted by the Goths at their leisure, and barbaric armies commanded every province, the cause of the Empire was not yet lost. A judicious policy might have utilized the mutual hatreds of the various tribes, and have put the able commanders, who were still in the service of Rome, at the head of formidable armies. But the weakness and obtuseness of Placidia led, on the contrary, to the loss of her finest general, her last free province, and a large proportion of her troops. Listening injudiciously to the malignant persuasions of one general, AEtius, she commanded the other, Count Boniface, to relinquish his post in Africa, under the impression that he meditated treachery. AEtius at the same time warned Boniface that the recall was due to suspicion, and the gallant officer was driven into rebellion.

He invited the Vandals to Africa, and soon

twenty thousand of the tall, fair-haired northerners, with a vast crowd of dependents and followers, spread over the province. Placidia discovered too late the deceit of AEtius. She was induced to send a friendly ambassador to Boniface, and the fraud was at once detected. But the Vandals could not be dislodged. Boniface was slain (432) in his struggle with them, AEtius was driven to the camp of the Huns, and Africa, the granary of Rome, was irretrievably lost.

The next blow that threatened the distracted Empire was an invasion of the Huns. Placidia cannot be held responsible for the subsequent calamities, for AEtius, strong in his alliance with the Huns, had forced his way back into power, and was the real governor of the Empire.

But the formidable task he undertook was made more difficult by a romantic and unhappy occurrence within Placidia's domestic circle. We have already spoken of her daughter Honoria, who came in disgrace to Constantinople in 434. The great distinction of the Constantinopolitan court, the possession of three royal virgins, seems to have excited the pious jealousy of Placidia, and she apparently designed that her court should not lack its Vestal Virgin. We are not told that any vow was imposed on the young Honoria, but she was reared with the discipline of a conventual novice, and given to understand that the exalted state of virginity was assigned to her. In 433 the title of Augusta was bestowed on her, in some compensation of her sacrifice. But the daughter of Constantius had thicker blood in her veins than the daughters of Arcadius, and the claustral regime--the restriction of attendance to eunuchs and women--does not seem to have been rigorously enforced at Ravenna. In 434 the seventeen-year-old princess was discovered to be in a painful condition, and was dispatched to Constantinople, and incarcerated in a nunnery by the indignant Pulcheria.

But the young girl had a spirit beyond her years.

She had heard of the formidable nation of the Huns, which awaited, in the neighbourhood of the Danube and the Volga, its turn to fill the Imperial stage; she had heard that the young and powerful Attila had recently acceded to the throne of that nation. In some way she secured a messenger who took from her a letter and a ring to Attila, offering him her heart and her dowry if he would release her. The girlish freak was destined to have terrible consequences for the Empire. The lady herself we may dismiss in a word. She seems to have been kept in close confinement in the East until about 450, sending fruitless messages, from time to time, to her romantic lover. Attila had sufficient occupation during those fifteen years, and was content to put her name on the lengthy list of his wives. When, in 450, he formally demanded her person, he was assured that she was married. It is not impossible that she was released on condition that she accepted a husband chosen for her.

But her end is obscure, and one is disposed to doubt if she would ever have resumed her liberty without joining the victorious Hun.

Placidia died in the year 450, leaving the astute AEtius to avert the oncoming disaster by an alliance with the Ostrogoths against the Huns.

For a quarter of a century she had had supreme power over the Western Empire.

It is, perhaps, only an indication of mediocrity on her part that she could not avert the blows that fell upon it during that period, but it was a calamity for Rome.

Her memory survived, in a singular way, for more than a thousand years. The pagan habit of cremating the bodies of Emperors and Empresses had been replaced by the Egyptian process of embalming, and Placidia had built a chapel at Ravenna for the reception of her body. There it sat, in a chair of cedar-wood, until the year 1577, when some children, thrusting a lighted taper into the tomb to see it better, set it aflame and reduced it to ashes.

Meantime, another Empress of the West had appeared.

In 437 Valentinian had married Licinia Eudoxia, the fourteen-year-old daughter of Eudocia, at Constantinople, and brought her to Italy. He had parted with a large slice of his Empire to Pulcheria and Theodosius for the honour, and is said to have held it lightly. The sequel will dispose us to believe his irregularities. A youth of eighteen at the time, frivolous, luxurious, and light-headed, he was content to enjoy the palace, and leave his mother, and then AEtius, to discharge his duties. Eudoxia could but idly follow the momentous movements of the nations, and appreciate the defeat of the Huns in the terrible battle of Chalons in 451; or shudder when, in the following year, Attila marched to the gates of Rome, demanding half the Empire as the dowry of his distant bride, Honoria; or when, in 453, the profligate Valentinian plunged his sword in the breast of his great minister AEtius. A grave personal tragedy was upon her.

The court resided generally at Rome, where Valentinian enjoyed the larger and faster amusements of a metropolis.

Here, in the year 455, he was stabbed by his soldiers, and a romantic story is told in connexion with his death. The story is rejected by a recent historical writer, Mr. Hodgkin ("Italy and her Invaders"), but Professor Bury has shown that it is probably true in substance. The full story, to which fictitious details may have been added before it reached Procopius, is that Valentinian, gambling heavily with the distinguished Senator Petronius Maximus, obtained his ring as a security for the money he had won. Maximus had a beautiful wife whom the Emperor desired, and he sent the ring to her with a summons to the palace. The unsuspecting lady was conducted to Valentinian's apartments, and outraged by him. For this crime, and in virtue of the general discontent, Maximus had him slain and occupied his throne.

Maximus was a wealthy Roman, of illustrious family, and peaceful and luxurious ways, so that we have little reason to doubt that an outrage on his wife inspired him with the thought of assassination. The further course of events adds authority to the narrative. His wife died very closely after the death of Valentinian, and he invited or compelled Eudoxia to marry him. In the obscurity and uncertainty of the records we are unable to understand the consent of Eudoxia, even under pressure. Some of the later Greeks affirm that he violated her. It is certain, at least, that she married him within a month or two of her husband's tragic death, and almost immediately afterwards sought to destroy him. Our authorities, late and uncertain as they are, do not lack plausibility when they affirm that he one day confessed that, out of love for her, he had directed the assassination of her husband. Rome had returned to evil days, and tragedy was brooding over its very ruins.

In a fit of repulsion Eudoxia secretly invited the Vandals to cross the Mediterranean and avenge her. Historians too lightly admit, in extenuation of her criminal act, that she had no hope of help from the East. The aged and upright Marcian was, it is true, intent upon the internal prosperity of his Empire, but it is extremely doubtful, as the sequel will show, whether the deposition of Maximus would have offered much difficulty, and Eudoxia was the niece of Pulcheria. Her vindictive act hastened the end of the Empire. Genseric speedily landed his fierce troops on Italian soil, and the Romans at once slew the sullen or remorseful Maximus and cast his mangled body in the Tiber. The further adventures of Eudoxia, interesting as they must have been, are compressed in a few lines. After fourteen days' pillage, the Vandals retreated once more from the stricken city of Octavian, laden with gold, silver, women, and all kinds of valuables. Genseric compelled Eudoxia and her two young daughters to accompany him.

They were detained at Carthage for seven years. The Eastern court repeatedly asked for their release, but it was refused until, in 462, the elder daughter, Eudocia, was married to Genseric's son. Eudoxia and the second daughter, Placidia, were then sent to Constantinople. Years afterwards--in one of the legends--we catch a last glimpse of Eudoxia, the last prominent Empress of the West. She is standing before the column of Simeon Stylites, asking him to come and live somewhere on her ample estate.

Eudocia lived for sixteen years at Carthage, then escaped to the East, and ended her life in Palestine. Placidia we shall meet again for a moment.

We turn back to the shrinking Empire of the West, to dismiss the last four Imperial shadows that flit about its ruins. The vacant throne was occupied by the commander of the Roman forces in Gaul, Avitus. He had married, since we know that Sidonius Apollinaris was married to his daughter Papianilla, but his wife was dead, and we need only say that, after he had enjoyed the Imperial banquets for a few months, he was degraded to the rank of a bishopric by the commander of the barbaric troops, with the consent of the disgusted Romans, and he died soon afterwards. He was followed by a worthy and able officer, whose rule might have illumined a more propitious age; but we find no Empress in association with him, and must pass over the four years of his earnest effort to redeem the Empire. After his death Libius Severus had a nominal and obscure reign of four years (461-5), and again we find no Empress in the scanty records.

The throne remained vacant for nearly two years, during which the Vandals harassed the miserable remnant of the great Empire. At length the chief commander in Italy, Ricimer, sought the aid of the Eastern Empire, and the alliance was sealed by the Eastern court sending one of its wealthiest and, by birth, most illustrious nobles, Anthemius, to occupy the throne. His Empress was Euphemia, daughter of the Emperor Marcian by his first wife. But her name, and the names of her father and her children, are all that we find recorded concerning her, and we need not dwell on the failures and quarrels, or the last faint flicker of Roman paganism, which characterized his inauspicious reign. Within four years he quarrelled with Ricimer, and his life was trodden out on the streets of Rome.

For a few months Placidia, the daughter of Eudoxia, then occupies the throne. At Constantinople, to which she went with her mother from her Vandal captivity, she married the wealthy noble Olybrius. He had fled from Rome when it was looted by the Vandals, and had little mind to exchange the safe luxury of Constantinople for its uneasy throne when Ricimer offered it to him. It is said that Placidia impelled him. It was a fatal adventure.

They entered Rome in the train of Ricimer's troops, but Olybrius succumbed to that atmosphere of death in a few months, and we have not time to discern the features of Eudoxia's daughter before she sinks into the large category of obscure Imperial widows. His successor,

Glycerius, a puppet of the chief commander, seems to have had no wife. A competitor appeared immediately, and he exchanged the uncertain sceptre of the Western Empire for the solid crozier of a bishop.

One faint and shadowy Empress crosses the scene before the curtain falls. Once more the Eastern court had provided Italy--which was now the Western Roman Empire--with a ruler. Julius Nepos set up his court at Ravenna, and had for Empress a niece of Verina, the Empress of the East. But the barbarian leaders of the barbarian army--the only army that remained in the service of Rome--resented the Eastern intruder, and marched on Ravenna.

Nepos fled ignominiously; and one reads with interest, though not without reserve, that he was put to death by his predecessor, Bishop Glycerius. The fate of his wife is unknown, and the last Empress of the Western provinces entirely escapes our search.

The tattered purple was offered to the commander Orestes. He refused it, and allowed them to place it on the shoulders of his young son (476). The name of this pretty and innocuous boy united, as if in mockery, the names of Romulus and Augustus. To later times his pathetic figure is known as Augustulus. His father was slain by the troops immediately afterwards, because he refused to distribute one-third of the soil of Italy between them. The Empire was now a mere phrase; Rome a plaything of the barbarians whom it had cowed for five or six hundred years. Odoacer, the latest leader of the troops, bade the child put off his purple mantle and begone, and some time afterwards--so low had Rome fallen that the year of this impressive consummation cannot accurately be determined--forced the Senate to abolish the Imperial succession in the West. Italy became the kingdom of a barbarian. Britain, Gaul, Germany, and Spain were turned into the battle-grounds of those fierce tribes who, after the violence and darkness of the Middle Ages, would in their turn scatter the seed of civilization over the earth. The gallery of Western Empresses was closed by the irrevocable hand of fate, and the long, quaint gallery of the Byzantine Empresses was thrown open.

* * * * *

FOOTNOTES

[1] The title "Empress" was unknown to the Romans. "Imperator" was a name of military command. The special use of it in connexion with Octavian and his successors was that it was given for life. The more novel title "Augustus" was extended to Livia, who later became "Augusta."

[2] Pliny places her birth in the year 54 B.C., but Dio says 57 B.C., and this date is confirmed by Tacitus.

[3] Improperly, because it is not a distinctive name, but common to the emperors. Livia and Octavia received the title of "Augusta" a few years later, yet even Livia is rarely known by it.

[4] "Non nisi plena nave tollo vectorem."

[5] Writers often convey the impression that Julia indulged even her most vicious inclinations in the Rostra, but Dio merely speaks of "revelling" and "carousing": oste kai en te agora kai ep' autou ge tou bematos komazein nuktos kai sumpinein. The emptying of a cup of Falernian wine in the Rostra, on some occasion of especial devilry or intoxication, may be all that is meant.

[6] Vol. V, p. 353.

[7] "Annals," v. 3.

[8] An apology should be made for retaining the nickname of the third Emperor, but it seems to be ineradicably fixed in history.

[9] Tacitus, who is followed by Merivale and other historians, makes Claudius also retire to Sinuessa. This is probably an error, as the Emperor fell ill and died at Rome.

[10] "The Life and Principate of the Emperor Nero," 1903.

[11] kai outo ge eauten dia pases tes arkhes diegagen oste medemian epegorian skhein: lxviii, 5.

[12] Duruy quotes Aurelius Victor ("Epitome," xiv) as saying: "It is impossible to say how much Plotina enhanced the glory of Trajan." The passage is really found in c. xxxix of the "Epitome."

[13] Gregorovius points out that the incident may have occurred at Rome, and that we have no positive proof that Sabina accompanied him on this journey. But the narrative of Spartianus seems to imply that she was in Britain, and we shall see that she accompanied him on his longer journey to the East. Duruy and other writers hold that the officers were dismissed for lack, not excess, of respect for Sabina, but the word "familiarius," coupled with a threat of divorce, seems to demand the interpretation I have put on it.

[14] See Dr. Bassani's little work, "Commodo e Marcia."

[15] The references on coins and inscriptions to Julia Domna have been industriously collected by Mary Gilmore Wilkins, *American Journal of Archaeology*, 2nd series, vol. vi. They do not add materially to our knowledge of her, but are so abundant that they show her to have been an Empress of exceptional prominence and influence. She became Augusta in the first year.

[16] I conclude that they had already come to Rome because Elagabalus, the son of Soaemias, was given serious consideration in his later claim that he was the son of Bassianus. He was born in 204, and, unless his mother had been in the palace before that date, the claim could not have been made.

[17] It is difficult to imagine Elagabalus beginning his appalling career at such an age, and Gibbon, calculating from the age given to Alexander Severus in the "Historia Augusta" at the time of his death, changes the age to seventeen. But the "Historia Augusta" is very commonly wrong in the ages it ascribes to Emperors at their death. Professor Bury admits that Gibbon is probably wrong, and we may follow Herodian.

[18] Ammianus Marcellinus tells us the one fact, Zosimus the other. Neither mentions her name, but we learn it from coins.

[19] Some writers have conjectured, from the fact that the legend "In Pace" occurs on the coins of Salonina after her death, that she became a Christian. The phrase is not found otherwise except on Christian monuments. Duruy does not admit the inference, and points out that she built a temple to the goddess of the seasons.

[20] Her name is variously given as Vitruvia, Victoria, or Victorina. Since it appears as Vitruvia where the "Augustan History" copies from the Acts of the Senate, and no Roman would corrupt Victoria into Vitruvia, I take it that it was originally Vitruvia, and was Latinized, or changed by her when she became Empress, into Victoria.

[21] It has been suggested that the fifteen months of Lactantius may date from their expulsion from the court of Maximin. This is hardly possible. Galerius died in May, 311, and Valeria was still in mourning for him, and pleaded his recent death, when Maximin sought to wed her. Maximin died in April, 313, so that the deaths of Prisca and Valeria cannot have been earlier than the summer of that year.

[22] The Greek original of the "Chronicle" is lost, and Jerome informs us that he has added many details in the Latin version which we now have.

[23] One of the most authoritative works on Roman institutions, Marquardt and Mommsen's "Handbuch," says this emphatically: "Ehen, bei welchen der eine Theil der Romischen Burgerschaft, der Andere den Latinern jungeren Rechtes oder den Peregrinen angehorte, sind nach Romischen Recht nicht gultig" (vii. 29). Goteke, in a special study of the subject ("Constantinum honeste et ex legitimo

matrimonio natum"), says that special edicts made it impossible for an officer to marry in the province in which he served. He believes that the effect of these would not be permanent, but he fails to consider Helena's disability as a *peregrina.*

[24] The question may be raised whether St. Augustine had not the case of Constantine in mind when, in his moral treatise "De Bono Conjugali," he refuses to condemn a man who, having a barren wife, takes a concubine in addition, to provide a family. It is clear, at least, that early Christian opinion was not fixed. Gibbon again improves upon Christian writers by holding that Minervina was an earlier wife, not a concubine, of Constantine; but, as Professor Bury points out, the document on which he relies does not apply to that Emperor.

[25] It is from the confusion of dates that I ascribe the words confidently to Jerome, and not Eusebius The words "ninth year" can only refer to the ninth year of the Caesarate of Crispus, or 326. The interval of three years has no significance in view of the confusion of dates.

[26] Gibbon, Professor Bury, and Mr. Firth make Zosimus coincide with Zonaras. The reader will see from my literal translation of his words that he differs very materially. He does not suggest that Fausta accused Crispus, or that she was really guilty of any misconduct; but he pointedly accuses Helena.

[27] Miss Gardner observes, in her life of Julian, that we do not know if Helena was older than Julian, But, while Julian is known to have been born in 331 or 332, since he was in his sixth year at the time of the massacre of 337, and died at thirty-two, Helena's mother had been murdered in 326.

[28] Philostorgius says that, as she lay ill with her malady, Constantius recalled Bishop Theophilus from exile, and he cured her. But Zonaras makes her die of this very malady, scouting the Arian miracle.

[29] The Alexandrian Chronicle repeatedly calls her Marina, and we have no coins to determine the full and accurate name. Cohen, at least, gives no coins, though Tillemont refers to them.

[30] Lib. xxviii. 1: He says that Gratian put a certain man to death "on the advice of his mother." Zonaras says that Severa still lived at the time of the second marriage.

[31] Gratian, the youthful son of Severa, had been clothed with the purple by Valentinian, "at the instigation of his wife and father-in-law," says the epitomist of Aurelius Victor, in the autumn of 367. On the other hand, Justina's brother was killed, in the service of Valentinian, in 369, The second marriage falls most naturally in 368.

[32] Yet St. Augustine, who was in Rome the year after the death of Gratian, says in his "Confessions" (viii. 2) that "nearly the whole nobility of Rome" still clung to the old religion.

[33] Hence Tillemont and others, who give these dates, must be wrong in placing the quarrel with Eutropius in 399. Philostorgius expressly says that she had two daughters in her arms when she appealed to Arcadius.

[34] See Professor Puech's "Saint Jean Chrysostome," 1891.

[35] The curious reader will find Chrysostom's surprising strictures of the clergy more than confirmed in the letters of Jerome, and his fierce denunciation of the monks borne out in Augustine's treatise on them.

[36] Gibbon makes her survive Chrysostom, and die in 408. But Tillemont has pointed out that the "Life of Chrysostom" by George of Alexandria, on which he seems to have relied, forges letters, and is quite unreliable. The earlier writers put the death of Eudoxia in 404.

THE END

Printed in Great Britain
by Amazon

53823910R10179